THE HUMAN ODYSSEY

Other Books Published

Biblical Hermeneutics: An Introduction

Called to Teach: The Vocation of the Presbyterian Educator, editor with William J. Weston

Exploring the Spirituality of the World Religions: The Quest for Personal, Spiritual, and Social Transformation

Living Wisely and Well in the Evening of Life: Foundations for Flourishing; A Spiritual Perspective

Lovescapes: Mapping the Geography of Love; An Invitation to the Love-Centered Life

Making the Bible Your Book: Content and Interpretation

Mindful Spirituality: The Intentional Cultivation of the Spiritual Life; A Book of Readings

New Age Spirituality: An Assessment, editor

The Radical Invitation of Jesus: How Accepting the Invitation of Jesus Can Lead to Living Faith and Fulfilling Life for Today

The Radical Teaching of Jesus: A Teacher Full of Grace and Truth; An Inquiry for Thoughtful Seekers

The Teachers of Spiritual Wisdom: Gaining Perspective on Life's Perplexing Questions, with Jamal Rahman and Mary Petrina Boyd

Traces of Transcendence: The Heart of the Spiritual Quest

THE HUMAN ODYSSEY

The Journey of the Soul in Perilous Times

by
Duncan S. Ferguson

WIPF & STOCK · Eugene, Oregon

THE HUMAN ODYSSEY
The Journey of the Soul in Perilous Times

Copyright © 2025 Duncan S. Ferguson. All rights reserved. Except for brief quotations in critical publications or reviews, no part of this book may be reproduced in any manner without prior written permission from the publisher. Write: Permissions, Wipf and Stock Publishers, 199 W. 8th Ave., Suite 3, Eugene, OR 97401.

Wipf & Stock
An Imprint of Wipf and Stock Publishers
199 W. 8th Ave., Suite 3
Eugene, OR 97401

www.wipfandstock.com

PAPERBACK ISBN: 979-8-3852-4320-4
HARDCOVER ISBN: 979-8-3852-4321-1
EBOOK ISBN: 979-8-3852-4322-8

VERSION NUMBER 040725

Unless otherwise marked, Scripture quotations are from the New Revised Standard Version Bible: Anglicized Edition, copyright © 1989, 1995 National Council of the Churches of Christ in the United States of America. Used by permission. All rights reserved worldwide.

Scripture quotations marked MSG are taken from *The Message*, copyright © 1993, 2002, 2018 by Eugene H. Peterson. Used by permission of NavPress. All rights reserved. Represented by Tyndale House Publishers.

The Journal records constant, one might say, obstinate growth, in step with the very slow rhythm of nature and grace. It is a growth in understanding and knowledge of God's purpose, and an increasing embodiment of that purpose in his spiritual and ecclesiastical office. God's desire for us, being eternal, keeps pace with us; it grows with us and we grow with it.

Pope John XXIII, *Journal of a Soul*[1]

---

1. Note that I have paraphrased the title given to Pope John XXIII's diary, understanding it as an extraordinary account of the journey of his soul and his quest to bring the life and teaching of Jesus and the ministry of the Christian church into the contemporary world. Across the years, his diary has been informative and inspirational for many and for me as I have journeyed through life in perilous times.

Contents

PROLOGUE
The Formative Journey of the Soul: The Odyssey of Life | 1

SECTION ONE
The Soul's Journey of Being Informed: On Finding a Spiritual Center | 19

CHAPTER ONE
On Being Informed: Living Wisely and Well in Perilous Times | 21

CHAPTER TWO
On Being Informed: Assessing the Alternative Ways to Well-Being | 37

CHAPTER THREE
On Being Informed: Endorsing a Spiritual Center and Embracing a Pathway of Faith | 57

SECTION TWO
The Soul's Journey of Being Reformed: Cultivating Spiritual Maturity | 71

CHAPTER FOUR
On Being Reformed: Understanding the Spiritual Life | 73

CHAPTER FIVE
On Being Reformed: Participating in the Practices of Spiritual Maturity | 88

CHAPTER SIX
On Being Reformed: Emphasizing Those Practices That Encourage Strength of Character and Guide the Ethical Life | 107

SECTION THREE
The Soul's Journey of Being Transformed: Engaging in Mission in a Troubled World | 121

CHAPTER SEVEN
On Being Transformed: Understanding and Endorsing the Divine Presence as Love | 123

CHAPTER EIGHT
On Being Transformed: Discerning and Cultivating One's Values, Responsibilities, and Spiritual Gifts for the Divine Mission in the World | 141

CHAPTER NINE
On Being Transformed: Finding Peace in a Troubled World Through Spiritual Awakening and Wisdom | 154

CONCLUSION
The Soul's Journey of Being Conformed: Following Jesus | 171

CHAPTER TEN
On Being Conformed: The Way of Jesus | 173

Bibliography | 185
Index | 191

PROLOGUE

The Formative Journey of the Soul
The Odyssey of Life

> It matters not how strait the gate,
> How charged with punishments the scroll,
> I am the master of my fate:
> I am the captain of my soul.
>
> William Ernest Henley, "Invictus"

The Contours of Our Journey

IT IS NO SECRET that the journey through life is hazardous for most of us and genuinely threatening for many in the human family whose way of life has been or is on the brink of being destroyed.[1] Even without these external threats of violence and the destruction of the infrastructure of our lives, our odyssey is still not easy. We also have the internal challenges rooted in our development as a person. It is no small task to learn how to live with peace and purpose across the life span. Full maturity does not come easily.

---

1. I write at the time of the violence in Gaza, the conflicts in the Middle East, and unrest in many parts of the world such as Ukraine. I understand that there is almost no time in history when there is a setting in which our way of life, indeed, life itself, has not been threatened in some way. Our journey is an odyssey, a spiritual voyage marked by many challenges.

Our odyssey is seldom free from the given and difficult demands of our immediate responsibilities, the high expectations of those in our circle of nearness, the confusing values of our culture, and the dramatic changes and conflicts in our time in history. As we seek to follow the way of mature responsibility, we are faced with a vast array of challenges. Many must struggle and some just give up because they cannot cope with the demands of their journey through life. The harmful social conditions surround them and fill their lives, and they come to this journey with an array of insecurities and needs, often a carryover from a difficult childhood.

We grow from birth into adulthood hoping that, in spite of our challenging environment (and sometimes because of it) and personal struggle to develop, we will still be able to become the person we were created to be and have the potential to become. Our healthy and informed mind, our sensitive and caring soul, our rich mixture of emotions, and our occasionally ill, though reasonably healthy body, will be our foundation. It is these dimensions of who we are and what surrounds us that must be integrated into a healthy and whole person, one who will then be empowered to cope in perilous times and live with a good measure of peace and purpose.

Our subject in this writing is how best to encourage and manage our growth and development in our challenging environment. We want to explore how we move toward maturity by learning how to live wisely and well in our journey of becoming. How is it that we move toward integration and wholeness, gain an understanding of who we are, reach a good measure of personal peace, and then find our place in the confusing circumstances of our life and in our world?

Our foundational premise is that one very important way we move toward health and wholeness in our odyssey is by the thoughtful nurture of our spiritual center, our soul. Looking back and learning from the odyssey of Odysseus, we know that our voyage will be marked by many changes of fortune as we engage in our intellectual, emotional, and spiritual wandering and growth. We stay on course by having a center, one that has integrity and is informed; this becomes our solid foundation for the life journey. As we step out and begin to wander, the mature soul becomes the compass of our journey as we move toward health and wholeness.

We will try to demonstrate how this journey toward maturity has the best chance of being successful, giving us the capacity to inform our minds, open and enrich our hearts, and maintain our physical health. As we travel, we will encounter a complex environment, draw upon our mixed inheritance from the family, and face the challenging social conditions in which we live. It is the soul, our spiritual center, which is able to guide and integrate the many dimensions of our growth and development. Our purpose, then, in this writing is to explore how to nurture our soul, move toward health and wholeness, and begin to flourish as we live wisely in our odyssey.

The values that guide us on this journey are deep faith, unvarnished truth, spiritual wisdom, and unconditional love. We understand the soul as the coordinating center which connects us to the ground of our being, ultimate reality, often called God, and how this healing connection and life-giving encounter become the foundation for our journey.[2]

The challenging conditions we face in our journey may occasionally cause us to lose our way in this odyssey of our soul that moves toward maturity. It is no secret that many of us do get lost; just turn on your computer, read the morning paper, watch the evening news, or talk with your next-door neighbor or your colleague at work if you need any confirmation. Getting through life with a heartfelt smile, inner peace, and becoming a responsible and healthy adult remains a challenge, but possible in many ways. One way it becomes possible is when, as we mature, we find, endorse, and cultivate a solid spiritual foundation for this journey of becoming.

On this journey, we need a foundation that sustains us, one that has the basic values that ground us and an outlook or worldview that gives us wise guidance. We will then be motivated in our growth toward wholeness, enabled to live with a good measure of peace, and to find and cultivate an informed purpose in life. From our foundational center we map a wise journey, traveling as a pilgrim grounded, informed, visionary, and committed.

The Meaning of the Terms We Use

As we begin to reflect and talk about this odyssey, it is important to have some clarity about the meaning of and the way we use a few descriptive words. In this domain and area of study—human growth and spiritual development—many words are used, and it is occasionally difficult to understand precisely what is being said. It often depends on which of the

---

2. Many of the people with whom I talk prefer not to speak of connecting with God, especially if what we say is expressed as a specific religious outlook. All too often, a specific religious orientation may be tribal, cultic, and exclusive, and not lead us to health and maturity. I fully understand and share this point of view, although I write out of a Christian center, which I hope is a healthy pathway, one that is inclusive and spacious in character. A spiritual center can be healthy and life giving, often because it is linked to a mature religious orientation. It need not be a particular religious orientation such as Christian, especially if it is exclusive in character. It is certainly possible to speak about ultimate truth or the ground of being as in forms of secular thought or in Asian religions such as Buddhism and Hinduism. See the thoughtful and scholarly book by Denise L. Carmody and John T. Carmody titled *Ways to the Center*.

disciplines of knowledge we consult, such as classic literature,[3] psychology, sociology, history, philosophy, religious thought, or just the evening news.

For example, we may get confused because these words are used and understood by us in our particular language and cultural frame of reference and then by others with a different language and frame of reference. There may be subtle shades of difference and even conflicts between the vocabularies of these different settings. More often, there is just a subtle shade of difference, even among those with a common language and heritage. Though influenced by the normative meaning of these words in our culture, we still give these words shades of meaning based on our experience, and others will give them a slightly different shade of meaning based on their context.

Soul is one of these words and, as I listen and observe how the term is used, I discover that it is being used in a variety of ways. I also observe that several other words are used in reference to soul, three of which are especially important in our discussion.[4] They are *spirit, self,* and *mind,* and they too need some clarification about how they will be used in this writing, giving special attention to their relationship to the soul.

We will use the word *soul* as a reference to that part of our identity and personality which guides us as we engage in our life work, in sensitive relationships with other human beings, and in our connection with the divine or ultimate reality. In our spiritual life, we say that it is our soul that connects us with God. Our soul clarifies our values, much like a compass, as we cultivate a meaningful and purposeful life. We will speak of the soul as having the capacity to connect us with the divine or center, help us establish authentic relationships, empower us in making good ethical choices, and then to find direction for an integrated pathway that gives our lives meaning.[5]

One often hears the comment, "She has a soulful relationship with God," meaning a deep and gratifying relationship with God. We might say as well, "She is soulful, one who is profoundly reflective and sensitive

---

3. See the two novels of Madeline Miller, *The Song of Achilles* and *Circe,* in which she brings to life the tale of the gods and goddesses and the kings and queens of ancient Greece, central to the human odyssey.

4. There are literally dozens of words that need clarity as we explore our spiritual pathway, and, as far as possible, we will be careful in their usage to explain their meaning and place in our spiritual journey.

5. We might say as well that our soul connects us with deep and profound truth, by which we often mean the divine or God. We know that not all people believe in a personal God who is ultimate truth; indeed, many don't, but they may still long for a foundational center that gives them a purpose and values, empowering them to cope with the complexity of their particular circumstances and navigate their way in the perilous times in which we live.

regarding values, relationships, and ethical norms." *Soul* is used in other ways as well, but in our use of the word, we will speak about how our soul is that dimension of our being that is spiritual and links us to the divine or ultimate truth, and that this connection enables us to engage in authentic human relationships, guides us in the formation of our ethical norms, enables us to cope with complexity and challenge, and gives us purpose in life. Our soul connects us with the divine or the ground of being, empowers us to discern and care about what is right and wrong, and is sensitive to the well-being of others. It is the immaterial essence and animating presence of connection, care, sensitivity, and purpose.[6] The mature soul empowers us to flourish.[7]

Another word, not unlike *soul*, that we often use in reference to what is very important to us in our life journey is *spirit*. In fact, *spirit* may sometimes be a synonym for *soul* in that it, too, is often a reference to that part of us which connects us to the divine and describes the kind of orientation and attitude we have in our journey. In Christian thought, the reference to the divine as the Holy Spirit is to speak about God as being fully present, empowering us to find a healthy way to live and to flourish. We understand Spirit as the divine presence and power, enabling us to live in a wise and healthy way. We often say that the quest for connection with the ground of being[8] is a spiritual quest, and we become more spiritual as we focus on our understanding of and connection with God or ultimate reality and then give time and energy to the quest for a consistent and firm linkage and relationship.

We will often use the terms *spirit* and *spiritual* in these ways, yet our lean is toward using *spiritual* as a description of our attitudes and the nature of our emotions in our spiritual journey. We often hear, "She has a great spirit about the project in which we are engaged," meaning a positive and hopeful attitude about it, or that she is being spiritual as she moves forward in her quest to live in harmony with and for the divine or foundational

---

6. The word *soul* may be used in other ways as well; it is one of those words that we use in several ways and a valuable word because it helps us talk about that which is so important to our well-being. We note as well that the word *soul* is akin to the word *self*, our true identity. Our inner life is not divided up into easily identifiable and separate parts, and we use these words to speak about the ways we function. We are not Legos, but putting them together may result in a single object that is easy to identify and which has a name with meaning.

7. Noted interpreter of religious thought Huston Smith gives us some guidance on the various ways these terms are used and their complexity in his book *The Soul of Christianity*.

8. *Ground of being* is a term often used by Paul Tillich, a theologian of the last half of the twentieth century, to speak about ultimate reality or the divine, God.

truth. To sustain our spirituality, we must engage in certain practices such as participating with others in a shared sacredness and in symbolic acts such as the Communion service. In addition, we nurture our spiritual center when we are alone, experiencing in the stillness and silence the presence of the divine, empowering us to transcend our personal needs and blocking our tendencies to allow life to frustrate us and cause us to resort to negative feelings such as anger. Rather, in the stillness, perhaps present in nature, we begin to transcend our needs to be in control; we pause, celebrate the beauty and depth of life, and sense God's unconditional love. We are not alone. As we rise to the events of the day, we find fulfillment in our tasks, let our frustrations subside, become slow to anger, are quick to forgive, and empowered to fulfill our responsibilities and to love others as God loves us.[9]

A third word, also starting with the letter *s*, is *self*, a more comprehensive term. We often use this word as a reference to who we are, our identity, the person who ponders life's pressing concerns, understands them, and makes decisions about them. We use the terms *myself*, *himself*, and *herself*, meaning and referencing a particular person. It is a more direct reference to our identity and that which has a gentle soul and a good spirit. For clarity, we may need to mention a fourth word, *mind*, and we will use this term in reference to understanding what has been, is, and will be. It is that part of us that thinks through options, reasons about them, gains an understanding of the journey, and then reflects on our situation in life and guides us in making wise decisions. It is our mind that enables us to know, understand, have informed relationships, and be in a thoughtful relationship with God or the ground of being.

These words and a few similar ones will occur in this writing, and I will try to be careful about their usage and subtle nuance, generally suggesting that it is the self or the person who has a soul, a spirit, and a mind, and who is or can be soulful, spiritual, and mindful.

A Perilous Odyssey

As we begin to speak about the soul's journey, it is wise to call attention right up front with how easy it is for us to get anxious and confused along the way

---

9. There are numerous books on spirituality. One helpful guide is titled *The Study of Spirituality*, edited by Cheslyn Jones, Geoffrey Wainwright, and Edward Yarnold, SJ. Noted social psychologist and scholar Jonathan Haidt, one who questions the existence of God, even has recommendations on the need for spirituality in his book *The Anxious Generation*, 201–18.

in our spiritual odyssey.[10] Our soul's journey takes place in perilous times, and we have to deal with the clutter and occasional chaos inside of us. It is the mature soul that guides us in the wide range of internal and external challenges in our lives and gives us direction in our complex and troubled world.

Contemporary life is perilous and many of us will get damaged or lost. One common cause of getting lost, confused, and anxious is that we may undertake our journey without a good foundation; we don't have or use a mature soul or a spiritual center, one that is authentic, enlightened, informed, and able to guide us and keep us on track. It is what motivates and empowers us for the journey. We need an enlightened and inspired soul to ground us, a foundational principle and center for self-understanding and guidance in our journey through life.[11] By speaking about a spiritual center, we are referencing that part of the person, the soul, that affirms and contains our values and beliefs, held so deeply that they engage the whole person and give shape to our identity and way of life. We speak of the soul as a base for self-understanding and that which guides our life decisions, our spiritual quest, our deep and true relationships, and our ethical behavior.

As I think and write about the journey, I find myself examining my travels and the pattern of life of those whom I know, especially those who struggle. I recently had a pastoral conversation with a middle-aged person who had vigorously pursued a life that would give him extensive income, connect him with persons of notable achievement, and place him in a significant category of recognizable importance in our culture. Unfortunately, his health deteriorated and he has now passed away. His marriage had failed, and he felt anxious and lost in his final months. The external goals of life, money, possessions, power, and reputation had not given him internal peace and happiness. His condition was akin to the rich young man who spoke with Jesus about how to have eternal life (Matt 19:16–22). Jesus explained to him about keeping the important commandments (to have faith in God and obey the commandments), to which he replied that he had done that: "'I have kept all these; what do I still lack?' Jesus said to him, '. . . Go, sell your possessions, and give the money to the poor, and you will have treasure in heaven. . . .' He went away grieving, for he had many possessions." Who am I to judge this young man speaking with Jesus, living in another time

---

10. When using the word *odyssey*, we are suggesting that our journey will be marked by many changes of fortune.

11. This point has been made by several modern scholars. The Buddhist word *mindfulness* is often used in reference to the journey of the soul, and the mindful course is to engage in careful thought, have a positive attitude, and the joyful spirit we need to have in reference to our journey.

and culture, and who had a life that was exceedingly difficult and complex? I was not there to understand his circumstances. But it does appear in this story that Jesus thought the young man needed to have a spiritual center, one that gave him deep meaning and wise guidance. He may have also discovered that amassing wealth, possessions, power, and a notable reputation were not ultimately satisfying. He had become distracted and moved away from a true spiritual center that may have led him to a deep and enduring peace. The point of the story is that we do need God or a spiritual worldview as our center and then we will more likely have the motivation, wisdom, and strength to deal with the complex issues of wealth, possessions, power, and reputation, and, indeed, with life itself.

In short, our primary thesis in describing this journey, our odyssey, is to maintain that it needs a spiritual center, which is to say that our soul must be in harmony with God or ultimate truth for us to find our true way. This relationship and linkage guides us on our journey and empowers us to flourish.[12] The soul connects us with God or ultimate truth as we travel, and the healthy soul listens to the presence of God and gains insightful truth and wisdom for guidance in the journey of life. We are maintaining it is our soul that is the center of the spiritual dimension of our growth, connecting us with a personal God or with a universal ground of being.[13] As we grow and mature, we nurture our soul, our spiritual center, with practices that keep us aware of our ethical values and attuned to the presence of the divine or the ground of being. As we do, we gain resilience and perspective.

We move through life sustained by spiritual practices and often with a community of support that is engaged in cultivating an ethos that gives a high priority to relating to God or truth, enhancing self-understanding, encouraging sound ethical behavior, and inviting us to a life of loving service. Our mature soul has this purpose and, as far as possible, it is grounded in and guided by universal values such as a commitment to health and maturity, to truth and integrity, to a life full of love and compassion, and to a dedication to ethical norms that guide and invite us to do our part in sustaining and working for peace and social justice.[14]

---

12. I am suggesting a broad understanding of a center, not a narrow and sectarian one.

13. Again, I use this term from Paul Tillich, a noted theologian of the previous century, whose perceptive theological outlook has carried over into the present. His use of *ground of being* as a term for the divine has the value of being universal, not attached to a period of time or a particular religious tradition, and it is at least partially removed from the common tendency to create God in our own image.

14. I am writing just after the election of the president, one who needs a soul full of integrity and compassion.

As we explore the many dimensions of our spiritual odyssey, we may draw upon a person from the past who epitomized in their life the deep and profound values and wisdom necessary for the journey. As we start, I turn to Saint Augustine, one of the Christian church's greatest theologians who, in a quite dramatic way, describes in his *Confessions* how he was getting lost in the journey of his soul. He then describes how he fundamentally changed his priorities and had a dramatic conversion. One day, when he was outside, he heard these words coming from a neighbor's yard: "And Thou, O Lord, how long? How long, Lord, will Thou be angry, forever?" He listened carefully, thinking the words were meant for him, and he wondered whether God would ever forgive him in that he had drifted away from a life of faith. He describes this experience in his *Confessions*:

> So, as I was speaking and weeping in the most bitter contrition of my heart, when lo, I heard from a neighboring house a voice, as of a boy or girl, I know not, chanting and oft repeating, "Take up and read; Take up and read." Instantly, my countenance altered, and I began to think most intently, whether children were wont in any kind of play to sing such words; nor could I remember ever to have heard the like, "Take up and read." So, checking the torrent of my tears, I arose interpreting it to be no other than a command from God; "Go, sell all that thou hast, and give to the poor, and thou shalt have treasure in heaven, and come and follow me."

He continued to read from Scripture: "'Not in rioting and drunkenness, not in chambering and wantonness, not in strife and envying; but put ye on the Lord Jesus Christ, and make no provision for the flesh.' . . . For instantly, by a light as if it were of serenity infused into my heart, all the darkness of doubt vanished away." Filled with guilt and confusion, he began a new journey, one with a spiritual center.[15]

It is important to add, as the account in Augustine's *Confessions* makes clear, that this spiritual center or soul needs cultivation and renewal in order for us to move toward maturity, a purposeful life, and inner peace. We are not born with a mature soul, but, much like our minds, our soul goes through a process of learning and becoming. Ideally, we will have, as we do with education to improve our minds, the opportunity for improving our spiritual life by deepening and enriching our soul and being inspired and empowered to live an ethical life. We are able to move toward a soul that gives us the capacity to connect with the divine, become transformed, develop responsible values, cultivate life-giving relationships, and engage

---

15. Augustine, *Confessions*, 170.

in a life of service. We then move out from this center into the world in the hope that our spiritual center will help us to be resilient, stay attuned to God or truth, to have integrity and be authentic, to have a good measure of peace, to flourish, and to contribute to the well-being of others.[16] Augustine was such a person in history who faced a particular challenge and responded to it in a wise way. He reflected on the journey of his soul and found the values that would become the foundation for the journey. They gave him guidance and empowered him on his journey through life; he cultivated a spiritual foundation that sustained and enriched him, and led him to a life of peace and service.

It is also important to stress that as our souls are in the process of becoming mature and responsible, there will be many risks and endless ways of getting sidetracked in this odyssey. We are not yet complete and, therefore, have a good measure of vulnerability. Our spiritual and moral center is in the process of becoming and not yet fully mature and secure. As we journey, we know we will be challenged and have few guarantees that our developing soul will enable us to cope and continue the positive journey toward full maturity. We need to recognize that we are still on the way, traveling on toward our destination of becoming mature, healthy, authentic, kind, and responsible. The spiritual journey of Augustine underlines the reality of the challenges in our spiritual odyssey.

The risks appear at every point in our lives. They are certainly present in our early life as a child, often in the context of the family (or lack of a family) with parents or their substitutes who may be unable to create a safe and secure home and to provide guidance and unconditional love. Again and again, Augustine refers to his mother as a model for him. We know her as one whose name became the name of a city in California, Santa Monica. She and her husband lived in Hippo, a city in North Africa near the shore of the Mediterranean Sea. It was where Augustine was born, and she has been honored for her spiritual devotion and for the way she guided her son. She is the patron saint of mothers, and she prayed for him as he journeyed, not always wisely, in his early years.

While grateful to my parents and their desire to provide a home environment that was safe and secure, I look back and see that my parents, given their own needs, were not always able to provide my brothers and me with a setting free from worry, loneliness, and neglect. Often there was a lack of care, and each of us had a measure of emotional insecurity. I know personally that when the family structure is dysfunctional, the child feels

---

16. Augustine, *Confessions*, 171. Note: there are more recent translations of the *Confessions* and the Scripture which is quoted.

lost and insecure and must struggle across the years to achieve health and wholeness.

The risks continue as we move from home into the culture of schools, and again, Augustine's life reflects this element of risk. This new setting creates challenges in that the schools are not intended to take the place of the family or to be fully equipped to provide the care and the nurture of a loving home. These early years of school are not always easy for a child. In fact, we may suffer as children, and often the risks become more serious as we move through the complex teenage years. The schools may help, but we are still liable to take the wrong turn, especially in adolescence when we begin the journey to independence and adulthood.

Looking back, we are usually grateful to those who have supported us and helped us get on the road to becoming a healthy, mature, and secure person, although not all of us will have this foundation. When we finish our years of schooling, we are then expected, almost on our own, to become mature young adults, often starting a new family and beginning a career. Yet we are still growing and gradually discover that the challenges will stay with us across our adult years and even into in the evening of life. We don't just arrive at the point of maturity and then stop our quest for inner peace; it remains a challenge across the years of our lives.

At the center of this process of growth is the challenge of becoming a mature adult, in part shaped by our family system, often a supportive community, the many years of education, and the challenges of early adulthood. As the process of growth continues, we look back and discover how we have been engaged in shaping our identity, forming a way of life, selecting and preparing for a career, securing the means of financial support, and in most cases choosing a life partner and starting a family. These developmental tasks are full of challenge, as Augustine learned.

He also learned that in the middle years there will be many demands, perhaps that of a challenging career, selecting a way of having financial security, being a wise parent if there are children, and becoming an integral and responsible part of our chosen community. A midlife crisis is not uncommon, and Augustine had what we might consider in our contemporary language a crisis, one he endured and then became a changed person, able not only just to manage, but to become a remarkable leader and scholar. In our final years, as he discovered, there continue to be risks and challenges, perhaps sadness and disorientation as we lose so much that has been dear to us. There may be an illness that slows us down, the loss of our parents, the loss of our role as a parent as children leave home and enter into adult life, a shift away from day-to-day engagement in our life work, and the possible loss of a life partner.

In the evening of life we are especially vulnerable and need to be prepared, wise, and creative. It is a distinctive phase of life, one in which we become increasingly aware that there will be an end to our journey. As we seek to enjoy time with others, we discover that we have lost some of those in our generation whom we loved deeply. Gradually, we discover that we need to prepare ourselves for the end of life.

Given these risks on our journey, we do need guidance and help from others. We also need to have resources within, to be guided by our soul, our spiritual center, taking shape in a family structure and a community of support. The mature soul will enlighten, empower, and comfort us as we move through life. Unfortunately, not all of us are able get the help we need when the risks in life intensify, and in our time, it does seem that the risks have intensified. We may discover that what we had counted on to sustain us and give us the foundations for the flow of our lives is more limited than we had hoped. We may have fewer resources to manage the complexity of our setting and, indeed, our rapidly changing culture and the world than we thought we would have.[17] We often move toward adulthood partially unprepared for these new realities in our changing culture and world. It is within this swirl of change and challenge that our soul goes on the precarious journey of becoming. We want to travel well and arrive at our true home of maturity and inner contentedness; for many of us, it is a spiritual journey that takes us to the place of knowing that we have lived wisely and are truly loved by God.

Deep in our consciousness, we want a good journey and hope to arrive at our preferred destination with a life full of love, peace, and purpose. We hope to flourish as we take on the task of living well in our final years. We observe and even know many people who have had or who are having a demanding journey and unable to cope in their later years. We observe many people who may be finding it especially difficult in their final years. We may have dear friends, for whom we care deeply, who are suffering in the evening of life, perhaps even parents or close relatives who were not prepared to manage dramatic changes and new realities. We see their suffering, want to help, and we often do so in caring ways. We may have learned from their journey about how we need to be prepared, how to stay on course, and then how to manage wisely our situation and the challenges in the evening of life. We may be able to help them as we draw upon our experience and give them sound advice.

17. Some are speaking of AI as containing the risk of causing us to lose our balance and mature outlook. See, for example, Mustafa Suleyman's *The Coming Wave* for a clear picture of this technology and its place in our future. There is even a new therapy model called Woebot that seeks to use AI as a source of guidance and healing.

We also learn, as we travel, that the journey of our souls will not necessarily be like those living in a different generation from ours. Our challenges are different from our parents, and our children's way will be different from ours. In fact, the world is changing so fast that we journey on a quite different pathway than the one from which we started; it is certainly different than those from the generations that preceded us. We become keenly aware that those behind us will have quite different challenges than the ones we face. We will need to find our way and have a foundation geared to our journey; the pattern of Augustine's life was different from ours, although he did face similar challenges. We learn that the journey of the soul will have subtle differences for each of us, and we will travel in many directions with an array of turns and roundabouts.

The Components of the Journey

There are many dimensions and components in this journey of our souls, ones which, if understood, may make our journey more manageable and more fulfilling. In a religious context, we underline that there is great wisdom in engaging in spiritual preparation for the journey. With guidance from family, friends, and our community of faith, we begin to ground our soul's journey in religious belief, spiritual practices, and the support of a caring community of faith. Having a clear understanding of our faith, our beliefs, wise spiritual practices, and a community of faith can be profoundly important along the way in the soul's journey.[18]

Those of us on a religious journey need to be informed about the ways that our faith will ground us, support us, and guide us. Our faith journey needs more than just having a vague emotion that occurs at critical times and that lingers from an exposure to the life of faith earlier in our life. Rather, it is an authentic and profound relationship with God and an informed understanding of the deep truths we affirm. Our religious journey must include at least a preliminary understanding of the way God has and continues to enter into human history and takes up residence in our souls. Emotions, as important as they are, do come and go and do not always sustain us in perilous and threatening times. For many, it is a profound and deeply personal relationship with God that becomes the foundational component in

---

18. I am fully aware of the secular nature of our time, and that fewer people are seeking a religious way toward peace and maturity. In fact, I find that some of what I hear in the religious context is cultic and exclusive and it turns me toward a more secular journey. I occasionally find myself using the categories of contemporary thought to describe my journey, sensing that they touch the deep realities of my experience in a better way. See the classic work of Charles Taylor *A Secular Age*.

our journey, giving clear guidance and enabling us to live wisely and well.[19] So, we must continue to learn and be better informed about our life of faith, or this faith commitment may fade from our consciousness and lead to the feeling of being lost and alone in the storm.

In addition, we also need to keep in mind that the journey of the soul involves all aspects of our lives, not just a small piece of our lives to which we give attention for a few minutes every other week. We need to remember that we are engaged in the cultivation and development of the whole person for all of life, not just a part of the person for one aspect of life. I begin with this holistic perspective, looking at the soul's journey as the journey of the whole person to be mature in all aspects of life. There may be quite specific spiritual components, and we underline that this part of our journey is best integrated with all aspects of growth and development in the many contours of our lives. The soul's journey is one that touches every part of us, all needing integration and inner harmony.

One integral part in the ideal journey of the soul is that it will usually have a clear destination, one that will help us to arrive at a place where we feel loved and secure in our family, our communal life, and have a good measure of peace and the gratification of a life well lived as we approach the end of our travels. We hope it will be one in which we feel fulfilled and at peace because of life-giving relationships, success in our vocation and career choice, and one that has had a good measure of joy and gratification in our day-to-day living across the years.

We are keenly aware that in our culture and location, such a peaceful destination may be difficult to find and sustain. Therefore, we cannot stress enough that we need to plan carefully for the journey to our desired destination. We can easily lose our way. For example, we may discover somewhere along the way that we have chosen the wrong destination and that new travel plans need to be made. In fact, as we pass through the stages of life, we will need to take time to reflect on our way and perhaps change some of our goals and patterns of life. We hope to find the destination best suited to our desires and needs, giving us assurance that we are on the right path, even if we still have to look at the map and make another turn. We are a traveling pilgrim.[20]

---

19. I want to acknowledge that there are many forms of a foundational center, some religious with a personal God, and others with of a deep sense of reality, the way things are, as for example in Buddhism and some forms of Hinduism. In our contemporary world, it is often just a sense of living in reality in an authentic way that becomes the foundational base.

20. See John Bunyan's classic book *Pilgrim's Progress*—a bit dated, but the challenges and principles are still present.

This same care must be given to the road we take and the pace of our travel. We want to arrive at the right time and in the best condition in order to feel comfortable and ready for the demands of a new location. As we journey, we know that the condition of the road, our responsibilities along the way, and the approximate time of arrival will profoundly influence our level of comfort and sense of security when we arrive. Careful planning along the way is essential. For example, if we envision our destination as that which includes our final years, we need to have a clear financial plan, one that will give us adequate financial resources in retirement. We may need to select the location of our retirement along the way, identify the housing we will need, give attention to the ways we will use our time, and find ways to be with those whom we love.

We will likely have traveling companions on our journey, some who help us and others who may be a burden. Will our family members, with all of their needs and differences of personality, travel with us and help us along the way? Will they live in close proximity so that we can be with them and count on them as we have needs? Are the members of our family nurturing and caring, or interfering and demanding, or perhaps just distant? Are they able to help us or do they, because of their health-and-wealth needs, expect that we will help them? How do we care for those who are where we were just a few years ago, perhaps beginning their journey? How might they want us to help?

Often on our journey there will be settings and places where we have been, full of warm and touching memories and profound learning, inviting us to return on a regular basis. In addition, there will be new settings filled with levels of beauty, inviting wonder, appreciation, and joy. My wife and I have one of those special places in central Oregon, a place of mountains and meadows, of rivers and lakes, and of snow and sun. Other sites may invite some sadness and even regret about a past experience. Our discussions with our travel companions will often be about our hopes, mixed with what we have seen, what we have experienced along the way, and the nature of what we may find as we arrive. There may be visions for a new trip, often with feelings of hope. We sense that we have learned how to travel and that we can be delighted and confident about a new adventure.

Our imaginations take flight as we travel, perhaps with a positive outlook, or there may be some anxiety and fear about the future. We remember, ponder our experiences, and have memories, some of which will be joyful, others that will evoke insight, and still others that may cause sadness as we reflect on past experience. We then begin to wonder about the future and hope it will bring joy, peace, and happiness. We may find that we often fantasize about what might be in our future, hoping there will be beautiful scenery and joyful experiences. We then remind ourselves that we need to stay in the present and be responsible.

Staying the Course

Quite often the journey of our soul will be undertaken with our family and friends, and as we travel, we hope and expect they will contribute to our health and happiness. Our lives are enriched as others share the journey with us. It is safe to say that the journey of the soul is most enjoyable, refreshing, and even healing and transforming in a loving and caring family and a community of friends. Yet we also know that some people are more inclined to travel alone (and some have no alternative but to travel alone), and find that a contemplative life filled with quiet meditation is a source of insight, growth, and deep joy. There is the spectrum of introversion and extroversion as we seek to find the best way to journey and finding our place on this scale will assist us as we travel.

There are times when we discover that members of our family and close friends may not be able to guide us as we travel. Their journey may be different than ours, and they may be too invested in telling us what is the right way for us to travel and what our destination should be. Once again, we will need to find that right balance, listening to those who are empathic and insightful and being cautious around those who want to control us. We need wisdom, understanding, and care.

Our soul, our immaterial essence and identity, filled with values and hope, may easily, although often unintentionally and inadvertently, become passive and confused on the trip, causing us to lose clear sight of the destinations of health, maturity, deep joy, and contentment. The soul's journey toward good health and maturity takes place in perilous times; we must be intentional and reflect on our journey in such a way that we are assured there will be loving guidance, promising directions, and life-giving destinations.

As we travel, we need to remember and even underline that our culture is filled with the promises of happiness if we only do what others say we ought to do. The promises may be very seductive, carefully hiding their artificial character. An evening of television is filled with promises that life would be better if only we bought what is being sold. We live in a giant market place, competitive and entrepreneurial in character, one with the goal of making money and the promise that happiness consists in the abundance of things possessed. There are shiny objects, exotic locations, beautiful people, and symbolic magic carpets that will take us to paradise. These promises are bound to have at least a measure of influence on all of us, even those of us who have a carefully nurtured spiritual center filled with discernment and good judgment.

It is our mature soul, our foundation of beliefs and our center of values, which will guide and empower us to stay on the course to joy and peace and fill us with love. The journey of our soul has taken us to a mature consciousness, empowering and sustaining us to become all that we have the potential to be. We then have the resilience to be able to take care of ourselves wisely and, as we are able, give ourselves in helping, healing, and nourishing others, and to lend a hand in creating a better world.

Questions for Reflection and Discussion

1. How would you describe the journey of your soul? Has it been a good one? Were there any problems along the way? How have you coped with the challenges in your odyssey?
2. What are your primary goals on this odyssey? What is your desired destination? Do you have a model for finding your way? What is it?
3. Who do you want to become? Are you making progress on the way? Do you have friends to help you?
4. What are the fundamental values that guide your life and inform your journey?
5. How do you sustain a hopeful spirit, given the conditions we face in our troubled world?

Key Terms and Concepts

1. Soul: One's spiritual identity, the immaterial essence and animating presence of a person who seeks a relationship with the divine or ultimate truth, the love of others, and guidance in ethical decisions.
2. Spirit: The animated or vital dimension in a person, usually reflecting attitudes, feelings, energy, and enthusiasm. Occasionally used as a synonym for soul in Christian thought and refers to the divine presence.
3. Maturity: The capacity to manage one's internal life well, even with troubling circumstances or conflicts; a wise posture and attitude that is able to manage the challenging demands of life wisely.
4. Journey of the soul: The pathway of life leading to one's growth toward maturity; how a person cultivates the connection with the divine or

truth and integrates foundational values across the span of life; an intellectual and spiritual outlook across time, often called an odyssey.

5. Peace: A term used to describe an inner contentment for an individual, and the outcome of wisely managing conflicts between groups or nations.

Suggestions for Reference and Reading

1. *The Confessions* by Augustine
2. *The Imitation of Christ* by Thomas à Kempis
3. *Man's Search for Meaning* by Viktor E. Frankl
4. *Modern Man in Search of a Soul* by C. G. Jung
5. *Pilgrim's Progress* by John Bunyan

SECTION ONE

The Soul's Journey of Being Informed
On Finding a Spiritual Center

> Again Jesus spoke to them, saying, "I am the light of the world. Whoever follows me will never walk in darkness but will have the light of life."
>
> John 8:12

THESE ARE THE APOSTLE John's record of the words of Jesus.[1] In them, Jesus teaches us that by following his example, one can hope to achieve enlightenment and be delivered from the blindness and emptiness of chasing pleasure, possessions, power, and recognition.

"Christ's teachings surpass all the teaching of the saints, and those who cling close to Christ with like spirit will find in his teaching hidden manna. Many hear the Gospel but care little for it because they are neither of like mind nor spirit with Christ. But those who wish to fully understand the words of Christ must strive to conform the whole of one's life after Christ's model."[2]

---

1. I am aware of the complex ways that the New Testament was formed, one which raises some questions about the actual words of Jesus and how they may have been preserved.

2. Thomas à Kempis, *Imitation of Christ*, 6. There are a multitude of books explaining the value of the wisdom in the teaching of Jesus. This book, by the German monk (1379–1471), is a classic and has been read across the centuries as a guide for those living the Christian life. Yes, the ideas do occasionally have the sound of his time, but they also have the ring of eternity.

CHAPTER ONE

On Being Informed
Living Wisely and Well in Perilous Times

Do not let your hearts be troubled. Believe in God, believe also in me.

John 14:1

The Model of Jesus

I DON'T WANT TO use the name of Jesus as a sort of trump card, taking all the tricks in the challenging game of life. I occasionally hear this promise in a sermon or conversation that God "will take care of everything if you just believe in Jesus and have faith." Very often, when I hear this comment, I sense and honor its sincerity, but often wish that the person speaking would also add that as we travel by faith, we will still face difficulties, and that our faith and study of the way of Jesus will empower and guide us on our journey and help us manage our difficulties and challenges. His life was full of them, and how he managed to cope and respond can teach us. Many do make this observation and offer good advice, and it is these wise souls whom we need to meet and to hear.

My study of Jesus reveals to me that he got it right about life, although I have spent a career trying to understand fully what he taught about managing life wisely and well.[1] There is the marvelous account in the Gospels,

---

1. I do take seriously the challenges of history, culture, and language study required

which describes the way that Jesus spoke about, modeled, and promised the good life during his time of nurturing his soul and preparing for his life work. He had left his likely vocation as a craftsman in the Galilee and traveled south for conversation and guidance from his cousin John, who had chosen the life of a prophet. Jesus found John in a rural area, east of Jerusalem, was baptized by him (John was called John the Baptist) in the Jordan River, and in this act, he reaffirmed his commitment to give his life to love and service. The record indicates that he heard the voice of God: "This is my Son, the Beloved, with whom I am well pleased" (Matt 3:17). Yet, even with this confirmation, he sensed that he still needed more reflection and contemplative preparation in order to undertake his mission in life.[2]

He traveled to a slightly different location and camped in a rocky desert area, not all that far from the flowing waters of the Jordan River and the Dead Sea. He sensed that he should continue to prepare for his life calling, a God-given vocation and one filled with extraordinary challenges. There, he devoted himself to fasting and meditation, preparing himself for his calling to love and care for those he would soon meet, help, heal, and challenge.

A personalized evil influence entered his life and said to him that there were at least three ways to orient his life which would give him all that he ever would want or need.[3] There were three promised choices and directions, which, if chosen, would have led him in the journey of his soul in a false direction and blocked his extraordinary contribution to humankind (Matt 4:3–11).

While meditating and preparing himself in a disciplined way in his wilderness retreat, he heard a voice, one that offered immediate food and rest with the promise that, since he was God's son, he could use his divine power to change the stones near him into bread, gratifying the needs of the body.[4] All he had to do was to call on his divine power and turn the stones

---

to enable one to better understand and interpret the recorded words of Jesus and those from different cultures and times in history who have endeavored to explain the words of Jesus in the manuscripts that we have available. There is the temptation, and many have yielded to it, to say that their reading and interpretation of the words of Jesus are the best and only ways to understand the teaching of Jesus. We may learn from them, yet we also know that the wise way to understand the teaching of Jesus is by engaging in careful scholarship, accompanied by sincere faith and deep humility.

2. So might we.

3. The reference to a personalized evil is translated as the "devil." I am not sure there is a personal devil in red pajamas and a pitchfork, but sense that there are some little devils in my life.

4. There is some debate among biblical scholars about whether there was an actual divine voice, or just the internal sense within Jesus of his options. I understand this account as occurring while Jesus is in deep meditation.

where he was standing into bread. He was tired and hungry, yet not fooled by false promises. He did not cut corners and stayed on course, saying, "One does not live by bread alone, but by every word that comes from the mouth of God" (v. 4). Jesus was needy and hungry, yet knew that he must follow the will and way of God, not yield to the subtle falsehood that peace and happiness come with immediate physical gratification. The stones were close and accessible, yet gaining reassurance from his perceptive and pure soul on its journey to maturity, he chose to ignore the stones and go in the right direction, to the heart and will of the God of wisdom and grace. Jesus knew that he still had work to do and to perform a circus act was not part of it.

Next, perhaps in his imagination, he was taken to a high place in Jerusalem, on the temple. He might have reflected on what he intuitively saw, throngs of needy people, and wished that he had the power to change the conditions that caused them suffering. The temptation, however, went in a different direction, suggesting power and glory for Jesus rather than caring for those who were suffering. We know that it is not hard, especially when filled with deep personal needs and anxiety, to let our minds reflect on different way of life and to fantasize about having more power and some control over a troubled world. It is easy to say "if only" as we look back upon the flow of our lives and what we wish could have been done in resolving similar challenges. The personalized evil one invited Jesus, as he stood on the highest point of the temple, to "throw yourself down" (v. 6), testing whether he could control God who would save him from sure death from the fall, and with this power, to make changes in the social conditions he observed. He could easily access God, he was told, and even have the influence to control God's will and way. Jesus replied, "Do not put the Lord your God to the test" (v. 7). Jesus underlined that he followed God's way, not what might be his own way sometimes disguised as the way of God. He did God's bidding, not pretending that God did his bidding. He worked for God, not God for him, and with faith and a pure and humble heart, he turned to God for guidance, not a fantasy of power.

And third, he was taken to a high mountain where he could see all the kingdoms of the world and was told that they would be his if only he followed the evil one.[5] He replied, "Worship the Lord your God, and serve only him" (v. 10). In a time of fatigue and hunger in a lonely desert region, Jesus viewed the centers of prestige and beauty in the world, resisted the lie

---

5. There is a high place in the desert mountains above the region of the Dead Sea that has a pathway to a cave, one with a view that oversees a vast region. Tradition has assigned the viewing point of Jesus to this high cave, with no real confirmation that it was the spot where Jesus could have viewed a vast region. But visiting this cave gave me a sense of what Jesus may have envisioned in his mind.

that having it all would bring peace and joy.[6] He would not have been taken in by all the scams we receive on our phones and computers. Jesus placed his faith in God, rejecting all the false promises that power and possessions bring peace and joy. He knew, on this journey of his soul, that doing God's will was the right choice and would bring wise guidance and deep contentment; he would stay attuned to and follow the will and way of God and not disobey the teaching of God.

The life of Jesus gives us the map for choosing the right direction for our soul's journey and destiny. We ground our growth toward fulfillment, maturity, and deep peace in a spiritual way, one based on finding God's will for the journey of our soul. Ultimate truth, the very ground of being, God's will and way, is our choice, not our immediate gratification or yielding to the false promises that happiness consists of having unlimited power, immediate gratification, and the abundance of possessions.[7]

I have learned so much from this story of Jesus and, for the most part, have attempted to follow the way of Jesus in my wilderness, one filled with many alluring yet suspicious promises. Perhaps we all receive false invitations at some point in our lives. I have occasionally failed in my response to these, saying yes to a phony invitation and taking the wrong path, sometimes causing internal struggle and deep pain. I may have endorsed the false promise of immediate gratification, given in to the unchecked quest for power, and thought that shiny and beautiful possessions would bring fulfillment. Yet, overall, I have tried to follow another way and the true promise, that to have faith in God and have a foundation for life based on truth and love will make life fulfilling. It is by placing our faith in God or our sense of unconditional love and ultimate truth that has the potential to make us a mature and whole person, the goal of our soul's odyssey.

As one on the journey, I often understand it and put it in context by a careful study and reflection on the identity, teaching, and compassionate life of Jesus.[8] I understand Jesus as the loving expression of God, the one who makes God's love visible, the one whose teachings *inform* us about the way, the one whose prophetic actions *reform* us and invite us to care about those who suffer, and the one whose healing and sacrificial ways have the capacity to *transform* us, empowering us to have integrity and to love. Jesus

---

6. He was not planning to run for president of the United States.

7. I have been taken by the writing of Ilia Delio, theologian and scientist, who beautifully traces the ways that we join with God in the flow of evolution and change, not sensing that we have the ultimate power. See *Unbearable Wholeness of Being*.

8. My study has led me to write two books, *The Radical Teaching of Jesus* and *The Radical Invitation of Jesus*. There are many great teachers and wonderful models of the good and healthy life, and I read them carefully and honor their teaching.

was an extraordinary teacher, a courageous prophet, and a compassionate healer. I have found that there is a way of life, a true odyssey, discerned in the example of Jesus, that will wisely guide and empower us on the journey of our soul.

The Challenges of Following Jesus in Perilous Times

There are many ways of following Jesus and, as one carefully reads about these ways in the New Testament and church history, there is inspiration and guidance. As we begin this process of learning from Jesus and following his teaching, it may feel a bit overwhelming; after all, he was Jesus, the Son of God. He lived with integrity, faithful to all that he taught. We may feel that we can't easily do it, given our many limitations. Yet he was also very human, and his example of living in perilous times has much to teach us about the odyssey of our soul in somewhat comparable and difficult times. His obedient faith, his extraordinary wisdom, and his deep commitment to a life filled with compassion give us a marvelous example to follow in the journey of our soul.[9]

As we seek to live as he did, we will focus on the ways that speak directly to how his life and teaching will guide us in the journey of our soul. Of course, as we do, we will face many challenges that have some similarity to the ones faced by Jesus. Being conscious of them as we travel will aid us in our journey.[10] Our first challenge, in this endeavor, is to be careful to take into account the full story of the life and teaching of Jesus and have this big picture in our hearts and minds as we, on occasion, take time to focus exclusively on only one aspect of the life of Jesus, risking some distortion. It may be easy for us to focus so intensely on one story or single teaching that we then allow this one concept to become the exclusive basis of our view, even distorting the meaning with our own preunderstanding. As we read the full story, we grow and our understanding matures; as we study and meditate on a careful reading with an openness to his many wise insights, we continue becoming what God wants for us to be. But if we emphasize just one aspect of his life and teaching, we run the risk of becoming narrow,

---

9. Franciscan priest and teacher Richard Rohr has addressed the invitation to follow Jesus in his life and many books; see *Universal Christ*.

10. I am aware of the many interpretations of the example and teaching of Jesus. Many are carefully discerned and helpful. Yet there are just as many that are narrow, exclusive, and driven less by careful study and reflection and more by the needs of the interpreter and his or her cultic community.

even judgmental, sectarian, cultic, tribal, and exclusive.[11] In order not to lose our way and to grasp the full implications of what Jesus has to teach us about our soul's journey, it will help us to have a comprehensive understanding of his life and teaching in our minds. We need to keep his extraordinary love, his unflinching commitment to truth, and his unselfish service in the cause of justice in front of us, and they should give us our map for the journey. From this more comprehensive understanding, we will find good ways, although not easy ways, to integrate his example and teaching into our learning and apply it to the journey of our soul. The Christian church does depend on informed and committed Christians, and the world needs them.

I have spent several decades in this process of integration and application of the life and teaching of Jesus, and from this experience, I want to underline a second often-mentioned challenge—namely, that to follow the life and teaching of Jesus is very demanding.[12] As I look back across the years, I am reminded again and again that I have not always followed his teaching with sufficient commitment and wisdom; there have been some inconsistencies and even failures. But I have found that as I stay attuned to God, sensing the presence of the spirit of God in my life, I then know that I am loved, have been forgiven, and now can be empowered by the spirit of God. From this full awareness of being loved truly and unconditionally, I have gradually moved toward becoming a person with more integrity and increased my capacity to live in harmony with the foundational values of Jesus. I now sense that I am being told to pick up my crutches and start walking. Being faithful, truthful, and loving others are on the top of my list and have become my agenda for each day.

At times, making this my daily goal, I still may miss the mark, in part because the description of the way of Jesus comes to us from a different time in history, a different language, and a foreign culture. I may not fully understand what is being said in an initial reading, and we need to be careful about our tendency to impose our preunderstanding on what we read.[13] Our

---

11. I have met those sincere people who say that Jesus was a healer and that healing is the primary way we understand Jesus. It might be wiser to say that Jesus lived in a particular way and in a setting when and where there were many ill people. He did care for them in remarkable ways, and we should reproduce those aspects of his compassionate love and make them an integral part of our Christian life. Healing was central to his ministry of compassionate love, although it is not easy for us to replicate his healing ministries, nor was it the only way he served.

12. "Well, of course," you might say. But following the way is incredibly difficult and complex, and we should have humility and openness to continuing to learn.

13. I was made keenly aware of these challenges of interpreting the life and teaching of Jesus in my doctoral studies at the University of Edinburgh. My dissertation was titled "Preunderstanding in Historical and Biblical Interpretation." I later wrote the

third challenge is to be careful not to make our understanding of his life and teaching exclusively fit our cultural norms and the specific patterns of the particular form of Christian faith in which we were raised and now practice. Not infrequently, we may even impose our view on others, believing it is "the" truth and they must accept it. There are many ways to live in harmony with the teaching of Jesus. With a prayerful and humble spirit, we continue to learn. We do so across the decades of our lives and keep on learning how his life and teaching may transform and enrich our understanding.[14]

We may find an outlook that is nurturing and works for us, but it is not likely the only way. With an openness to learn, we begin to discover a fourth challenge, that of our tendency to judge those who do not fit our particular patterns of practice and understanding. On occasion, I see this careless pattern in human behavior and observe the irony that those who know less are more prone to judge, and those who know more are humbled by the beauty and breadth of wisdom and truth. They then become reluctant to judge. It is wise to be open to and guided by the lives of Christians who have put their faith in different languages and other forms of expression. With this additional understanding, we avoid the all-too-easy tendency to slip into the mode of judgment, assuming that our way is the only way and others should live as we do. Protestants do judge Catholics and conservatives do judge progressive liberals, but this pattern of judging those whose understanding is slightly different from ours is risky, often harming the relationships. So, we humbly approach God and know that our understanding is an approximation and needs to continue to grow and develop.

As one fortunate to have been with many Christians in different parts of the world, I have continued to learn and become more accepting of alternative views, allowing them to add depth and expand my learning. I am so grateful for the welcome I have received by Christians in other parts of the world, many in religious communities quite different than my own. They have taught and inspired me by their example, their beliefs and practices,

---

book *Biblical Hermeneutics: An Introduction*, suggesting some guidelines for interpreting the Bible.

14. Unfortunately, there are those who have lost balance and perspective in maintaining that Jesus has given us, by his life and teaching, the model of the spiritual life. When I see or hear those who claim that their interpretation is the only truthful one, I carefully withdraw. Often these views tend to be more about the one speaking than about Jesus. Our views of Jesus need to be the product of devotion and also education in order to offset imposed and mistaken views, sometimes expressed in the limited cultural patterns that have shaped the one who is speaking. We can learn from a quote often attributed to Einstein: "The more I learn, the more I realize how much I don't know."

and by their writing. This exposure, read with a critical eye, has enriched my way of being and living.

I affirmed in the prologue that to study and understand the life and teaching of Jesus is a very good way to be informed about a wise and healthy journey through life. Of course, we, on this journey, will travel with prior understanding and receive information and guidance within the framework of our learning and traditions. But with careful study, an open heart and mind, and within our community of faith, we are better able to learn and receive God's message of love and guidance. We are given, in our soul's odyssey, an expanded and deepened understanding of the life, values, and teaching of Jesus.

While affirming the values of Jesus in this life-giving study of his life and teaching, I also acknowledge that there are other great teachers in different religious traditions who also give us light as we walk along the dark paths of life. Our fifth challenge is to recognize that we have chosen the Christian way framed in the contours of our country, language, and culture, and we also know that God speaks many languages across cultures and historical eras. God's love is universal and available to all. We need to keep in mind that there is wisdom in many corners of our planet, and there are descriptions and options for life's journey and healing in many cultures and historical eras. I am able to learn from them, as they may be able to learn from me. One of my best friends is a Muslim Imam and we learn from one another.

I have also learned that my choice of the way of Jesus is to acknowledge and accept that I have not chosen an easy journey; it certainly wasn't for him, and so we repeat that making the odyssey of our soul patterned after the example of Jesus is going to be demanding. He did not say that the Golden Rule was easy. "In everything do to others as you would have them do to you; for this is the law and the prophets" (Matt 7:12). Nor did he say that loving others would be simple and uncomplicated. In fact, it is said that the way of Jesus has a narrow gate (Matt 7:13). Only a few will find it and enter into the discovery that unconditional love is the essence of the soul's journey. He teaches that doing to others as I would have them do to me is the good and noble life.

The person we become is inevitably shaped by our profound needs, the idiosyncrasies of our growth and development, the negative as well as the positive currents within our history and culture, and the conflicted realities and outlooks in the cultures and nations of our world. Our soul—that is, the person we are, our essence or true self, the values we hold dear, and the direction we chose to follow in life—will be a partial product of our environment with all of its truth and goodness, but also with its harsh and debilitating realities and falsehoods. It is not easy in our culture (or world) to become a truly healthy and mature person, one with integrity and compassion, dedicated to lending a hand in the formation of a mature and life-giving society and world. We need a foundational center and a fully realized and healthy identity in order to manage the challenges of contemporary life. We need to be formed by the spirit of God, coming to us in all the ways we can understand, whether we live in Kenya or Kansas or Kathmandu.

Beginning Our Odyssey

These are perilous times in which we take the journey of our soul; the negative realities of our social setting, culture, and world are present with us. Their presence is dramatically illustrated, as I write, by the conflicts in Ukraine, the tragedy in Gaza, the threats in Iran, and the unrest in many places in the world and in the Middle East. Not long ago, my wife, Dorothy, and I were on a cruise that began in Athens, stopping at other sites in Greece, and an historic island in the Mediterranean. We then sailed on to Istanbul, Turkey, with a stop in Ephesus along the way. We noted that the location of Istanbul on the globe is the dividing line between Asia and Europe and the not-too-distant location of the troubled country of Ukraine. Istanbul is not adjacent to Ukraine, yet it shares a region in middle Europe on the Black Sea, and we were reminded once again of the profound human suffering just northwest of us in Ukraine and in the conflicts in Israel. We asked in our hearts and minds why the Russian invasion was happening. How could such an aggressive action improve the lives of the Russian people? Or anybody's life? What values and convictions could lead a powerful nation to kill innocent people in such a destructive way? How were the souls, the inner life of the people, being impacted, and how would the personhood and identity of the children caught in the middle of this conflict be affected, influenced, and harmed? We ask many of the same questions about the violence in Gaza and the Middle East.

We understood that the leaders of Russia were on their misguided quest to restore the Soviet Union. We also know that even this questionable goal could have been pursued without the nearly total destruction of Ukraine. Perhaps the Russians could have moved in another direction, even aiding in the development of Ukraine without the violence and heavy cost of human life. Was it necessary to kill so many and cause the souls of the Ukrainian people to be so profoundly harmed and filled with fear and even hate, leaving an emotional scar on their souls for the rest of their lives? And was it necessary for Hamas to murder people in the region of Gaza, and for this to ignite military action from Egypt to Iran?

Now, as I write, we are asking a whole range of questions about the conflict in a vast region. How will its continuance improve the life of the citizens of Israel and the surrounding Arab nations? What will this intense suffering and ever-present fear do to the inner life of the Palestinian people who understood and claimed Gaza as their homeland? Will fear and discouragement be their lifelong companions? We ask the same question about the Jewish community in Israel. Will there be a residue of lifelong anxiety and insecurity for the children of all those engaged in the war? Yes, Hamas reignited the conflict and caused great suffering, but might there have been other ways to resist the violent action of Hamas, perhaps a more limited retaliation aimed directly at the militant organization that would not kill and injure so many innocent Palestinians. Such an action may not have run the risk of being expanded into a regional war. We ask, as the military action expands across a vast region and there are the deaths of thousands of innocent people living in their homeland, whether there is a better way to resolve the deep differences that have existed for years in the region. Should the life and welfare of humankind be our deepest value, rather than violent war, killing innocent people in order to gain an advantage in what seems like an endless conflict? There are better ways of living together.

The Bonds of Peace

Our aims and goals for our trip to this region of the world had several components. One for me was to retrace some of the steps of the apostle Paul and learn more about the region in which he travelled and engaged in his ministry. For example, we visited the ruins of Ephesus, walked on the ancient steps of the arena where he had preached, and paused to reflect on his visit. We were inspired by the extent of his travels and the goals of his journeys. Later, following his travels to the region, he—perhaps with a colleague[15]— wrote to the Ephesians and to other newly formed churches in the region: "I therefore, the prisoner in the Lord, beg you to lead a life worthy of the calling to which you have been called, with all humility and gentleness, with patience, bearing with one another in love, making every effort to maintain the unity of the Spirit in the bond of peace" (Eph 4:1–3).

We returned home, resumed our lives, and hoped that there would be peace in that region of the world. It wasn't long before we observed the break in the bond of peace in a location on the southeastern corner of the

---

15. I am aware that Paul may have had some assistance in his writing.

Mediterranean Sea just north of Egypt. As mentioned, Hamas, an aggressive organization seeking liberation for Palestinian people located in the region of Gaza in the south of Israel, unleashed an attack to the north of them in Israel, killing many innocent people. There was a strong and aggressive response by the government of Israel, causing untold misery. Now there is expanded violence and the threat of a larger conflict among the nations in the region.

I lack the experience to say what should be done in the quests for justice and peace by all sides in such a complex setting. I am just a past visitor, with some learning about the region. I may not fully understand all of complexities of the situation, given my background and heritage in another part of the world. Yet, even as one observing from a distance, I wish both sides had found another way to continue the quest to maintain a safe and secure haven for Jewish people, while restoring the rights of the Palestinian people, giving them a safe location in their homeland. The leaders of Hamas did not think that peaceful ways and words would work in changing the aspirations of the Israeli leadership and believed that only violence would catch the attention of the Israeli leaders. It did, with disastrous results! We all fear that both sides have just made their problems more severe and that the violence will continue to cause great suffering.

One wonders if those causing so much suffering might have found an alternative strategy for accomplishing their goals, one that would carefully and diligently negotiate a peaceful settlement to this long conflict, perhaps going to the two-state solution. Might there have been a way to provide a safe home and country for persecuted Jewish people over the centuries, while still respecting the indigenous homeland of the Palestinian people? To be sure, this vision and quest for peaceful coexistence is surrounded by a long history, difficult issues, and intense feelings. Yet we still ask what reason could possibly justify the killing and suffering of so many innocent people.

Part of my responsibilities in my work within the national offices of the Presbyterian Church (USA) in the decade of the 1990s was to support a remarkable elementary and secondary school in the Galilee, the Mar Elias Educational Institutions, founded by the well-known Melkite priest, Abuna Elias Chacour. Over just a little more than a decade, I had the privilege of visiting the region and supporting the school, seeing it develop into one of the finest educational institutions in the region of the Galilee and, indeed, in all of Israel. Abuna (Father) Chacour's vision was to respect the need of the Jewish people to have a safe haven in Israel/Palestine and to honor the need of the Palestinian people to receive an excellent education and live out their lives in a safe and secure homeland. For him, it didn't seem like too much to ask of these two groups of people, Palestinians and Jews, to work diligently to secure such a goal.

I was deeply taken by Abuna Chacour's vision, and, as far as possible, I endeavored in my work to help realize this wise and compassionate hope by providing the resources that were available to me to offer. I was profoundly moved by the hope of many Palestinian friends that they could find a way to live in peace with their Jewish cousins, perhaps even in two adjacent states. It almost goes without saying that I was motivated by the Jewish-Palestinian prophet from Nazareth, living in the first century, who said, "Blessed are the peacemakers, for they will be called children of God" (Matt 5:9). We might say, "Profoundly contented are those who find nonviolent ways to overcome conflict and to create social realities that empower those with differences to find peaceful solutions. This is truly the work of God." Jesus may have said it better.

It was the enlightened and divine-centered soul of the prophet and teacher from Nazareth, Jesus, and the missionary from Tarsus, Paul, who believed that all of humankind are the children of the God of love and deserve to live in harmony and peace. Our goal in these pages is to reflect on how the journey of our souls in perilous times may be patterned after the enlightened souls of the Prince of Peace and the teaching of his missionary follower, Paul of Tarsus. How might following the model of Jesus and the teaching of Paul lead us to lives grounded and motivated by compassion and justice? How might their example empower us to continue the sacred work of healing and reconciliation in perilous times? How might it help disenfranchised groups and even troubled nations to find solutions to conflicts and to pursue ways to create a social order that nurtures justice and seeks a peaceful life for all?

We turn now in an effort to inquire about ways to overcome the damaging consequences of the forces of violence and how to navigate through the destructive forces of our world in order to inculcate and restore the values of peace and reconciliation. Our focus will be on finding ways to move away from the harm caused by violence, although always in the background, to a setting in which there is a peaceful environment in which all can flourish. It must be based on our values of truth, love, peace, and justice. It must honor our gifts and talents and empower us to become people of wisdom and compassion. The setting must honor our very soul so that it may be formed by love and justice and without the fear that drives us to resort to systematic injustice and destructive violence. Violent warfare should almost never be the means by which humans seek to find solutions to their differences.

Rather, we should join with others who seek to find peaceful ways to create a more just and humane home, country, and world. Our emphasis will be on nurturing the souls of those whom we serve and to create a climate of peace and hope. We know that there are many other strategies, some of which would say to us that our goal is naïve and will hardly make a difference. You can't change the outlook and pattern of violence of Hamas or the current government of Israel with conversation and references to hope and peace.

Perhaps there are elements of naïveté in our strategy, and we must continue to learn about all of the realistic peace strategies. We nevertheless follow the prophet and teacher from Nazareth in seeking to help those who serve the cause of peace to cultivate deep faith in God, seek compassionate wisdom for those in their circle of nearness, and to pursue a strategy that is committed to the truth and integrity in all aspects of life.[16] Our goal is to support the profound commitment to create a caring environment for all those who continue to live in the region. We want to lend a hand in Israel/Palestine, and perhaps the best way for many of us who cannot be on the ground in these conflicts is to be primarily concerned about how we educate and nurture the souls of all those in every corner of our world who want to join us in seeking a just and compassionate society and a world of peace.

Models of Human Development and Spiritual Formation

Across the centuries, there have been a wide range of models in both the study of human development and for practices in spiritual formation. They have not always been linked or integrated—that is, there have been a number of suggested patterns for spiritual formation, as well as a range of models of human development, and only on occasion have they been integrated or viewed as having a common base and shared goals. I have discovered in my study of these models and in my own personal experience that there is a great deal of commonality among those who begin with a spiritual foundation and those who start with a developmental psychology understanding. At times, those articulating these theories of human growth and development have carefully articulated differences, suggesting, for example, as in the case of Sigmund Freud, that the religious component in human growth and development is often a superstitious element and an escape from facing reality. It has also been the case that those articulating a spiritual pathway of growth and development have ignored and at times even rejected more secular, although accurate, descriptions of human development.

My lean is toward finding an integrative pattern, allowing for diversity, and then finding and integrating the common threads that provide an

---

16. Was Jesus naïve? Or was he profoundly wise?

insightful theory of human growth and development that has a spiritual component, even a spiritual center. The goals in this quest are to find accurate patterns of growth that lead to health and maturity and avoid those that tend to be narrow, sectarian, exclusive, and controlling. The assumptions we make and the language we use in describing these pathways to health and maturity may differ, with some starting from a classical base, e.g., Freudian/Jungian in the psychological domain or Franciscan/ Roman Catholic in the spiritual domain, and others using more contemporary models.

A full integration of these outlooks, the secular and the religious on human growth and development, may not be altogether possible, but the effort has been judged to be very important by many. The books on this theme are extensive. Full agreement may not be reached on metaphysical foundations, but there may be more room for integration when the goal is to use these outlooks and methods in ways that lead to an emphasis on healing, health, justice, and peace. There are and have been models, rooted in these goals, which have let some of the debate about foundations and starting points subside. I am grateful that those with a psychological starting point and those with a spiritual starting point have found common pathways to maturity; common ground has been found.[17] For example, there is a profound effort at integration classically expressed in the works of William James and Carl Jung. I have been influenced by the stages-of-development model, and have found the more secular model in the work of Erik Erickson used and expanded in a spiritual way by James Fowler to be a positive way of integration that has led to a personal understanding of spiritual growth toward health and healing.[18]

Our task then is to review some of the ways across history that leaders in the Christian church have used to inform and transform their followers, preparing them to be spiritual leaders who are engaged in creating a more just social order and peaceful world. As we learn from these models of suggested patterns and pathways, we want to engage in finding ways to integrate the spiritual models and the contemporary models and patterns of human growth and development. We move now to a review of some of the ways that various Christian denominations and collaborative groups have chosen to address the challenge of living wisely in perilous times, ways that have

---

17. I have gradually been giving my personal books to university libraries, and in arranging these contributions, I have found that I have at least a hundred books that base their theme on the integration of spiritual and psychological insight. The bookstores are full of them.

18. It is important to acknowledge that the theory of stages of life has been challenged and been subject to scholarly criticism; it is not currently in vogue, although I find it helpful. See Fowler, *Stages of Faith*.

the potential to enrich the lives of those seeking a spiritual center, many of whom will then engage in creating a more humane and just social order.

Questions for Reflection and Discussion

1. In what ways might the life and teachings of Jesus give us an ethical pattern to follow in our lives? If so, what might be its components?
2. What were the most basic values of Jesus, guiding him as he engaged in his ministry?
3. How much does our background (family, location, culture, time in history, etc.) shape the way we think and live our lives?
4. Do you think that military violence ever works as a method to preserve the spiritual values and the moral and ethical life of a country?
5. In what ways, if you were the president of the United State, would you guide the country's foreign policy in the Middle East?

Key Terms and Concepts

1. Golden Rule: The teaching of Jesus that we should behave toward others as we want them to behave toward us.
2. The Way of Jesus: A term used by the first Christians that emphasized that Jesus was guided by the fundamental values of truth, love, justice, and peace, and that we should follow his example.
3. The bonds of peace: The deep conviction that there are fundamental values, which, if commonly held, will preserve peace. What are its components for individuals, regions, and countries?
4. Palestine: The name of a region on the eastern side of the Mediterranean Sea (Middle East). It has been given the status of a country, but Palestine has been reduced in size as it has shared the region with Israel.
5. Israel: The name of the country on the eastern side of the Mediterranean Sea (Middle East), one viewed as being the homeland of Jewish people.

Suggestions for Reference and Reading

1. *Blood Brothers* by Elias Chacour
2. *The Historical Jesus: The Life of a Mediterranean Jewish Peasant* by John Dominic Crossan
3. *Jesus and the Politics of Roman Palestine* by Richard A. Horsley
4. *Jesus Through Middle Eastern Eyes: Cultural Studies in the Gospels* by Kenneth E. Bailey
5. *Jesus: Uncovering the Life, Teachings, and Relevance of a Religious Revolutionary* by Marcus J. Borg

CHAPTER TWO

On Being Informed
Assessing the Alternative Ways to Well-Being

Thomas said to him, "Lord, we do not know where you are going. How can we know the way?" Jesus said to him, "I am the way, and the truth, and the life."

John 14:5–6

Educational Models Within the Christian Church: Past and Present

I WANT TO SUGGEST several approaches used by the Christian church across the years for cultivating a deep and profound spiritual life in and for its members. There are many approaches, and they have varied greatly in that the church is a world church with approaches to this mission which partially reflect the many settings and cultures in which the individual churches were founded and located.

I offer this brief summary with an awareness that, as we engage in the journey of our soul, we do so in ways with which we are familiar and have been placed before us by those whom we trust. So, our odyssey will have many regional distinctives and in the early stages will reflect the assumptions of our time and place. It was certainly so as I began my journey. I was invited to place my faith in God and follow the pathway of Jesus, although the understanding of God and the pathway of Jesus had high school language and a California look. It was where I grew up and where the youth group and church that guided me were located. The framework was a kind and caring youth organization that placed a strong emphasis on friendship and a supportive community, one that suggested the simple steps of reading Scripture, joyful singing, personal prayer, and attending a weekly gathering of other high school students beginning their spiritual journey. It was the right approach at the right time for me, and I look back in gratitude for the care and guidance I received.

It was during my university years that I was able to deepen my faith and explore the more complex intellectual questions regarding faith and the challenge of sustaining a life-giving faith in a rapidly changing and perilous world. My understanding of the ways of deepening my faith and understanding my journey began to expand. One exposure I had, and an important one, was the way my simple faith could be understood and expanded by integrating it with the university courses I was taking in human growth and development in the social sciences. I became persuaded that the way a mature person is understood in the disciplines of human growth and development and what it means to be a mature Christian have much in common, although they were not identical. In fact, I learned that teachers and scholars in both domains have learned from one another, and the learning has deepened and nuanced the way maturity is understood and described. I am so grateful that my journey contained both the simple faith of following Jesus in a life of love and the profound insights of the disciplines of human growth and development. Jesus and Jung could be integrated. It was and is a combination that has provided me with a foundation for the journey of my soul.

One other fine source for understanding healthy growth and development was the way that the other religions of the human family were moving out of their regional settings in Asia and the Middle East and becoming studied, even endorsed, by many thoughtful people in the West. For example, I found myself very interested in the religious thought and practice of the native people of the world. Living in Alaska for several years gave me the opportunity to gain an understanding of the religious thought of Alaska natives. In particular, I was moved by their deep personal understanding of nature and the ways that the seasons and the natural surroundings of their world had sacred meaning. They saw with some clarity the presence of the divine in the beauty of their mountains, lakes, and rivers, and the dramatic seasonal changes gave them a pattern for life.

Still another major source of my reflections came to me through the travels to many parts of the world and the opportunity to observe and participate in the thought and practice of several other religious traditions. I was fascinated by their thoughtful belief systems and the deep commitment I observed in their practices. With many others, I found myself reading the books of the Dalai Lama and Thich Nhat Hanh, and found the writing of John L. Esposito, a non-Muslim, on Islam informative and even fascinating. As I traveled through Asia and the Arab countries of the world, I carefully observed the spiritual practices of people in these religions. On returning home to my work in higher education, I was asked to teach the course in world religions and did so with a better foundation and great interest.

It was during my years of graduate study and my work with students as a campus minister that I began to reflect more deeply on the Judeo-Christian belief that humans were created in the image of God. It is a concept that understood that humans have within them the positive qualities of maturity such as basic consciousness, self-understanding, ethical norms, and the capacity to love and serve. I learned that one part of the journey of the soul was to draw upon this image and cultivate the qualities of its presence. I discovered a wonderful affinity between the spiritual qualities of "faith, hope, and love" (1 Cor 13:13) and the way maturity is understood in the social sciences.[1] In time, I realized that my own faith tradition could be enriched by doing the hard work of comparison and integration.

As we do this integrative work, we are invited to ask, How might the Christian theological understanding of spiritual growth, the social scientific understanding of human growth and development, and the rich traditions of the religions of the world be brought into a common frame of reference and deepen our understanding of this very important domain in our understanding of ourselves and the world around us? And then, how might we suggest programmatic initiatives that could be extremely helpful and valuable to those who are seeking a spiritual way? Each of these descriptions of patterns of growth have distinctive features and vocabularies, yet there are many similarities as they describe ways to encourage growth toward maturity.

In the context of Christian spirituality, the description of the ways and means to maturity have the elements of the Bible's recording of the history of the Hebrew people and the new dimensions that were present in the life and teaching of Jesus and his followers. Many of these ways and means have been put in the modern clothing of the social sciences, compared with the

---

1. There is a vast amount of literature on this integrative work. Most recently, Dr. Lisa Miller of Columbia University, in her book *The Awakened Brain*, has engaged in this integrative work. Another resource for me has been the extraordinary writing of Ken Wilbur, a person who has done the work of integration as well as anybody I know. See his book *Religion of Tomorrow*.

other religions of the world, and are now models currently being used by the church.[2]

These patterns in the Christian literature of the church have been studied and practiced worldwide and have a long history. Indeed, almost every denomination or branch of the church across its history has unique features, has a specific identity, and a special set of concerns for educating its members. Even a local church may have some distinctives in that it exists in an historical era, a specific setting with cultural norms, belongs to a larger frame of reference such as a denomination, and has a measurable size and class structure with guiding pastors and priests who have their own heritage and training.

Yet it is possible, as one studies these several models of Christian growth and development in these diverse churches, to place them in families while still being sensitive to differences linked to their beliefs, history, and culture. As I place them in families, I do so primarily on the basis of their historical and theological legacy, yet I also recognize that they have drawn upon other religious traditions and contemporary methods and strategies of human growth and development to educate and nurture their members. These models, past and present, influence and partially shape the identity of a church and the active life of its members. Given this collaboration, the larger church community has had and continues to have several goals in the mission of empowering their followers to become spiritually mature and whole. I want to mention five:[3]

Goal One: Understanding the essential content of the faith: As one who has served the church's ministry in education,[4] I have become especially sensitive to how important the ministry of education was and is in guiding its members to and on the pathway to the mature, responsible, and fulfilling life. At the center of this educational mission was and is the goal of helping people of all ages to understand the biblical message of God's good creation, God's entrance into human history in the stories of the Hebrew Bible, and

---

2. The religious models are often integrated with more secular models, and rightly so in that spiritual models and secular models share a common understanding of the dimensions of human development, although may use a different language. It is wise to remind ourselves that truth speaks many languages. Once again I would point to the work of Ken Wilbur, e.g., *Sex, Ecology, Spirituality*, although he is just one among many who are doing this important work.

3. There may be dozens of these approaches, each having subtle and distinctive features.

4. I served primarily in the domain of church-related college/university education with some participation in theological education. I also briefly served in congregations with responsibility for middle and high school education and have been a keen observer of the education of children in the church.

the special place of the life, teaching, and ministry of Jesus and the way that he modeled and gave guidance for the ways to pursue a mature, ethical, and spiritual life. These areas of knowledge are the primary content of the curriculum used in the mission of Christian churches for cultivating the spiritual life of its members, with the term *spiritual formation* often used as a category of the way one becomes spiritually mature.

Goal Two: Understanding how this guidance for spiritual maturity comes to us in the Bible: Drawing upon this awareness that the content of the Bible provides spiritual guidance that leads to maturity, I want to provide a few examples of the ways this guidance comes to us in the several types of literature in the Bible, and how at times it may even be harmful if not taught with sensitivity and historical understanding.[5] The second goal of spiritual formation, then, is using the Bible as the textbook and the foundational curriculum for spiritual formation. In order to accomplish this task, the church must read and use the Bible with great care; the literature is very complex and there are the challenges of interpretation.[6] The literature spans several centuries, reflects the worldview of the era, has many authors, and describes events that come from different countries, cultures, and languages. In addition, there are several genres, ranging from history to poetry, from wisdom to story, and from exhortation to ethical guidance. Further, this material in the Bible generally comes to us in our language, our culture, and through our religious heritage, and it may easily be misunderstood and misused as it moves from its original language and culture to contemporary life.

These different types of literature and their interpretation through translation make learning the content and spiritual message of the Bible and the church somewhat difficult.[7] The Bible is a composite of literature from different times and places. This literature has a faith orientation, and

---

5. Across the centuries, the Christian church has engaged in the mission of guiding its members to become mature and live an ethical life. Occasionally, mistakes have been made in this endeavor when the church has become exclusive and cultic, imposing ways for its members to change their behavior and conform to a tribal pattern. On the whole, however, the church's ministry has led most of its followers to the mature life with the capacity to love others as they need and want to be loved.

6. My doctoral dissertation at the University of Edinburgh centered on understanding how our prior knowledge of and assumptions about life and history shape the way we interpret the Bible. The first point was "a lot." Therefore, I take just a bit more space on this point in that the Bible can be used and abused.

7. There are many teachers in the Christian church who say that the message of the Bible is quite simple: God loves you and this love is expressed in biblical history and the coming of Jesus. There is some truth in this statement, yet as one goes beyond the simple affirmation, the task of becoming spiritually mature may become complex and demanding.

we have some preunderstanding that may guide us in positive ways, but it may also cause some distortion of the essential message of the Bible. There is, for example, the historical accounts of how the Hebrew people interacted with the regional governments, yet this history is not present for us in a purely descriptive form based on the methodology of critical historical study. It comes to us rather as a faith statement expressing the presence of God's engagement in the history, and it comes to us in what is believed to be the unfolding story of God's way of entering into the world. We read these stories in faith, although we also listen to the critical historian who must engage in study with a rigorous methodology and assign causes and outcomes on the basis of the historical record, not necessarily using the material exclusively to guide people of faith. "Joshua Fit the Battle of Jericho," a lively little song, is often used with children. Yet, looking at the text, there may be ways of understanding different from the way it is sung to children in our churches. Did Joshua just invade Jericho or did he take an action that was rooted in God's guidance? We live with the challenge of hermeneutics, which is to discern what truly happened and then how it might give us guidance for our journey of faith.[8]

As we read about God entering into human history in the Bible, we discover a great deal of material that speaks to political and military events and issues that are given a particular point of view based on the assumptions of the interpreter. Often there is a favored side, and it describes the complex interaction of competing nations with a goal that is given by the author.

In these accounts, there are reflections on nature, history, the formation of groups of people, and complex human relations. The biblical literature addresses the extremes of deep peace and profound suffering, how to manage stressful situations, and ways to celebrate the joys of life. There is much to learn about life from this literature, yet these accounts were written from a cultural and faith perspective and come to us from preunderstanding of ancient cultures and different languages. They are written in several genres, and as we read them through our faith perspective, we must do so in a careful and informed way, avoiding the risk of using the material in a distorted and occasionally even a harmful way, not uncommon in some of our churches.

The undergirding message is that God has been and is a guiding presence and invites loyalty to and faith in the teaching. There is the recurring theme of God's unconditional love for all of humanity, present in the Psalms of the Hebrew Bible and uniquely expressed in Jesus. It is in the New

8. Hermeneutics is the complex process of understanding the best ways to interpret ancient literature and how this literature crosses time into a new era with meaning for the present.

Testament that we view his life-giving ways, read his profound teaching, and are given an account of his unique expression of love, given special meaning at the end of his life.

In the Hebrew Bible, there is the story of creation, the journey of Abraham and Sarah to Israel/Palestine, the emancipation from slavery in Egypt under the leadership of Moses, and his teaching of the Ten Commandments. As time passes in different locations and intrigue, we are introduced to the place of the law in securing justice, the wonderful stories of the biblical characters including King David, the adventures of Esther becoming a queen, and the quest for peace and justice in the teaching of the prophets.[9]

The New Testament tells the story of Jesus and the ways in which his life and teaching can inform and motivate us to live a compassionate and wise life, a theme that is amplified in the Epistles. There is a profound understanding in the New Testament that God will not forsake us; there is a life-giving message of hope as we live in perilous times. However, as we read, we take into account that there is a faith dimension and point of view in what was written, one that goes well beyond just listing events or writing history. The literature has a simple message, yet one that invites the critical work of the scholar of history.

Goal Three: Understanding the context: The Jewish people of faith and the Christian church in its several manifestations have sought to make the biblical message quite contextual, sensitive to the reality that the synagogues and the churches undertake in their mission of nurturing their members in a particular set of historical circumstances, many of which are perilous. In particular, the educational mission of the church seeks to provide a spiritual message that empowers believers to understand and commit to a faith orientation that enables them to live wisely and cope with the challenges of contemporary life. The church and the synagogue use the Bible to educate their members with an informed and personal faith that gives them a road map for their demanding and complex journey. The Bible guides the leaders and members of the religious communities to have a faith orientation that is informed and relevant, one that provides perspective on local problems, regional and international conflicts, current political realities that divide the country, and dramatic climate changes that are profoundly threatening.

In addition, the church and the temple are called upon to be a source of prophetic challenge and wisdom and to comfort those with deep anxiety about the troubled times in which we live. Even the children in the church are able to grasp the church's mission to aid those who suffer from limited

---

9. See Marilynne Robinson's extraordinary interpretation of Genesis in her book *Reading Genesis*.

income, experience poverty and hunger, and face prejudice and even the threat to their lives. The stories of Jesus have a message that is engaging for children, and he told his followers to let the children come to him. The adults of the church are able to have deep empathy for those who suffer and are able to identify with the way that Jesus gave special attention to these populations.

This dimension of the church's mission in education has provided guidance to its members about how to manage in settings of great suffering, including devastating poverty, widespread hunger, the lack of basic resources for a healthy life, and the way to address injustice. The church, in order to be faithful in its mission to care for those who suffer, is necessarily drawn into these serious problems at almost every level and needs to educate its members about how to help those who are disenfranchised, or, in many cases, those who have had to cope with and address profound social problems. It has often done so, as mentioned above, with the remarkable stories of the way Jesus cared for those who were poor and suffered from hunger and disease.[10]

Goal Four: Prophetic education: An integral part of the educational mission in the local congregation is to inform and guide its members on how they might lend a hand and help the people who suffer from these harmful conditions. It should engage in sensitive ways, using the resources of the church to urge those in power to seek peace in settings that are threatened by corporate violence and change the social conditions in settings where people suffer from injustice. Hence, the church's mission in education was and continues to be prophetic in its mission. Undergirded by the deep and comprehensive values of shalom, the church's mission in education teaches its members how to use its influence with those in positions of power who could influence social structures and find peaceful solutions to solve the deep divide between nations and militant factions.

I have become increasingly sensitive to the reality that many of those who lead nations and corporations often used methods of communicating their mission and products with mis- and disinformation.[11] This tendency is omnipresent, and the educational mission of the church in its prophetic role is needed to challenge these false and interest-driven descriptions of the harsh realities and forces in the world in which we live. As far as possible,

---

10. See, for example, the insightful books *Jesus and the Politics of Roman Palestine* by Richard A. Horsley and *The Practice of Jesus* by Hugo Echegaray.

11. This situation is a current social problem that carries great risk for our society. See Tim Alberta's book *The Kingdom, the Power, and the Glory* for an account of the misguided beliefs and actions of Christian nationalism.

the church's mission is to provide authentic and accurate information in order to face directly these harsh realities and challenge the false interpretation of them. It almost goes without saying that Jesus spoke directly to those in power and urged his followers to speak honestly and act with integrity.

Goal Five: Serving the common good: As I traveled internationally in my work in the church, I become increasingly aware that the church's educational mission was taking place in a world largely controlled by those who are advancing their self-interest rather than serving the common good. There are certainly exceptions to this situation, yet we see daily how governments and certainly global corporations are guided by few of the universal values of peace, compassion, justice, and an equitable sharing of wealth. Those guiding the educational mission of the church, with others from many other national and international groups, were called upon to give attention to and question the self-serving strategies of leaders, corporations, and countries. In fact, the contemporary context is much like the church's mission in education of the first generation of the church with teachers such as the apostles Paul and John who had learned from Jesus how to challenge those in power profiting from unjust ways, and articulate a way for the church to be a voice for those who suffer and the need to resist and change unjust social structures.

The church's educational mission across history has had to affirm and demonstrate the church's deepest values, ones rooted in the great stories of the Hebrew Bible, the life and teachings of Jesus, the redemptive character of his last days, and the apostles' interpretation of these events. How might the values of commitment to the truth, just social structures, and programs of compassion and care become a strategy for addressing a world in crisis? Part of the educational mission of the church was to articulate and model these values, defend them, and demonstrate how they could take form and shape in tangible programs. Many of these programs can be within the educational program of the church, although this ministry often was in the form of influence, as the church helped to shape the values of the leaders and the culture in which they lived. The authentic voice of compassion, peace, and justice needs to be heard.

Strategies for the Church's Mission in Education

The church's mission in education and spiritual formation across history has taken shape in a variety of ways given the realities in the settings in which the church worked. The mission has been grounded in the belief that the Bible is its primary resource. Because the church has been and is diverse and complex, several different approaches to its educational mission have been needed and used. I have placed these strategies for education and transformation into five families, noting as well that these families may not fully describe and contain the vast array of approaches to assist its members to be informed, to mature, and to understand the story of God's engagement with humankind. The mission of the church has been as varied as the several cultures in which the church was present.

Sacramental: Across the centuries and in the present, one widely used model of Christian nurture and development, especially in the Roman Catholic Church, is one that is called *sacramental*.[12] A *sacrament* is understood to be a sacred rite in which God is present, and that the believer encounters God and is nurtured by God's spirit by participating in the rite.

The sacrament, as the central component in spiritual practices, may come to the community of faith in the cultural norms of the present or patterns of the past. The celebration has had differences over time and in different locations, but it nevertheless remains central to Roman Catholic worship and nurture. The Catholic Church is global and, therefore, has a rich diversity of beliefs and practices, often influenced and shaped by the presence of the culture and history of the region in which it serves.[13] I keenly remember being present in a Roman Catholic worship service in New Delhi, one that had chants, singing, and even some dancing that was Indian in expression, yet universal in its undergirding beliefs. It has been my great privilege to have been in worship services in nearly every continent, and I have had warm feelings as I have tried to be a participant rather than just a detached observer. What I did learn was that most of the churches in the Roman Catholic tradition, although quite diverse, did include the belief in the sacramental approach, one that affirms that a true believer encounters God in the sacrament and is transformed by this encounter with the divine.

The Roman Catholic approach to guiding its participants in Christian growth and development has had and continues to have diversity, yet there are common elements across history and the diversity of cultures. While some of these regional churches have become more progressive in spirit, they are still guided by the doctrines articulated in the Council of Trent

---

12. The educational mission of the Roman Catholic Church has many dimensions and strategies and is certainly not limited to those which are sacramental in character, although it is that part of the church which has fully developed a sacramental model.

13. See the list of beliefs and practices in the entry titled "Roman Catholicism: The Roman Catholic Church and Its Theology," in Patte, *Cambridge Dictionary of Christianity*, 1079–103. This article carefully traces the contextual beliefs and practices in the Roman Catholic Church in the different countries and continents.

(1545–1563), although modified or at least restated by the Catholic Church several times since the Council.[14]

There have been enormous changes in regional cultures and ways of understanding the world, not the least of which has been the worldwide rise of the scientific understanding of all that exists and the strong intellectual current that sets aside religious views and turns to a more secular and evolutionary understanding of the world. The worldwide Catholic Church has had to respond, guiding regional churches with a new articulation of the beliefs and practices, carefully expressing them in the context of secular modernity and the particular culture in which the congregations exist.

The common and surprising element in the Catholic world, even with these great changes of understanding and the diversity of responses to the modern/postmodern world, is that the churches still affirm the sacramental character of its primary religious rites. They continue to believe that the sacramental practices have the presence of the divine in them and are more than mere symbolic expressions or general observations that God cares about the world. The sacraments, central to Catholic worship and practice, are believed to be transforming because one truly encounters God in them, and they are the way that Christians hear the divine voice and are transformed.

The sacraments are undergirded by a catechism or statement of beliefs, one that began with the Apostles' Creed and was supported by the Decalogue (Ten Commandments), and the Lord's Prayer. These resources are supported by timely and regional statements of faith, designed to bring the faith to the lives of those in different cultures, using the Bible as the guide for sermons and community life. The distinctive cultural norms are present in different parts of the world, although there are common elements, rooted in the belief that the sacraments have within them the saving power to sustain and transform the believer. Christian growth and development in the Roman Catholic Church are cultivated in many ways, yet participation in the sacraments and religious rites that confer special graces are central to the goal of empowering Christians to engage in a spiritual life that leads to spiritual maturity.

The creedal beliefs or statements of faith (catechisms), the ethical teaching articulated in the Bible, the Ten Commandments, and the ethical life and teaching of Jesus in the Christian Bible are also central to Christian growth. With an awareness that a few descriptive words will not fully articulate the sacramental view, it is important to underline that there are many

---

14. The current pope, Francis, following two or three progressive popes, has continued to have a progressive style and cares deeply about the mission of social justice.

other forms of ministry that are integral to the Roman Catholic Church as it guides its followers in spiritual growth and development. The heart of the Roman Catholic view is that God is believed to be present, that the believer is profoundly grateful for God's healing and nurturing presence, and that one receives God's presence in a deeply devotional way as one participates in various ministries of the church.

The affirmation and authority of the faith of the apostles: There is a related second pattern of beliefs and practices designed to nurture spiritual growth and practice, one that is present in the Orthodox tradition of the Christian church. It is that branch of the church which was formed in eastern Europe with its center in what was then Constantinople and is now Istanbul. This branch of the church formed because there were some deep differences held by Christians in central Europe with the church leadership in Rome. A schism occurred in AD 1054, one that came about as a culmination of these disagreements. These Orthodox Christians argued that the Roman bishop (the pope) did not have full authority over the life of all of the church, and that regional bishops were better able to guide the church in the particular settings in which they were present. The authority for clarifying the true beliefs and practices of the church community is best guided by regional bishops.

The Orthodox Church understood its articulation of faith and practice as being the original apostolic faith and that its decrees reflected an uninterrupted living tradition of true Christianity. There were both theological beliefs and patterns of discipleship that were partially different from those in the Roman Catholic position, the theological ones having to do with Christology and the practices focusing on using the vernacular language in the liturgy. Deep down, there were the convictions that the authority for orthodox rites and practices was regional rather than central, and that the rites and practices were apostolic, expressing the beliefs and practices of the original apostles.[15]

The Eastern Orthodox church continued to emphasize the centrality of the sacraments (rites) and remained committed to the ethical teaching of the Ten Commandments and the teaching of Jesus contained in the Gospels and amplified by the apostles, and especially Paul in the Epistles. The Orthodox Church's way of being Christian may be described as a quest to trust and follow the original teaching of Jesus and the apostles, being careful about how it understands authority by giving power to regional bishops, and being faithful in the ways its churches honor the sacraments and guide

---

15. See the article on eastern Orthodoxy in Doniger, *Encyclopedia of World Religions*, 309–10.

their members by affirming the apostolic message. A second word then on our list is *authority*, giving it to the original apostles and being committed to their teaching. The church nurtures its members and guides them in their development by being true to the original group of apostles that were with Jesus. The key word for them, and for many other Christian groups, is where truth is lodged, and in their view, it was present with the original group that was with Jesus. The authority for the ways the churches guide and educate their members is by the careful process of preserving and teaching the original message of Jesus.

Saved by faith: A few centuries after the break of Eastern Orthodoxy from the Roman Catholic Church, there was another major division and a third development within Christianity called the Protestant Reformation. It, too, came about because of different ways of understanding and interpreting the Bible and practicing the Christian faith. This movement rooted its break with the Roman Catholic Church and less so with the Orthodox tradition over how one is justified and becomes righteous before God by faith. There were many leaders of the movement, although the names of Martin Luther (Germany) and John Calvin (Switzerland) are central.

Martin Luther (1483–1546) focused his reform on how it is that we find and make peace with God; and it was his own struggle to find peace of mind that became a motivating force in shaping his understanding. He said, drawing upon his own dedicated and soulful attempt, that it is not possible for us in our own strength to be fully righteous before God. We have an inner nature that is in many ways sinful and we cannot measure up to the righteousness expected by God. Yet we are judged and then declared righteous by faith in the redemptive acts of Jesus Christ. Being righteous before God is not a human achievement but a free gift from God, and as we receive that gift of grace grounded in the unconditional love of God by faith, we are transformed and empowered to live the Christian life. He argued strongly for this deep truth, and it became the center of the Protestant Reformation.

John Calvin (1509–1564) largely endorsed the views of Martin Luther, as did several other Reformers. As a scholar and preacher, Calvin continued the Reformation emphasis on salvation by faith in the redemptive events of Jesus. As with Luther, he emphasized that we lead the Christian life by being faithful, empowered by the spirit of God, rather than exclusively by our own efforts. This outlook reflects the true interpretation of the New Testament, which is the authoritative guide to belief and practice. As we are transformed by faith, we then gain guidance by the authoritative New Testament, not by a gathering of bishops or the historical creeds, although many of the creedal statements of faith may be helpful. It is by faith that we have inner peace and become transformed. Being truthful and loyal to the teaching of the Bible is the essence of being Christian.

The Free Church: Experiential with a distinctive identity: In part, influenced by Martin Luther and John Calvin, the Reformation expanded and took shape in Europe. It was not long before those who were shaped by the reforms in Europe emigrated to America and other parts of the world, bringing their new faith orientation with them. There were many expressions of presence of the church's teaching in the Protestant movements, and they became an integral part of life and thought of this new country. However, as one might expect from the revolutionary spirit of these settlers in America, there was not always agreement and collaboration between these new religious groups. The Puritans, for example, were quite firm that their understanding of Christian faith was the way to believe and practice.

This situation was made even more complex when a variety of groups broke off from the Roman Catholic and Reformed denominations. It was a setting in which people, shaped by deep conviction and a revolutionary spirit, formed their own version of Christian beliefs and practices. Often, in these new movements, there was an emphasis on having a true spiritual experience of the presence and power of God. This became another way for the Christian church to take expression, as separate and faithful groups challenged some of the authority and teaching of a central church body and found their own way of understanding how their Christian faith may affirm its beliefs and provide direction for Christian living.

A common name that is attached to these many groups is the Free Church, and these groups were committed to their distinctive features, but shared a deep belief that one's religion must be experiential, not just loyal to a particular sectarian expression of the faith.

In addition to focusing on a deep experience of God's presence, they often had another dimension of their faith that gave them a more distinctive identity. I'll mention just two examples of this larger movement, and there were several others, many of which had quite distinctive features, and many of them continue to be active in the present. One group, well-known as an active part of the larger Christian movement, is the Baptist Church. Originating in Europe, this movement is now understood as largely a mainline Protestant denomination in the United States, in Europe, and other parts of the world. In its earlier formation in the seventeenth century, the Baptists put an emphasis on free will and the choice of an individual believer to place faith in the saving events of the life, death, and resurrection of Jesus. This was the way to salvation and growth in the spiritual life.

As the sectarian movement grew, it continued to emphasize the need for individuals to have a conversion experience of divine grace. The theological foundation for their beliefs was pretty much in line with the other Christian movements, although what did distinguish them was the need for a conversion experience, based on biblical authority and the liberty of the individual conscience. The sacraments were practiced much like the other mainline Christian movements, although they were viewed as a symbolic and worshipful event rather than the full experience of the divine presence. The authority for belief and practice as a Baptist was local, in the congregations, and there was a commitment to understand all Christians as having a ministry. There was ordination for special callings to ministry, and it occurred within the local congregation, although recognized by the denomination.

The inclination to reform continued, and there were others who participated in more sectarian movements. They had distinctive beliefs or practices which gave them their identity. For example, there was the movement of the Friends, often known as the Quakers, who had no clergy and met silently in small groups, quietly waiting for the leading of the Holy Spirit. The Quakers continue to be an active movement, often understood as the leaders of the quest for peace within the larger Christian community.

There were other movements within the church, often motivated to find the "true" teaching of Jesus and the apostles, some stressing ethical patterns of life and many seeking ways to be more spiritual. One representative group illustrating this tendency became known as the Brethren, with historical roots in Germany. There are now other representative groups stressing the need for a deep and true spirituality, ones that tend to remove themselves from the society. They place an emphasis on maintaining their distinctive Christian way of life by separating from mainline culture and emphasizing a dedication to living a spiritual life apart from the negative influence of society.[16] They stressed the separation of church and state and encouraged a deep personal faith, simplicity of life, and a commitment to peace.

These small groups were somewhat diverse in their origin, practices, and beliefs, yet were integral to the larger Christian movement although distinctive in their spiritual practices and beliefs. In fact, many of their practices were already present in the Christian churches, yet these Christians sensed the need to remove themselves from "the ways of the world" and be separate in order to sustain their distinctive way of life.

---

16. In fact, there were many movements, often separate and maintaining their own authority for determining correct belief and practice.

The worldwide Christian community has manifested itself in quite diverse ways and often has emphasized alternative ways to deepen its Christian life and to educate its members with a range of approaches. These smaller groups, often separate from the mainline Christian community, have the following features:

1. They often placed a strong emphasis on one aspect of Christian belief and practice, such as the need to have a salvation experience, as in the Baptist movement, or to live apart from mainline society in order to cultivate and maintain a true spiritual life. These groups have felt the need to remove themselves form the mainstream of life in society, living in a community of believers, and preserving and advancing one's spiritual life. Frequently, these movements have their origin either in the native and indigenous traditions or from groups that have recently immigrated from another country and maintained the distinctive beliefs and practices of their heritage. Others, claiming they are the true expression of the way humans relate to God, have certain fundamentals that must be affirmed.[17] The fundamentalist movement continues in many parts of the world, and some of its views are now advocated and taught in evangelical churches, with less emphasis on separation from the culture and a desire to preach and teach the apostolic and biblical faith.

2. They have emphasized a need to be led by the spirit of God, often having an experience which confirmed their beliefs and was devotional in nature. The Methodist movement is mainstream, although some of its members felt a need to remove themselves from mainline Methodists in order to stress true spirituality. The Nazarene Church is an example and represents a group that felt that the heart of Christian faith was to have an additional experiential transformation by the spirit of God called sanctification, a description of how one is filled with the presence of the spirit of God. There was another group, often called the Holiness movement, which understood that speaking in tongues was a manifestation of the Holy Spirit, a special divine experience. This tendency is present in the Assembly of God churches, viewing these experiences as a divine gift and the mark of spirituality. It is shared with many other churches who represent quite a large movement called Pentecostal that emphasizes the spontaneous presence of God's spirit in their lives. The worship in these churches tends to be charismatic

---

17. For example, they stress that the Bible is divinely inspired and has no errors, the literal virgin birth and resurrection of Jesus, and that one can only be saved if they endorse the substitutionary atonement of Jesus dying for our sins.

and participatory, with many of those in attendance experiencing glossolalia, or spontaneous utterance, and an anointing of the Holy Spirit in the ministries of healing.

3. These movements tended to value life-changing experiences that placed them in harmony with God. It may have been a "got saved" or "know the Lord" experience of going forward to the front alter in the church in order to be saved.

4. These groups may have had a particular belief that gave them their identity, such as the Quakers with the practice of being quiet to let the spirit of God move in their presence and their deep commitment to peaceful solutions to deep conflicts. There are also many churches that have a particular heritage and culture, such as the Black Church with its emphasis on a deep faith, nurtured by distinctive music, forceful preaching, and a commitment to a just society.

5. They were often sensitive to the issue of authority, saying that the authority was the Bible, or particular parts of the Bible, that authorized them to govern their affairs and arrange their beliefs in a particular way.

Liberal and progressive: I want to mention another movement in the development of the Christian faith that chose a distinctive direction in a desire to be an expression of the church that was vital and life giving in a setting that was rapidly changing and increasingly secular in tone. It was present in the nineteenth century,[18] reached its mature form in the twentieth century, and is now actively engaged in articulating faith in contemporary ways. These tendencies have nearly always been present in the worldwide church, and they have been called by several labels, the most common of which is liberal, although the title of progressive is also frequently used. The spirit of this movement is to guide and urge the church to be relevant and influential in a troubled world, working for peace where violent wars have broken out, the formation of just society, and to enable dedicated Christians to understand their faith in a way that is integrated with a contemporary understanding of the world. This movement has embraced the careful historical scholarship of the Bible, acknowledging it as a source of guidance for faith and practice, but not infallible by divine inspiration. Often there is the reference to Jesus as the model for living faithfully. It has supported ways for Christians to find an authentic way to live responsibly in the new world that is being born

---

18. Many people could be mentioned as providing the foundations for the liberal progressive movement; Friedrich Schleiermacher's book, *The Christian Faith*, was especially important.

almost daily. The presupposition of the liberal movement is that it is wise to modify belief and practice in the Christian faith in a way that makes the message relevant as it encounters a new and changing world. It is acceptable for the Christian faith to restate beliefs in reference to the profound changes in history, the rise of new worldviews, and even a new understanding of Jesus that has come about because of historical scholarship.

Our categories of the ways that the Christian church has sought to guide and educate its members in growth and development are:[19]

1. Using a sacramental approach, stressing the actual experience of the presence of God in sacred rites (to heal and save)

2. Trusting the authority of the original apostles in order to find the best way to guide belief and practice (to know)

3. Affirming that the heart of reconciliation with God is based on faith rather than exclusively on human effort (to grow)

4. Stressing the need to have a life-changing experience of faith and having a distinctive identity in mission (to empower)

5. Seeking ways to restate and live the faith in response to society's needs and the changing world (to serve)

We turn now to an exploration of the best pathways for an individual to find a spiritual center and to embrace spiritual practices that encourage a healthy pattern of belief and practice that leads to maturity.

Questions for Reflection and Discussion

1. Of the several views within the Christian church about how one matures and is transformed, which one do you think is the most persuasive and effective? Least persuasive and effective? In what ways?

2. Do you agree that the Christian church needs, at least partially, to restate its theology in reference to how a person grows and develops? If so, in what ways? Do you consider your views as conservative, moderate, or progressive?

---

19. There have been ways the church has been modified and reformed across history, and these five families may not be inclusive or viewed as adequately described; my hope is that the categories will be close to the truth and provide understanding of the differences in the expression and practice of the Christian faith.

3. In what ways do you think that having a religious faith is healthy, and in what ways might it be harmful? Is there a light and dark side in religion?
4. Do you think that the Christian values of truth, peace, compassion, and justice provide a good foundation for an ethical life?
5. What steps are you currently taking that have the capacity to increase your health and well-being?

Key Terms and Concepts

1. Prophetic: A point of view and behavior that encourages making changes in social structures that are harmful and promotes those based on justice.
2. Sacramental: The view, often associated with religious beliefs, that certain ceremonies and rites enable one to be in the presence of the divine.
3. Faith: A human experience that contains certain beliefs and practices that empower a person to be in harmony with the divine.
4. Sanctification: The condition of a person who has religious faith that enables them to be holy (set apart to do God's will) and live in harmony with the divine.
5. Integration: In our case, a careful study of different understandings of human growth and development and, indeed, other worldviews that invites comparison, the identification of common ground that can be shared; often linked with our formation of Christian theology and belief.

Suggestions for Reference and Reading

1. *The Awakened Brain: The New Science of Spirituality and Our Quest for an Inspired Life* by Lisa Miller
2. *The Christian Faith* by Friedrich Schleiermacher
3. *Contemplative Prayer* by Thomas Merton
4. *Listening for the Heartbeat of God: A Celtic Spirituality* by J. Philip Newell

5. *The Religion of Tomorrow: A Vision for the Future of the Great Traditions* by Ken Wilbur

CHAPTER THREE

On Being Informed

Endorsing a Spiritual Center and Embracing a Pathway of Faith

Meanwhile Saul, still breathing threats and murder against the disciples of the Lord, went to the high priest and asked him for letters to the synagogues at Damascus, so that if he found any who belonged to the Way, men or women, he might bring them bound to Jerusalem. Now as he was going along and approaching Damascus, suddenly a light from heaven flashed around him. He fell to the ground and heard a voice saying to him, "Saul, Saul, why do you persecute me?" He asked, "Who are you, Lord?" The reply came, "I am Jesus, whom you are persecuting. But get up and enter the city, and you will be told what you are to do." The men who were traveling with him stood speechless because they heard the voice but saw no one. Saul got up from the ground, and though his eyes were open, he could see nothing; so they led him by the hand and brought him into Damascus. For three days he was without sight, and neither ate nor drank.

Acts 9:1–9

On Being Christian: The Need for a Thoughtful and Heartfelt Commitment

I HAVE DISCOVERED THAT it is quite difficult to make and sustain a religious commitment and pursue a spiritual life, one that is based on the steady participation in the spiritual practices, a good measure of discipline, careful thought, consultation and worship with other pilgrims in a community of faith, the wise study of helpful literature, and practical participation in the mission of the church. I occasionally envy those who, perhaps because of their life history, have an easy time with a healthy pattern of spiritual discipline. Perhaps they have fewer questions and live in a life-giving context where there is support for a dedicated faith. They go about life with a deep trust in God's guiding and sustaining presence, remain firm in their beliefs, live faithfully in the ethical norms of their community of faith, and practice caring for others in healing and loving ways. There may be the occasional doubts or questions, often provoked by a challenging event, a broken relationship, or an exposure to an alternative way of thought. But they bounce back and find comfort and guidance in their faith while only needing to make a slight modification in their pattern of spiritual belief and growth.

I have been in the camp of slight modification in my journey of faith, both in terms of discipline and especially in the area of beliefs. With some questions, I have read church history and find reassurance in the historical practices of the church in honoring those who have engaged in some modification of belief and practice. The Christian church is quite diverse and has had to accommodate those with different histories, cultures, and languages. The church has endorsed and answered many of the questions, although I have had some pretty steady doubts. Overall, I have felt supported and able to reaffirm my deep belief that God speaks all of the languages of humankind and honors a thoughtful mind and good heart. I may be a case in point in regard to the church's willingness to accept those with questions.[1] I have not always found it easy to stay with unquestioned loyalty to a creedal statement, after discovering it was clearly a product of an earlier time and filled with the assumptions of a different era and culture. These statements of faith or creeds abound in the larger church's reflections across time and history. Much of the worldwide church is creedal and has been guided by the statements of faith.

On occasion, I have had some discomfort about remaining in the Christian church, not doubting the emphasis on love and justice, but

---

1. The church has struggled with how to honor diversity, and in some cases, those with slightly different beliefs and practices have found themselves in conflict with other Christians and even told to leave a particular church community.

wondering why it wasn't and isn't consistently practiced by those in the Christian family. In particular, it has not always been easy to affirm fully every phrase in the creedal statements.[2] Some of my good friends have suggested that my middle name should be Doubting Thomas; I am so grateful that Thomas and his questions were welcomed by Jesus.[3]

For example, in a career in teaching history and philosophy along with courses in my primary field of religious studies, I have had to reflect on the writing of Nietzsche, Darwin, Marx, Freud, Bertrand Russell, Sartre and a whole range of other nineteenth- and twentieth-century authors.[4] The works of first-rate scientists, such as Stephen Hawking and Richard Dawkins, raised questions that couldn't easily be ignored. I have often wondered if there really was Someone upstairs.[5] Along the way, there also have been a few critics of the Christian faith who maintained that there was no firm basis for belief in God. People such as Christopher Hitchens and Sam Harris wrote books about why belief in God was not defensible.[6] And "upstairs" is so vast with the earth just a speck of sand on the endless beach of the cosmos.

Human suffering, too, enters into these reflections, and I wonder why a loving and all-powerful God would allow it. Why is there so much suffering? How did Hitler get away with it? And where is God in the "holy" land as people in Israel fear terrorist groups and Palestinians in Gaza flee for their lives? Why do so many human beings suffer from hunger and sickness? Why has the church occasionally been unresponsive to human need and suffering? I reflect on these questions and arguments, and then my responsibilities press for attention and I move on. But in the recesses of my mind, I still ponder the questions and continue to explore the foundations for a life of faith.

Those with profound questions in our current century, from slightly different perspectives, ask if a religion, even one that is a product of clear thinking and careful scholarship, has a firm basis for belief. They ask, Is it credible? with some intensity. The questions and the suffering continue as representatives of postmodernism probe whether any metaphysical position, given preunderstanding, can be a credible basis for faith. Might it be

---

2. Brian D. McLaren addresses this concern in his book *Do I Stay Christian?*

3. See John 20:24–25.

4. I now struggle with more contemporary thought, which is often critical of a religious outlook.

5. See McGrath, *Big Question*, 5–8.

6. Harris, *End of Faith*, and Hitchens, *God Is Not Great*.

the case that nearly every philosophical and theological starting point is filled with unproven and, on occasion, questionable assumptions?

I do not doubt that Jesus lived a remarkable life of faith, was a model of love in his ministry, and was courageous in his last days, even as he was mistreated. I admire his courage and deep faith. But the resurrection accounts, the sort of capstone of Christian faith, invite me to wonder about the array of miracles in the Bible and in Christian teaching. Do miracles really happen? Or was it just a way for people, prior to the scientific and historical-critical methods, to speak about what could not be easily explained in a prescientific culture? Further, in my exposure to many of the world's great religions and their teachers, I occasionally wonder if there is one religious outlook that is more accurate in the recording of its historical foundation and has more integrity and credibility in stating its basic beliefs than another. Perhaps learning from all of them is a good idea, especially in the fields of spirituality and ethics.

I do not have a complete and satisfying answer to all of these questions, although I have thought, spoken, and written about them. So, with honest and real questions, I still find myself in the house that Jesus built, and I would like to share how I have managed to stay in the Christian family, endorse a spiritual center, and embrace a pathway of faith.[7] What follows is both biographical and, I hope, a well-grounded and logical argument for belief in God. I know that others may be where I have been and where I currently reside, and perhaps my pathway, hardly original, might provide some guidance as they believe, embrace a religious outlook, and find a spiritual pathway.

Across the years of my ministry and teaching, I have engaged honestly and with some credibility in answering the faith questions that surface in some communities of faith and certainly in institutions of higher education where I have served. I want, very briefly, to share a pathway of honest struggle and changing faith, one that I hope is thoughtful and has merit. How might one make a thoughtful Christian commitment in a confused and suffering world without ignoring most of the hard questions regarding faith and belief? Perhaps I have ignored some of them, but I have tried to be well-grounded and informed as I have struggled to stay in the Christian family. I have done so guided by three primary patterns of life and thought:[8]

---

7. It has not always been easy, yet being honest with the questions and doubts has made my life more authentic and responsible. I have learned to value the questions as I walk the pathway of faith; they have invited me to dig deeper and live with humility; I journey in faith.

8. Each with several subpoints.

1. Honestly acknowledging and caring about the realities of suffering and evil that fill our world and wondering where the loving God might be.
2. Continually struggling with the intellectual questions of endorsing a Christian worldview: is there a credible way to articulate the place of faith?
3. Living faithfully by the values of truth, love, peace, and justice, values that were central in the life and ministry of Jesus. On this issue, I feel grounded.

On Being Christian: Living with the Questions

I began rethinking the foundations of my Christian faith early in my career as a campus minister assigned to work with students in a large public university. This setting in the late 1960s and early 1970s was one filled with those who were asking a number of hard questions. There was an unpopular war in Vietnam, the full expression of new thought and counterculture behavior that came with the decade of the sixties, and pronounced doubts about presidential leadership in the nation. Old and established ideas and values were questioned and traditional American Christianity with a community church that served coffee after the service to straitlaced church members was not where students were on Sunday mornings. Most were just getting back to their rooms after a long night of partying, arguing, and loving.

I soon realized that I needed to be a bit bolder in my strategies if I were to minister to students. I realized that I had to meet them on campus, not expect them to come to a setting that felt traditional and was often boring for them. I also had to find ways to suggest that the life of faith was counterculture and that Jesus led some first-century hippies. In fact, Jesus was about as counterculture as they come.

What I sort of knew, but became fully aware of the more I studied his life and thought, is that Jesus was a radical, cared deeply about those who suffered, took on the religious establishment, and spoke directly to those who were running the show and allowing all sorts of injustices to occur. He sort of invented the hippie movement, although he may have been a bit more thoughtful and responsible than some of the students with whom I was working. I was pleased that the students were beginning to understand Jesus as a person who cared deeply about those who suffered from disease, poverty, and injustice, and then started a counterculture movement that questioned the way the government and the religious establishment were functioning. Some of the students did have profound faith and mature suggestions for change and renewal, both for individuals and for corporate structures. These students were open to understanding the life and teaching of Jesus in ways that connected with their life and values. They discovered that his agenda was to invite those whom he met to be transformed by a new outlook and pattern of life and to challenge dated social systems that kept people in poverty and without access to a good life.

What I taught, and I hope lived, was a message that Jesus was profoundly relevant, both to individuals and existing social conditions. He, in fact, really cared about human suffering (lepers on the side of the road) and the evil that was present in the social systems (he was not intimidated by Roman soldiers or high priests or Herod's sons, or by the Sanhedrin, or Pilate's Roman government). The world may not have seen or ever will see a person with so much integrity and compassion, wisdom and courage, sensitive love and the capacity to identify with those who are ill and disenfranchised.

Jesus Got It Right

As I have thought about my faith orientation and the relevance of the Christian faith, I have found ways of staying involved in the mission of the church because the church affirms that Jesus got it right.[9] Who else might have cared for the woman caught in adultery (forced by a man in power) and said, "Let anyone among you who is without sin be the first to throw a stone at her" (John 8:7). The men walked away. Who else would have overturned the tables of the money-changers who were not giving a fair exchange rate to poor believers who came to the temple to give alms? Jesus replied, "'My house shall be called a house of prayer'; but you are making it a den of robbers" (Matt 21:12–13). Who else would have healed two blind men, sitting by the roadside without food? "Moved with compassion, Jesus touched their eyes. Immediately they regained their sight and followed him" (Matt 20:34–35).

I stay in the Christian family in part because I am profoundly taken by the way Jesus lived and what he taught. I know that when I go to church, I will not find the human Jesus there, but I will find his legacy there, what he said and what he did, and people who want to follow his example. He

---

9. There is a vast literature on this topic, and good and gifted people have sought to remain in the church while articulating faith in more contemporary ways. See, for example, Bass, *Christianity for the Rest of Us*; McLaren, *New Kind of Christianity*; and Wolsey, *Kissing Fish*. There are several other authors, a bit less popular in their writing, who dig deeply into the profound questions of contemporary faith. At a deeper level, see Küng, *On Being a Christian*.

did care about the realities of suffering and the evil that fills our world, and then the Christian church was founded on his life and teaching by his followers. The members of this new movement were there to follow him in the quest to create a more just and humane world. Look carefully and you may find churches who carefully embrace his values; there are many, and I have sensed some responsibility, often introducing the bold and courageous agenda of Jesus through teaching in the churches where I have been active.

The Church Articulates Its Beliefs

A second reason I try to stay loyal to the church is because it is a vast, worldwide organization that does try to make a case that Jesus really was an authentic messenger of God. Generally, churches and their related educational ministries try to answer the intellectual questions that surround this worldview and state their beliefs in careful and honest ways. In fact, I am often engaged in this task, in part because I need to feel reassured and have had to reflect on these questions because of my years in university settings where smart people raised hard questions. I have not been free from doubt. I continue to live with the intellectual challenges of staying in the Christian faith; it is not easy to prove the claims and belief systems of the Christian faith, yet I honor those within the Christian family who work on these questions, and I travel with them.

While not an intellectual challenge, I do occasionally feel challenged and turned off when I see Christians acting foolishly while arguing for and defending views such as Christian nationalism. We do live in a country where there is the separation of church and state and where there is a need to respect all people. Across history, there have been several movements of sincere Christians with misguided views. The Christian church does not always get it right; neither did the disciples of Jesus, but they didn't walk away. Members of the family will have differences, as they have had from the beginning, but who they are and what they believe are not a full expression of the Christian church; they are just those who struggle to get it right and put it together in an understandable way in their setting.

Some Christian groups may miss the heartbeat of the Christian faith by focusing on the wrong issues. Some members of a local church may have a few off-the-wall ideas. I can cope with these as I keep the teaching of Jesus to "love your neighbor" (Matt 22:39) in front of me. I don't walk away, and I continue to look for good ways of supporting and clarifying Christian beliefs and practices. I stay with it and occasionally suggest views and ways of affirming the faith that are not held by the majority of Christian churches.

I am not a conservative fundamentalist[10] or a fundamentalist liberal, but one on the way who tries to help with the challenges of understanding and believing.

I expect if I had been deeply wounded by those in the church or the formal structures of the church, I might want to retreat from active participation. Yet I do know that misunderstanding and unfair treatment are not the Christian faith, but they do exist in the church. I was deeply hurt once or twice during the twelve years I worked in the national offices of one denomination, and I tried to say that my hurt was not caused by my belief or the structures of the denomination, but more likely because of my carelessness or incompetence, detected by those in positions of power and leadership. To walk away and find healing for these hurts is not to walk away from Jesus or the church, which tries to be true to the original teaching of Jesus and forgives those of us who make mistakes.

I also stay in the church, not always because it is intellectually sound in articulating its beliefs, or because it never makes mistakes in administrative practice, or because everybody in the church is always loving and understanding. I stay in the church because it affirms the values of truth, love, peace, and justice, and attempts to live faithfully, expressing these values day to day, as Jesus did.

The Church Struggles to Live Its Faith

I stay in the church also because responsible and thoughtful Christians have from the beginning attempted to be true to its best teaching and continue to struggle with the hard questions that surround belief and practice. The church has not been passive, but has engaged in finding ways to be helpful, informed, wise, and relevant. Across the centuries, those who led the church have not ignored the hard questions. In fact, the early church was thrown into an array of beliefs and patterns of behavior that put these new Christians in a minority, and they had to be diligent about defending and sustaining their new orientation. The first Christians received some help from having fine teachers who were unafraid to argue with contrary belief systems and support the ethical norms of their new faith. From the beginning, they understood that the life they had been invited to live would not always be an easy one. They encouraged and helped one another. Perhaps

---

10. I do think that *fundamentalist* is a good description of this conservative movement and wish that they had not claimed the term *evangelical*. *Evangelical* means "good news," and the current fundamentalist movement in this part of the Christian church claims to be that part of the church which has good news.

the most telling influence on their beliefs and practices was the way that Jesus boldly faced a prevailing worldview and patterns of behavior, ones he resisted and restated with great wisdom and courage.

As he began his public ministry, he encountered those of his own faith tradition, Judaism, whose leaders saw him as a renegade if not an infidel. Even in the present, there are those who find the life and teaching of Jesus less than engaging, or too engaging. It is these renegades with whom I often speak and who are one of the primary reasons why I stay in the church that follows Jesus. There were many beliefs and practices that he challenged, and his response to them gives me guidance and courage. I also note that his challenge to the beliefs and values he encountered may have had less to do with the actual content of these beliefs and values and more to do with the way the beliefs and values were expressed and taught.

For example, he often had to restate and illustrate the nature of God's love. In the beatitudes (Matt 5:1–16), Jesus spoke about a personal God who loves and restores rather than one who judges and condemns. On several occasions, he spoke about the reign of God (often translated as "kingdom") and underlined that God is not like an insecure, judgmental, and uptight king. Rather, he speaks about God as one who welcomes the poor in spirit and affirms that those who mourn will be fully cared for by God. In fact, the poor in spirit will have the full presence of God, those who mourn will be comforted, and the meek shall have all of the goodness of Mother Earth. God will honor and empower those who seek God's will and way; those who hunger and thirst for righteousness will be filled with God's presence; the merciful will be treated with mercy; and the pure in heart will see the fullness of God's love. It is this kind of teaching that keeps me on board the ancient ship of faith.[11]

As one reads these several teachings of Jesus in the Gospels, one discovers a Jesus who teaches that God loves the pilgrim who may not have all the answers and even the one who is full of doubt and struggles with life. God does not condemn and discriminate on the basis of sectarian belief and practice. Rather, God invites us to come, to be enlightened, and to experience the divine presence, feeling a deep and true love and expressing it, even to those who are the most difficult to love.

We also note as we read the Gospels that Jesus resisted some of the practices of the religious leaders. In his judgment, some of them had become narrow and legalistic about the ways they interpreted what was called the Law, and sometimes more inclusively the Law and the Prophets. Jesus understood the law as a guide for following God's will, and, on occasion,

---

11. Although close to the life rafts.

challenged the religious leaders who had made the law a burden rather than a blessing. There is a passage in Mark 2:23–28 that illustrates the way Jesus understood the law as given to guide one in leading a mature and healthy life. In this passage we read that the disciples picked some grain to eat on the Sabbath day, even though this grain was set aside for the fasting priests to eat following the Sabbath. Jesus is called into account by the religious leaders; picking and getting sustenance from this grain would have involved working on the Sabbath and eating grain set aside for religious leaders. Jesus resists the challenge of the priests and reminds them that the Sabbath was set aside for the health of human beings, a time for rest and recovery. It was not a violation of God's will to feed the disciples on the Sabbath; they were hungry. And there was plenty of grain to feed the Pharisees. The Sabbath law was made for the good of humans, not to confuse them about appropriate behavior. There are several other incidents of this kind regarding the Sabbath, understood by Jesus to be a blessing as a day of rest, not a stern law that prevented being sensitive to the needs of others. Jesus remained a faithful Jew, although he taught and acted in a way that fundamentally challenged some of the Judaism of his time.

It is interesting that the apostle Paul takes on the question of how it is that one can have a good measure of comfort and security within the new church. Like Jesus, he did not turn away from his Jewish heritage, but added to it.[12] He provided his contemporaries with good reasons to be in the fellowship of believers. What was important to him was how to defend a new addition to Jewish faith, one that included understanding the life and death of Jesus as a way to be truly faithful to God. Yes, he does say that the life and death of Jesus is a model of how to please God.[13] He does it very carefully, addressing both belief and practice. In regard to belief, Paul makes the case that the expected Messiah, important to the Jews of his time, had in fact come; Jesus was the Messiah, and therefore the believing community needed to follow Jesus.

His arguments are both theoretical and practical. It is in the letter to the Roman church and to some extent in the letter to the Galatian Christians that we find an illustration of his careful reasoning. In short, Paul argues that Jesus is the expected Messiah and a new orientation to faith is necessary.[14] He maintains that the heart of the Jewish faith is that one can be

---

12. The focus for Jesus may not have been so much dying for our sins in order to gain acceptance by God, but living with integrity, faith, and love, as expressions of a true commitment to God!

13. See Paul's argument in the early chapters of the letter to the Romans, chapter 2 in particular.

14. Paul's arguments are somewhat complex, although understandable in a general

faithful to God by following the Jewish law, often accompanied by a range of traditions that have been added to the law in order to be sure the law is understood and applicable in all aspects of life. One remains accepted by God as one is obedient to the law.

He then maintains that this system of belief and practice needs to be refined by a faith orientation that endorses the life, teaching, and events of the last days of Jesus. The faith orientation will bring the believer into full acceptance by God and will be the basis of a personal walk with God, a relationship that is transformative in character. The teaching of the law and the prophets will continue to guide believers, and as they have faith, they will be guided and empowered by the Holy Spirit, God's full presence and enabling power to live a faithful life.

On Staying in the Church

For the most part, the many families of the church have been faithful in their belief that God was present in the life and teaching of Jesus and the events of the Easter weekend. Yet, because of history and culture, these families have not always agreed on every detail. Nor have different families of the church and their members always been faithful in belief and practice. In the present, there are additional challenges for the churches, some of which are expressions of a new articulation of beliefs, and others that have to do with integrating what was called the Way with the ethical and social concerns of contemporary life.

As one looks at the Christian faith, and especially its contemporary manifestations in different cultures and settings, it is easy to spot places of inadequate articulation of foundational beliefs and even easier to point out the church's failure to be wise and have significant influence in advocating and leading the human family in the quest for international peace and social justice. I find these realities all too true and at times, especially as I age, I wonder if faithful participation in worship and service in the church is worth it or even a good way to help correct injustice and relieve human suffering. I have discussed at length with many contemporary Christians about whether to stay active in a church is worthwhile. For the most part, I have found an agreement among thoughtful people with a history in the church that we must remain active in the church's mission and learn how to live with the questions and the occasional failures.

Some people, of course, and maybe with good reason, are unable to stay active in the life of a local church. Perhaps they have been hurt in some

---

way; they are a bit more elusive in detail.

way or just found that the local congregation near them is not healthy and without inspiring worship. They may sense that there is a failure on the part of the members to engage in dedicated service, or they may find that the culture of the church is exclusive, tribal, and cultic. Many of my friends have said to me that it is just a waste of time; the church is not informative and inspiring, and it is not worth my time and energy. I do understand all of these concerns and I often identify with them. But deep down, I call on these four reasons to stay involved:[15]

1. With some doubt and responsible study, I stay in the church because, for the most part, it continues to have ministries that care for those who suffer, ones that challenge the mis- and disinformation that fills our sources of information, and those who seek to address injustice and evil in the world.

2. I stay in the church as well because there are those in the family of the church who have addressed the complexities of belief, and yet can affirm that there is a God of love who is the Creator, one that has been present in the history of the human family, and was present in the extraordinary life and final days of Jesus. I find myself in this circle of friends.

3. In addition, the Christian faith provides one way of putting it all together, a comprehensive worldview that helps me integrate the various strands of reality. Not everyone needs this integrated and comprehensive understanding, yet I find it very reassuring, even if there are further questions about its authenticity.

4. I stay in the church because it gives me a community of love and invites me to be responsible in a life of service.

I remain in the Christian church even if it is a challenge. It has been a good way to be and to become, following Jesus.

Questions for Reflection and Discussion

1. What is the most attractive feature of your church, or an ideal church?
2. If you were the pastor of a congregation, how would you try to guide your church in a way that helps the congregation face the contemporary challenges to faith both in their setting and in our world?

15. And many other reasons, of course, such as the quality of the worship and the means of providing opportunities for service.

3. In what domain or area do you feel most challenged in your life of faith?
4. How do you think your church should relate to other denominations and other religious traditions?
5. If you were to write a book that you hoped might be helpful to contemporary Christians, what would be your subjects?

Key Terms and Concepts

1. Liberal: In the religious context, liberal generally means that it is possible to rethink and restate the beliefs and practices of the church to make them more in keeping with the contemporary world.
2. Orthodox: Maintaining foundational beliefs and practices such as the Christian church affirms in its beliefs about Jesus and the values of truth, love, and peace. There is also a major branch of the church called Orthodox.
3. Spirituality: Committing to a way of being, believing, and acting, most frequently in a religious context. It usually contains engagement in practices such as prayer and contemplation, which cultivate a deep sense of peace and purpose.
4. Postmodern: The shift in contemporary culture that maintains that previous foundational starting points in the modern world for claiming a true outlook on history and indeed all of life are filled with indefensible assumptions that need to be questioned.
5. Evangelical: The view that there are certain beliefs and practices that are "good news" (literal meaning), and were in the traditional pattern of belief in Christian thought and should be continued, and in most cases, not changed.

Suggestions for Reference and Reading

1. *Birth of a Dancing Star: From Cradle Catholic to Cyborg Christian* by Ilia Delio
2. *Christianity for the Rest of Us: How the Neighborhood Church Is Transforming the Faith* by Diana Butler Bass

3. *Do I Stay Christian? A Guide for the Doubters, the Disappointed, and the Disillusioned* by Brian D. McClaren
4. *Kissing Fish: Christianity for People Who Don't Like Christianity* by Roger Wolsey
5. *Original Blessing* by Matthew Fox

SECTION TWO

The Soul's Journey of Being Reformed
Cultivating Spiritual Maturity

> O God unto whom all hearts lie open
> Unto whom desire is eloquent
> And from whom no secret thing is hidden;
> Purify the thoughts of my heart
> By the outpouring of your Spirit
> That I may love you with a perfect love
> And praise you as you deserve. Amen[1]

---

1. Johnston, *Cloud of Unknowing*, 43.

CHAPTER FOUR

On Being Reformed
Understanding the Spiritual Life

> By contrast, the fruit of the Spirit is love, joy, peace, patience, kindness, generosity, faithfulness, gentleness, and self-control. There is no law against such things. And those who belong to Christ have crucified the flesh with its passions and desires. If we live by the Spirit, let us also be guided by the Spirit. Let us not become conceited, competing against one another, envying one another.
>
> Galatians 5:22–26

The Apostle Paul's Ministry to the Gentiles

WE ARE EXPLORING HOW to travel through life in a wise and mature way, one filled with "the fruit of the Spirit." Our trip is complex and it includes traveling through many locations and staying in several camp sites, some of which are nurturing and others that could easily lead us astray and cause some discomfort. For us to arrive home, we need to be *informed*, using our mind to gain a knowledge base and learn about the best routes to the good life. We also need to be *reformed*, often correcting the direction we think might lead to happiness and fulfillment, but proves to be false, taking us to destinations that are harmful and self-destructive. We need guidance and direction. We also need to be *transformed*, renewed and empowered to travel on healthy pathways that lead us to those destinations which are nurturing and inspiring.

We are suggesting that an essential part of being guided and empowered is to invite God's presence into our lives and then to meditate and contemplate in a spiritual way on the journey of our soul. It is our soul that gives and sustains our values, contains the needed wisdom to find our way, provides the inspiration to travel well, and helps us stay on course in a life of peace and purpose. It was the apostle Paul's mission and strategy as he ministered to the new Christians in the region of Galatia and the Greek city of Corinth. Drawing upon his own experience and his understanding of the regions, he sought to inform the new Christians in Galatia about how it is that one can journey wisely and well, especially in an environment that is not conducive to supporting a healthy way and nurturing the spiritual life. We can learn from his teaching to the new Christians in the region of Galatia and other locations such as Corinth, which had a new church and questions about how to organize the church and to live wisely and well in their new Christian faith.

The context in which we live, not unlike Galatia and Corinth, tends to be filled with misleading values and makes false promises. We are told daily as we turn on the television that happiness consists of the abundance of things possessed, that fulfillment comes with immediate bodily pleasures, and that meaning in life is realized by gaining power and importance in the eyes of others. We live in a diverse and complex environment filled with misinformation, one that is ever changing and perilous.

Paul's Message to Us[1]

Our goal is to find a pathway to the good life, one based on the life and teaching of Jesus and filled with inner peace and compassion for those who travel with us. It is essentially described in the ministry of the apostle Paul in Galatia and Corinth as we read his guidance in his letters to these churches. We need to study many of the subjects in these letters in order to be better informed about having a healthy journey of faith. They come from the heart and mind of Paul, fresh from his ministry in these areas within the Roman Empire. They reveal the challenge and the complexity of establishing new churches and guiding their members on how to live the Christian life in complex, and even dangerous, settings.

---

1. There were several other new churches which received letters from Paul, and they too give us a good pattern of how the church was developing and how to stay on course.

The setting in which we live is as complex as were the ones in the regions of Galatia and Greece, maybe even more so. The guidance drawn from Paul's letters may not speak in detail about our complex setting; we live in a different culture with a different language, and face contemporary problems. Yet the letters do suggest essential ways of coping with the challenges of our journey.

Paul does describe in his letters that the first step in finding our way is to cultivate a deep spiritual life, one that invites the presence of God into our lives and that takes into account the complex environment in which we live. It was this strategy that was the heart of the ministry of Paul, and in many ways, though with slightly different language, it describes the pattern of the ministry of Jesus.

The passage in his letter to the Galatians, quoted at the beginning of this chapter, provides the foundation: "Now the works of the flesh are obvious: fornication, impurity, licentiousness, idolatry, sorcery, enmities, strife, jealousy, anger, quarrels, dissensions, factions, envy, drunkenness, carousing, and things like these. I am warning you, as I warned you before: those who do such things will not inherit the kingdom of God. By contrast, the fruit of the Spirit is love, joy, peace, patience, kindness, generosity, faithfulness, gentleness, and self-control. There is no law against such things" (Gal 5:19–23). There is a clear contrast between the two ways of life, the one self-seeking and chasing false pathways to fulfillment and the other being filled with the spirit of God who brings us peace and purpose and the very power and presence of a loving God.

As I look carefully at the setting where my wife and I live, I discover that there are some healthy norms and values. All is not dark and dreary, although there are certainly traces of the negative behavior described by Paul. In my setting, I find that there are people who truly care for one another, have sufficient income to sustain a comfortable way of life, and have mutual respect for and warmly receive the visitor or stranger or minority person. Even in cases in which there is racial and cultural diversity, there are healthy and mature ways of affirming all who live in our circle of nearness. We are especially pleased that there are many good schools, a general respect for one another's property, attractive, comfortable, and safe housing, and governments at different levels that seek to sustain a just and humane context. A good and healthy life is possible for us.

Yet there are traces of harmful behavior in settings close to us, ones where there are homeless people and many who are unemployed and experiencing debilitating poverty. There is a measure of fear about one's health, and schools that are less than adequate for children. Life is difficult for some who live in our environment, and there is an abundance of mis- and disinformation. Our political life, for example, is conflicted and has dimensions which are threatening to our future.

A somewhat comparable situation, although perhaps with less healthy and life-giving conditions, was present for the first generations of Christians. As their new orientation and values changed their way of life, they had to find the best ways to live in a setting where their new faith and values where honored. There was poverty, crime, and many who had alternative beliefs and lifestyles. There was an abundance of situations where there was injustice, often with a wealthy and powerful class in charge and where the majority were poor and disenfranchised. The gospel (good news) spoke to these issues and concerns.

It was also the case that the new faith initially attracted Jewish people who were able to connect with and affirm the life and teaching of Jesus, viewing it as part of God's ongoing care for the Jewish population. In fact, most of the first Christians where Jewish and were guided initially by Jesus and later by Paul and other Jewish leaders. There was an active Christian church in Jerusalem that was led by James, the brother of Jesus, one that existed side by side with the Jewish synagogues.

The new church had to find ways of relating to the Jewish community. It was the primary context in which Jesus engaged in ministry. But it wasn't long before the new faith expanded well beyond the Jewish community, in part because of the missionary work of the apostle Paul. In this expansion, a new outlook and vocabulary were required. The new community of faith had to find good ways to live with those who were not part of the Jewish context and had quite different beliefs and ways of living.

Paul, as a young Jewish Pharisee, led the initial effort to resist the new church's understanding and strategy to remain within Judaism. He understood the Christian message as more universal, reaching out to gentiles, not just supporting those people in the Jewish population who were following the radical prophet from Nazareth, Jesus. The book of Acts summarizes this situation, after describing the stoning of Stephen, an early Christian leader: "That day a severe persecution began against the church in Jerusalem, and all except the apostles were scattered throughout the countryside of Judea and Samaria. Devout men buried Stephen and made loud lamentation over him. But Saul [he later changed his name to Paul] was ravaging the church by entering house after house; dragging off both men and women, he committed them to prison" (Acts 8:1–3).

The early Jewish Christian community did not have an easy and trouble-free start. Saul continued his persecution of these new Jewish Christians, moving his base for persecution to Damascus. It was there, during his threats against the disciples of Jesus who understood him as Lord, that Paul had a profound conversion experience. It is described in the book of Acts: "Meanwhile Saul, still breathing threats and murder against the disciples of the Lord, went to the high priest and asked him for letters to the synagogues at Damascus, so that if he found any who belonged to the Way, men or women, he might bring them bound to Jerusalem" (Acts 9:1–2).

It was in that conflicted setting that Paul experienced a dramatic shift in his loyalties as a result of hearing in his mind and heart the voice of Jesus, asking why he was persecuting the new Christians. For three days, he was without sight and fasted, sensing that his condition was an act of God. In a quite profound way, Paul shifted his loyalty and became a Christian missionary, a new role that was confirmed by Peter, the leader of the Christian movement in Rome. This transformation of Paul was reported to the church in Jerusalem, with many of the new Christians rejoicing and others still a bit suspicious. Sensing within himself the complexity of his situation, Paul chose to spend an extended time in personal retreat, needing to understand more fully his shift in beliefs and to nurture his soul. His whole life, his sense of who he was, his very identity, his values, his beliefs, and his vocation were fundamentally altered. Paul's heart and mind were transformed and his soul matured. He had opened his mind and heart to the spirit of God, the very power and presence of God.

The place of his retreat and its precise length of time are not known in detail, although it was an extended period of time. Later he returned to the region and became a missionary to the gentile population, a shift of the church's strategy and one that gave him a new identity and way of articulating his new faith.

While there were other new Christian churches being formed, many in Jewish settings, it was the ministry of Paul all across the Roman Empire that gave the church a more universal dimension, not limited to the Jewish population, and welcoming and receiving people with a variety of backgrounds and nationalities. It was during this retreat that Paul confirmed his calling to minister to the gentile population. To pursue this calling, he had to gain approval at a gathering in Jerusalem, which he received. Joining with other new Christians such as Barnabas, he became a missionary to the Roman Empire with a new message that what Jesus did and taught was a life-giving foundation for all people. He understood his responsibility to give new insight and guidance to gentiles about their new faith and the journey of their soul.[2]

---

2. The story is in many ways how the Christian faith became a new religious orientation, one related to the Jewish faith, but extending it and in time essentially becoming a new religion.

Paul's Ministry to the Roman Empire

Paul, often with companions, traveled across the Roman Empire and finished his ministry in Rome. As he traveled, he would occasionally write letters to keep his colleagues who were also followers of Jesus inspired and informed. It is in these letters that we grasp how his understanding of faith was passed on to those from a variety of settings, countries, and cultures with profound differences. One of his letters was sent to the Christians in Galatia, more a territory in north central Asia Minor than a single city. It had an active and diverse church community, one that he helped to start. He writes to them about their faith, giving encouragement and also guidance about the differences of understanding of this new religious outlook that was present in this first generation of Christians.

At the heart of the differences was the way the Jewish understanding of faith was rooted in a belief in and worship of the Jewish God, Yahweh, and in obedience to the law contained in the Hebrew Bible. Paul affirmed this foundational belief in God, yet gave more detail in his ministry about how the new Christian understanding of faith focused more on a relationship with God and was grounded in the life and teaching of Jesus and the redemptive events of his last days.[3] The law still had a place in one's faith journey by providing ethical guidance to the believer, yet this new orientation was more centered on the personal connection with God, based on the mission of Jesus. It was a relationship that empowered the believer to live by faith and to be led by the spirit of God. It emphasized the transformation of the central core or soul of the person, which empowered the new believer to live in harmony with the values that undergirded the law. These new Christians, both Jews and gentiles, rejoiced in God's unconditional love and felt called to dedicate themselves to the spiritual life. The law still had its place in guiding the believer, but it was less of a legal obligation and more of the natural flow of the new life of the Christian who had been transformed by faith and filled with the spirit of God.[4]

---

3. I do not mean that the Jewish faith did not teach that God was personal and loving, a Being with whom a relationship was possible. Paul, however, chose to make this aspect central to his understanding of faith.

4. The Holy Spirit was understood as the power and presence of God in one's personal life, and indeed in the life of the new Christian community, soon to be called the church.

The Meaning of the Life of Faith, Hope, and Love

Paul's full understanding of the meaning of faith developed as he reflected on his new orientation following his experience in Damascus and his time of retreat and reflection on his new faith. There were at least four components of his new faith orientation. The first is that it was a divine gift that enabled a personal connection with a loving God. This understanding was certainly influenced by his Jewish background, yet for him it was an orientation based on his new understanding of the spirit of God, that God is indeed present in the believer's life. This orientation was not the final product of doctoral studies complete with a dissertation or the end of a disciplined retreat, but more of an encounter, a life-giving experience that he sensed and believed was the guiding and empowering presence of God. Later, as he wrote to new Christians in Corinth, he said, "Therefore I want you to understand that no one . . . can say 'Jesus is Lord' except by the Holy Spirit" (1 Cor 12:3). God takes the loving initiative and becomes fully present in the new believer, and the soul of a newly converted person is transformed.

He goes on to affirm that our responsibilities in the new Christian church will be determined by spiritual gifts that we are given by the spirit of God: "Now there are varieties of gifts, but the same Spirit; and there are varieties of services, but the same Lord; and there are varieties of activities, but it is the same God who activates all of them in everyone" (1 Cor 12:4–6).

Faith, Paul teaches, comes to us as a gift as we open our hearts and are transformed by God's loving presence, the Holy Spirit. It follows from this new relationship with God that we are then given the grace to lead a spiritual life. The second component of faith, following from the initial gift of transformation by God, is to act in accord with God's teaching. Our faith becomes active, a life of faithfulness, which is to say that we are to act in accordance with the values and norms of our new calling. We have a new orientation to life, one rooted in the reality that we have a personal relationship with God. We are then guided and empowered to live in accord with the values of our new orientation and become faithfully engaged in using our God-given gifts in the activities of the new community of the church. In short, we are to be faithful in loving others, and we do so by using the gifts and talents we have, understood as the way that God endows us to minister in a loving way (1 Cor 13).

A third component of faith is believing trust—that is, as we sense the presence of God in our lives, we become aware of our gifts and talents given by God. This awareness not only gives us a hopeful outlook, but also the motivation and capacity to sustain a life of faith even in the presence of challenge and hardship. Paul certainly knew, as he wrote his letter to the

Corinthians, that God's spirit would sustain them in difficulties. Paul's new life as a Christian was difficult, demanding, and dangerous. He reassures these new Christians, whose lives may also be difficult and demanding, that they can trust the God of love to guide, empower, and sustain them, even in a challenging environment.

The fourth component of faith is to cultivate a theological understanding of their new faith, one grounded in the ways that God has come to the human family across the centuries and now in a special, unique way in the life, teaching, and work of Jesus. God has come to the human family in the person of Jesus, and it is his life and teaching about compassion, the model of his faithful obedience even to the point of death, and the life-giving presence of God's spirit that will guide and transform us. It will enable us to be the person and persons whom God will use in the mission, people with integrity and truthful in all they say and do. We are called to truly love all those who come our way, engaging in the mission of justice that seeks a more humane world for all those who suffer and are disenfranchised.

The Life of Hope

There is a wonderful gift that emerges from the life of faith. As we place our life in faith on the very ground of being, the foundation of all that exists, upon the God of creation who created us in the divine image, and the God who is all loving, we then become people of hope. Our faith becomes our forward-looking virtue and blossoms into the positive experience of hopefulness. Paul's summary of God-centered life is expressed for us in the Corinthian letter: "And now faith, hope, and love abide, these three; and the greatest of these is love" (1 Cor 13:13). Hope is the way we sustain our lives, filled as they are with threat, hardship, and the deep fear that we may not be able to manage our own well-being, the multitude of our responsibilities, and the threatening and perilous setting in which we live.

Often, given our busy and demanding lives, we easily forget or set aside the ground of hope. We may get overwhelmed with responsibilities, feel impotent, and then unable to cope with the conditions of our lives. Perhaps it is illness, broken relationships, lack of friends and a supportive community, a shortage of money to have what we need, aging and the threat of death, and even a divided country that may threaten our way of life. It is easy for us to feel discouraged as did the first generation of Christians. Paul reassures them and us that followers of the Christian way can be hopeful.

As we read about the lives of those who have gone on the journey of faith before us, we can be inspired and guided by them; they have managed the challenges of life in their time and place. There are, of course, the great heroes and heroines of history and our faith communities. Abraham and Sarah might have lost hope as the traveled west to a new land, yet "going without knowing" (Heb 11:8) they arrived. Moses might have given up in facing the power of the Pharaoh, yet he led the people of Israel back to their homeland, just a step ahead of the chariots of the Pharaoh. Esther might have lost faith in the court of the king of Persia, Ahasuerus, yet she emerged as a queen. And Jesus, dying on the cross, says, "Father, into your hands I commend my spirit" (Luke 23:46). From their stories, we learn that their heart-filled hope in God sustained them.

Their hope, and the hope of many facing discouragement and great danger, has several qualities. We are unable to name them all, in part because we weren't there and can only read about their experience, but the stories tell us that their hope had a solid foundation. I'll mention just three components of this foundation:

1. The first and most obvious one is that they trusted in the loving God who is all powerful, beyond time and above the ebb and flow of human circumstances. They believed that this new and hopeful God-centered life would be fulfilling and life giving. Further, they believed it would continue through their descendants as they passed from their human condition in a particular time and place into the eternal and unconditional love of God. Those who were with Jesus on Friday, almost losing their faith, were later reassured by the Christian belief in the resurrection of Jesus and the continuation a new form of being and way of living in the presence of God.

2. Second, they have become for us the tangible example of those who were given responsibilities to guide and secure their future life and the life of those whom they served. They trusted that their sense of God's leading and loving presence would continue in the midst of change and struggle. Moses did lead the people of Israel out the bondage and slavery in Egypt; even the Pharaoh could not stop them. More personally, even Mary, who lost her most remarkable son, sensed that he continued to live in the hearts and minds of his followers who would continue his mission.

3. Third, we need to understand that it is not always the case that we will be led immediately to what we consider to be a safer and life-giving environment. It is more likely that our hope will be present for us in the midst of challenge; it is there because hope also has an eternal dimension. The hope we have may not always be fully realized in our

time and place. Life's challenges may in fact continue. It may not take us to a carefree life, but lead to the deep conviction that to do what needs to be done, what is right and good, may be a process in which we are sustained by hope. Our hope is that what is good will eventually come to be, that to be faithful is the start of the way, and that I will rest in God's love as I labor in faith. We do not lose hope because of our immediate circumstances; our hope is the presence of the eternal loving God in the midst of challenge.

The Life of Love

The apostle Paul, in his early, perhaps first letter to the Corinthian church,[5] not only urges them to cultivate their faith and to sustain their hope that one day, all will be well, he also speaks poignantly about how we live the life of faith and have hope in the present. We place our trusting faith in God and have sustaining hope in the loving and all-powerful God in the challenges of each day. We need to cultivate a sense of God's presence; as we do, we will be filled with a sense of purpose, be empowered, and have personal peace. This attitude of trust will guide us on the way and fill our daily lives with faith and hope. We are still here in real time and a tangible place, and our list of problems is often longer than our list of blessings, and even in these conditions, and especially in them, God will give us the peace that passes understanding (Phil 4:7).

There is one other foundational value that Paul provides to believers in the midst of daily struggle; it is God's unconditional love for us and the invitation to love others as an expression of God's love. This assurance of God's love comes to us in many ways, and Paul underlines it in the letter to the Corinthian church, the struggling new congregation in the less-than-nurturing coastal city in Greece. These new Christians, many from the lower classes, were struggling with how to organize their new church and what should be its foundational values. Neither the task of determining the leadership roles and the structure of the church, nor its teaching on how to live as a new Christian were easy to determine and express. In response to these challenges, Paul, the founding missionary of the Corinthian church, not only has extended visits with them, but also writes to them, and, of course, to us as well. The first letter, and there was likely more than the two that we have, summarizes his extensive work in the congregation.

---

5. These letters were not sent to the Corinthians as a first or second letter nor were they placed in the convenient form that we have with chapters, paragraphs, and verses.

As he concludes one of his visits to them, he writes to them and says, "But strive for the greater gifts. And I will show you a still more excellent way" (1 Cor 12:31). This comment follows his remarks on the complex issue of spiritual gifts (what they are and who has them) and the guiding principle of their fellowship (one body and many members).

He is trying very hard to help them get their act together, no easy task in a port city filled many ways to lose one's way. Several concepts and principles may have come to him, and they obviously did as one reads the two Corinthian letters of Paul, and we know that there was likely another one that appears to have been lost or may have been partially attached to one of the two letters that have been preserved.

I am fond of his closing comments in chapter 12 of the first letter, with the straight forward introduction, "And I will show you a more excellent way." He is getting to the heart of the matter of how new churches get organized and provide spiritual nurture. He does underline the point that regardless of how you organize, you must understand your beliefs and mission; they are foundational. Then it is possible to create a new community of faith.

He teaches them that there is one value that is foundational for all that you are doing. No matter how you come down on your beliefs, organize your administration, and engage in a variety of activities, you will need to do so with agape love. He knows that just to say "love others" would not be sufficient; this advice too easily becomes just another platitude. Paul does take into account how difficult this command is to follow because it is comprehensive in scope. Later, in his second letter to the Corinthians, he underlines again that living a life of love is very demanding. We are often too weak to be consistent in our loving. He writes to them about his own struggle to be a loving person, suggesting that he had one serious problem that hindered his work, although he does not reveal what it is.[6] "Three times I appealed to the Lord about this, that it would leave me, but he said to me, 'My grace is sufficient for you, for power is made perfect in weakness.' So, I will boast all the more gladly of my weaknesses, so that the power of Christ may dwell in me. Therefore I am content with weaknesses, insults, hardships, persecutions, and calamities for the sake of Christ; for whenever I am weak, then I am strong" (2 Cor 12:8–10).

He continues his encouraging letter: "So we do not lose heart. Even though our outer nature is wasting away, our inner nature is being renewed day by day" (2 Cor 4:16). "So we are always confident; even though we know that while we are at home in the body we are away from the Lord—for we

---

6. Many scholars suggest that Paul may have had some physical disability.

walk by faith, not by sight" (2 Cor 5:6–7). "Therefore, knowing the fear of the Lord, we try to persuade others" (2 Cor 5:11). "All this is from God, who reconciled us to himself through Christ, and has given us the ministry of reconciliation" (2 Cor 5:18). We no longer live exclusively for ourselves, but for others and seek their welfare. Paul provides this theological foundation for the ethical life of the Christian; it is a life of faith, hope, and love.

Paul underlines that agape love as "the greatest of these" (1 Cor 13:13), the three ethical principles. He offers in the well-known chapter 13 in 1 Corinthians a description of agape love. He is keenly aware, after living with the new Christians in Corinth, that they need to sort out their ethical values. Corinth was a coastal city, one filled with an array of ways to entertain sailors, and these new Christians were unsure how to organize their new church and had some conflicts in their effort to organize their new fellowship in such a context. He wants to guide them, and he provides them with the basic principles of how to live together in their new community of faith. In his first letter, he reaches the point in his guidance that should be the cornerstone of how they should live together in a challenging context.

He says that agape love is the preeminent value in the ethical life of the Christian. "And now faith, hope, and love abide, these three; and the greatest of these is love" (v. 13). The first paragraph of his description of love is to compare it with the other inherent values of the culture. In that the vast majority of the people did not read, they generally got their information and guidance from listening. Speaking to and for others was a very important foundation of this culture. Paul acknowledges that oratory has high value, but underlines that "If I speak in the tongues of mortals and of angels, but do not have love, I am a noisy gong or a clanging cymbal" (v. 1). If love is not present in our speaking, we are just an annoying sound. We are just making noise, not being helpful.

He also affirms that love is even superior to the discernment of mysteries and knowledge, affirming that love must guide our discernment of the mysteries of life and our search for knowledge that will guide us. It is all too easy to speak of mysteries that may carry secret knowledge and to use this knowledge as a form of power to control others and discriminate against them. Love must guide our use of knowledge. He goes on: even if we pretend to be generous and give away all our possessions, we must do so sincerely with the motivation of love or we will not accomplish our goal of helping others. Even if we sacrifice our body for a cause and then boast about it, we accomplishes nothing. Love must be the undergirding motivation of our behavior; it is the preeminent ethical value of the Christian, as it was for Jesus.

Therefore, Paul continues with a description of love. He wants them to understand. Love, he affirms, is practical and has an action or performance clause. He begins by saying that love is patient; love does not cease loving when the other person whom we meet fails and acts in a way that is unhealthy and annoying. Love continues to place value on the person, even when it is very difficult. Who of us has not faced this challenge? In fact, we will likely face the love challenge daily. It happens when we accept the difficult person as one who is on the way and we offer kindness and a nurturing spirit. It is difficult for us to love those whose behavior is annoying and threatening, those who are boastful and arrogant. Perhaps this behavior is driven by their deep needs, and our careful comments to and acceptance of them will be healing.

In fact, true love does not always insist on its own way, and is not irritable or resentful when another person speaks and suggests ways of moving forward or solving problems. Love does not just tolerate or rejoice in wrongdoing, but with care and sensitivity seeks to find the truth. And, as this process takes time, love patiently bears with the holdup, believing that the good and truthful way will be found. Those who love have patience with the complex process that leads to a good end.

Paul goes on to affirm that love is permanent: "Love never ends" (v. 8). Other behavior and actions may cease, and as one engaged in the pursuit of knowledge, I have learned that much of our knowledge is time bound and comes to us in the guise of our language, culture, and time and place in history. Prophecies come to an end and our knowledge is partial, "for we know only in part" (v. 9). In fact, as I look back across the decades, I realize that some of my understanding was partial and has come to an end. I understood, and to some extent still understand in part, but trust the work of God's presence in my life, knowing that in time I will fully understand as I crossover to the full presence of God.

So, the foundation of my life is my trust in the unconditional love of God; faith abides as does hope. They sustain me, guide me, and give me comfort. And I am reassured that my final resting place is in God's eternal love which abides forever. This is the way to journey through perilous times and find our way.

Questions for Reflection and Discussion

1. How would you describe the apostle Paul's way of ministering to the new churches at Corinth? Galatia? What were his goals in these visits?

2. What do you think is the most important ethical value in your life? What should be the most important values in the life of church?

3. How do you understand the meaning of faith? On what do you base your faith and find assurance that your faith has a good foundation?

4. At this time in history and in our location, are you hopeful and positive in your outlook, or a bit discouraged and do not know how to find a way to be genuinely hopeful?

5. Do you find it relatively easy to love others, or is it a continual challenge, especially to love others whose behavior goes against your values?

Key Terms and Concepts

1. Holy Spirit: The very presence of God who abides in our lives and is active in the church and the world; the power and presence of God.

2. Corinth: An ancient Greek city on the southeast coast that was visited by the apostle Paul in his travels as a missionary.

3. Faith: A dimension of human experience that places its confidence and trust in a way of believing and acting; often with confidence and trust in God.

4. Hope: A way of being that is positive about the future and finds comfort in the prospect that life will be good.

5. Love: A term with a range of meanings often associated with an attraction to another person or a positive experience or a beautiful object. In some cases, love may be expressed in an unconditional way, caring deeply for the welfare of another or others.

Suggestions for Reference and Reading

1. *Becoming Adult, Becoming Christian: Adult Development and Christian Faith* by James W. Fowler

2. *In Search of Paul: How Jesus's Apostle Opposed Rome's Empire with God's Kingdom* by John Dominic Crossan and Jonathan L. Reed

3. *On Being a Christian* by Hans Küng

4. *Paul* by Günther Bornkamm

5. *Wholehearted Faith* by Rachel Held Evans

CHAPTER FIVE

On Being Reformed

Participating in the Practices of Spiritual Maturity

> Finally, beloved, whatever is true, whatever is honorable, whatever is just, whatever is pure, whatever is pleasing, whatever is commendable, if there is any excellence and if there is anything worthy of praise, think about these things. Keep on doing those things that you have learned and received and heard and seen in me, and the God of peace will be with you.
>
> Philippians 4:8–9

Keep on Doing These Things

THE APOSTLE PAUL WAS careful when he left a local congregation to be sure that these new Christians would continue to grow in their faith. One way he used to encourage them was to send a letter after he left, one giving careful guidance on how they should continue their journey toward spiritual maturity. He reminded them of their commitment and provided counsel on how to stay on course. At times he addressed specific concerns, perhaps a difference of opinion among the leaders or how to organize the new church. Often, he urged them to engage in the practices of spiritual formation in order to keep their faith vibrant, and then he would remind them to lead an ethical life in a social context that did not encourage a life of compassion and a concern for the welfare of others. Frequently, Paul is quite specific about a problem or a concern, and he spoke directly to the leaders of the church about maintaining the appropriate spirit and attitude.

The letter to the Philippian church provides us with a good record of the way he worked with the new churches. The city of Philippi, located in northeastern Macedonia, was named after Phillip II, king of Macedonia. In an earlier period of history (359–336 BC), Phillip led this region with a firm hand. This goal of ruling firmly and expanding the kingdom was passed on to his son Alexander the Great, who greatly expanded the kingdom. After Alexander's early death the kingdom was vulnerable, and by the time of Paul's arrival, about AD 50, accompanied by his two missionary colleagues Silas and Timothy, this area was under Roman rule.

A new church was formed by these mission workers and was in an early stage of its development. Paul, in his letter to this new church, was eager to encourage the leaders to expand the church. He suggested to them that they take into account the history of the region and the unique context in which the church was located. In fact, it was generally Paul's strategy to aid new churches in their growth by first understanding the context and character of the setting in which these churches were founded. It was his way of helping them to address both the specific needs of members of the church and also how the new church might have a part in creating a more humane and just setting in which the church was located.

Paul's letter to them begins, as did most letters of that time, by identifying himself as the sender and, in this case, also acknowledging Timothy, who was with him in the initial visit. Next is the salutation or the sending of good wishes (grace and peace) to the leaders of the church, with Paul using the label of *saints* for the leaders and members. In referencing the leaders, he uses words generally translated as "bishops" and "deacons," identifying specific leadership positions.

As Paul moves more directly to the substance of the letter, he reminds them that they are in his prayers. Paul clearly had a close and warm relationship with the members of the church; he is sincere in his compassion for them. The content of his prayers, which he provides, is a good reminder of how we might pray for those whom we love and are distant from us. His prayerful remembrance of them has these dimensions:

1. He is grateful for their good work and reminds them that this good work will continue because God's grace is present in this work; it will not totally be on their shoulders. God will not cease guiding and empowering them. It is a paragraph of encouragement. God is with them.

2. Paul joyfully remembers being present in their ministry, feels deep concern for them, and prays that mutual love will continue to be present as the church develops. It is a paragraph of reassurance, that God's omnipresent love is the heart of the church's ministry and, he remarks, that he even sees love among the prisoners in the Roman prison where he is located.

The Phases of Spiritual Formation

Paul then gives them a report on his activities and shares with them the hardship of missionary work. He notes that he is now in prison for proclaiming Christ "out of love" (Phil 1:16), the only right way to share the message of God's love. There is a measure of irony in his observations in that he has been working with the motivation of love, yet he has still been arrested. No good deed goes unpunished.

He acknowledges the difficulties that the new Christians faced in Philippi, which are not unlike his own. He then moves into what is now classified as the second chapter of the letter, which focuses on the foundation of the mission and the motivation to continue in the spirit of love.

The current circumstances in our churches have some similarities with the circumstances of these new Christians in Philippi. Of course, there are many differences as well; they did not worry about climate change and the interruption of the flow of life because of computers and artificial intelligence. It was not an electronic age, and there were no bombs that could wipe out millions of people and destroy the good earth on which they lived and depended. But there were some developments in their setting that have a similar ring to ours, such as how to deal with the government (Roman in their case), a fickle and unjust economy, poverty and hunger, the lack of quality education, and the presence of injustice.

In addition, there is, from this era and location, a different worldview than ours, and it is a concern of Paul's in that he knows that the worldview of the leaders of this new church will influence the formation of their faith.[1] He is aware that other religious traditions and practices are present and will have some influence on the way the Philippians put their faith together, and, of course, there was the comprehensive shadow of the Roman empire. There

---

1. Paul was quite conscious of the assumptions about life and what is most important in the hearts and minds of those with whom he worked, and while not referenced as a *worldview*, it was generally part of his strategy to understand how those whom he served thought about what was important and how they viewed their context, their historical circumstances and, indeed, all of reality.

was the reality that human life may have been more at risk in their time than ours, although for different reasons. Their expected lifespan was certainly lower than ours, especially for those of us who live in a developed country. Paul, in his writing, assumes the harsh realities of their lives as he writes. He is very aware of their struggle and has a concern for them as he remains in a Roman prison. In his ministry to them and in his writing, he suggests several ways for them to live wisely and well given their new faith and the challenges of their environment.

I want to underline four phases of spiritual formation that Paul either assumes or speaks about directly in his letter. As we read this letter, we learn how Paul guides this new church and its members regarding how to cultivate a deep spiritual way, one that will help them manage their challenges and give them guidance as they move into the future. What he writes speaks directly to Philippians, yet has relevance in our time as he outlines a pattern of faith development. It is important to note that Paul's guidance on faith development, although expressed in slightly different language, is also present in the Gospels as these beautiful works of literature describe and explore the spiritual life of Jesus.

The first stage in spiritual formation present in the ministry of Jesus and in Paul's teaching is that our Christian faith is often the product of a genuine *conversion* and then becomes more mature as the new convert is present and active in a local church or a group of others committed to the life of faith. Paul illustrates this point by drawing upon his conversion that took place in Damascus, a setting where he was actually persecuting Christians (Acts 9). It was a quite dramatic conversion in that it directly followed the stoning of a young Christian leader, Stephen, and while Paul was engaged in arresting the new Christians in Damascus because of their new faith. Following his conversion, Paul was likely surrounded by those whom he had persecuted and who now rejoiced in his conversion.

Following this experience, Paul may have had moments of loneliness and perhaps felt isolated from these new Christians because he had persecuted many of them. Yet he does acknowledge in his writing that he was accepted by the new Christian community. He expresses deep gratitude about being with the new Christians in Philippi who now share the commitment to nurture their new faith and cultivate a deep spirituality. Paul had a profound conversion, and he was able to begin his Christian journey supported by the community of other new Christians in Damascus.

Jesus, of course, carefully selected a group of disciples with whom to share his mission, and the Gospels tell us the amazing story of how this group of disciples were taken with Jesus and converted to what was to become the Christian faith. They dropped what they were doing and, even though it meant that there would be significant changes in their lives, followed Jesus and joined with many others in this new Christian mission. They traveled together and supported one another, although life was not easy for them. But there was conversion and inclusion, a new way of life and a supportive community.

Paul, following his conversion, had the support of his coworkers, although later he was somewhat isolated in prison. Yet he calls attention to receiving support even in prison, and he expresses gratitude for this support in his letters. He frequently calls attention to those groups in which he has belonged and which had nurtured and sustained him. Before being imprisoned, he had traveled as a mission worker and frequently had partners who joined with him. Timothy and Silas and a few others joined him in mission, and he deeply appreciated their company; it was a life-giving fellowship.

He frequently references how he prays for others and has deep gratitude and love for them. He writes to the Philippians: "It is right for me to think this way about all of you, because you hold me in your heart, for all of you share in God's grace with me, both in my imprisonment and in the defense and confirmation of the gospel" (Phil 1:7). He is especially thankful for this community of people because they supported him during his imprisonment.

I can remember the early months and years of my pilgrimage as a Christian, how I had ventured into this faith journey with a clear conversion, but without much background or past attendance in a church. In my new faith, I did long to meet and be with others who could teach me about the life of faith. There were several different groups, both church and parachurch, that were part of my early years of faith. They welcomed and guided me and put their guidance in a simple form that I could understand. At times, I had some suspicion that their guidance was almost too simple and needed more study and depth, but now, looking back, I realize how they patiently taught me how to cultivate and sustain my new Christian faith.

One of these groups emphasized that there were four basic practices that nurtured the faith of a Christian: fellowship, study (primarily the Bible), prayer, and service or ministry. I incorporated these four practices into my life, and they did help to sustain me. I especially appreciated the one called fellowship; my association with others in the journey of faith was essential to my growth. Weekly, I joined with other Christians to learn and be inspired by the new life of faith and love.

Paul, in this letter to the new Christians in Philippi, also speaks with great sincerity about the need for study which I understood as reflection on what I had done, what I now believed, and how it would guide my life. A second sustaining practice for me, in addition to the support of a community of faith (*koinonia*), was *reflection*, and I did reflect on my new faith, its teaching, and the ways it gave me guidance for the direction of my life.

Paul writes to the Philippians, "And this is my prayer, that your love may overflow more and more with knowledge and full insight" (1:9). I needed to understand the depth, breadth, and width of my new Christian faith, and not unlike Paul, I diligently sought to understand the Christian faith and experience its wisdom and richness. With deep gratitude, I was brought into an association of Christians, many in the church fellowship and some with positions of leadership in specialized ministries in parachurch groups. I look back with some amazement about the ways I was surrounded by wise and kind mentors.

In fact, I so appreciated this learning that I began to think about a possible career in ministry. It required that I would need to rethink the flow of my life and perhaps consider a call to ministry. I did and, after graduation from my university, attended seminary. Following graduation from the three-year seminary program, I accepted my first formal call to a position in campus ministry, one based in a local congregation near a large public university.

Gradually, I began to feel that I was on my way to learning about the many dimensions of and the nature of ministry. In addition, I was very much at home with this appointment because it was in the context of a university, a setting and culture in which I felt comfortable. The university setting for ministry enabled me to begin to integrate the world of faith in the church and the world of learning in a university setting. I continued my study of the Christian faith and grew in my understanding about how the Christian faith could be credible in a university setting that valued the quest of truth. This integrative task became a lifelong calling, and I knew I needed more study of how faith and knowledge might be connected, integrated, and honored.

Nearly five years later, and with an appreciation of my Scottish heritage, I went to the University of Edinburgh and earned a PhD in theology. The religious studies program had several tracks or emphases, with two tracks in theology, dogmatics and apologetics.[2] I selected apologetics because it invited reflection about how a thoughtful faith enters into dialogue with the intellectual currents shaping our new world.

I now had two overarching descriptions of how I might expand and deepen my understanding of faith, honoring the first stage of *conversion* and then associating with a thoughtful Christian community. With the assistance of this community and more education, I continued to *reflect* on

---

2. The word *apologetics* has slightly changed in its meaning and is less focused on defending the faith and more focused on understanding faith in the context of a secular culture, as well as a postcolonial awareness and global understanding.

how my faith can be informed and contribute to the critical discussion of how our world can survive and even thrive in perilous times.

I was often in discussions with other Christians about my dedication to reflection about the Christian faith and was often counseled not to be too intellectual. Dear and caring people pointed out that while faith and knowledge are connected in marvelous ways and worthy of study, I should give the same level of attention to my soul as I did to my mind. I listened carefully to these gifted and faithful friends. I soon discovered that there was a quiet revolution taking place, nearly worldwide, that was rediscovering and embracing what was called spirituality.[3]

I wanted to learn about spirituality and did, but also discovered that one understands spirituality best by engaging in its practices, not just reflecting on the subject of spirituality. I had developed some modest spiritual practices, such as Bible study, preparation for teaching about faith, and the occasional times of quiet reflection and prayer. Yet I sensed a need to go deeper, and the third word of my spiritual formation became *contemplation*. I did reread the Gospels and realized that Jesus took time to be alone, to reflect, and then go beyond reflection to contemplation, our third word and stage of spiritual formation.[4]

In order for him to maintain his center of faith and life calling, he often left the disciples and crowds which surrounded him and retreated to a place where he could engage in private devotion and nurture his mystical encounter with God, one filled with love and light. One of these quiet occasions occurred as he traveled with his disciples from the region of the Galilee down to Jerusalem. They paused as they began to draw near their destination. Jesus, sensing that it was a time for a possible climax to his ministry, felt the need to be prepared. Luke writes that he "went up on the mountain to pray. And while he was praying, the appearance of his face changed, and his clothes became dazzling white. Suddenly they saw two men, Moses and Elijah, talking to him. They appeared in glory and were speaking of his departure, which he was about to accomplish at Jerusalem." It is a bit difficult to understand fully this experience, and it is only reported, not fully explained, in the Gospel of Luke 9:28–31, 35–36:

---

3. I read widely in the field of religious thought, the urgency of caring for the earth, the challenge of creating a just and humane world, and the ways to cross over in collaboration with other religious traditions. I read works of the Dalai Lama, the writing of Thich Nhat Hanh, and those Christian writers who are exploring the way we understand God and cultivate the spiritual life in a new world.

4. Thomas Merton, an American who led a monastic life, spoke often about contemplation. See his books *Contemplation in a World of Action* and *New Seeds of Contemplation*.

> Now about eight days after these sayings Jesus took with him Peter and John and James, and went up to the mountain to pray. And while he was praying, the appearance of his face changed, and his clothes became dazzling white. Suddenly they saw two men, Moses and Elijah, talking to him. They appeared in glory and were speaking of his departure, which he was about to accomplish at Jerusalem. . . . Then from the cloud came a voice that said, "This is my Son, my Chosen; listen to him!" When the voice had spoken, Jesus was found alone. And they kept silent and in those days told no one any of the things they had seen.

The prevailing explanation of this brief stop along the way and the remarkable experience had by Jesus and three of his disciples, is that Jesus had been in deep contemplation about his mission and how it might reach a climax when they arrived in Jerusalem. It was a dangerous undertaking, and Jesus, in what is called the transfiguration, heard the voice of God say that he was on the right track. On the mountain, he contemplated about his coming visit to Jerusalem and saw it as a time for which he must have a deep and profound spiritual foundation in order to be sufficiently alert and wise to manage its complexity with care. On the mountain, his mission was confirmed by a profound affirmation and deep spiritual experience. Even his disciples, who observed the transfiguration, were awed and amazed; it was a profound spiritual experience linked to the history and values of his faith (Moses and Elijah), yet pointing to the future. He sensed he heard the voice of God and knew he was on the right track.

There will be moments when we may have contemplative experiences, ones shared with our spiritual companions and which reassure us that we are truly in touch with God and fully present in the divine will and way. We will ponder these experiences, perhaps share conversations with those who have had similar ones, and value them as a way of deepening our faith and gaining the reassurance that we are going in the right direction. Contemplation is our third stage in our spiritual formation.[5]

Many of those saints who have gone before us have made a slight distinction between our third word, contemplation, and the additional stage of spiritual practice, *meditation*. As one engaged in some of these practices, I do sense that there might be a time when the focus is not on doing, thinking, feeling, or prayer with words, but on being centered, quiet, open, and when the words of explanation are not present. It is a time when one is in

---

5. For a thoughtful description of contemplation, see the medieval work of the unknown saint, translated by William Johnston, *The Cloud of Unknowing*. See as well the work of Richard Rohr and his colleagues on contemplation, *Contemplation in Action*.

the state of being beyond purely rational thinking and explanatory words, yet open to truth.

This meditative experience is present and taught in most of the world's great religions, and perhaps it is more central in Buddhism than in other religious traditions.[6] It is the practice that goes beyond contemplation to a heightened awareness of the divine or ultimate truth and in which one senses a deep and peaceful calm. Those who use meditation as a central component of their religious practices usually have a prescribed set of steps or means of reaching a certain calm, sometimes using a mental repetition such as the Jesus Prayer. In Buddhism, one goes through the stages of arriving at the place of total calm and, on rare occasions, reaches the stage of perfect peace called nirvana. Within the Christian tradition, there is the practice of centering prayer that leads one into a quiet calm in the presence of God.

Spiritual Practices Within the Dimensions of Faith Formation

The great religious traditions of the human family have an array of spiritual practices that are taught in order to guide the seeker to a more profound and mature spiritual life. I have benefited from them and remain so grateful for the privilege of being present and guided, not just in my own Christian faith, but also by other religious traditions. In fact, it may be in the areas of spirituality when we do join with others with a different faith orientation, going beyond being polite and actually engaging with them in spiritual practices that nurture the soul. Meditation is certainly one of those practices, and another is in the field of ethics where people commit themselves to the causes of peace and justice and care for those who have been left behind or out in the rush of contemporary life.

Within the Christian faith, several different approaches and practices have been used to assist the seeker to deepen and expand one's faith. I want first to say a brief word about approaches to deepen one's spirituality within the larger Christian family, and then turn to specific practices that enable one to get there and stay there rather than just arrive and leave. I have had the opportunity to cross over some of the artificial barriers that inadvertently cut us off from those in the Christian family who have a different origin and set of beliefs and practices. I have been nurtured, not only by my

---

6. See, for example, the writing of Jack Kornfield, an American Buddhist, *Wise Heart*. See as well another book by Richard Rohr, *Naked Now*, in which he explains patterns of quiet and "learning to see as the Mystics see."

Protestant Presbyterian and Reformed heritage, but also by those from other Protestant groups, the Roman Catholic and Orthodox traditions, and the many who might be thought of as representing the Free Church traditions.

A couple of decades ago, a thoughtful and inclusive Christian author, Richard J. Foster, wrote a book titled *Streams of Living Water: Celebrating the Great Traditions of Christian Faith*, describing the essential spiritual practices of seven slightly different traditions of the Christian faith.[7] I want to borrow from him his thoughtful and careful description of these seven traditions and place them in the context of our quest to understand better how we reach our goal expressed in the title of this chapter, "On Being Reformed: Participating in the Practices of Spiritual Maturity."

The first one he mentions is titled "*Imitatio*: The Divine Paradigm."[8] The thoughtful assumption of this approach to Christian formation is that we follow the example of the life of Jesus Christ, an approach that also includes and incorporates his teaching.[9] At first glance, this affirmation has great appeal, although as one seeks to follow this path, there are some sharp turns and steep hills as we walk. One of those, obviously, is to how to adequately understand the example of Jesus, carefully discerned from reading the Gospels. As we read these accounts about Jesus, they may sound on the first reading or hearing to be relatively obvious and easy. We receive advice that is straight forward: Go to a quiet place, sit still and read about Jesus, follow his teachings, and be open to God's presence.

But, in fact, while this advice has some merit, it is not so easy to understand the spiritual practices of Jesus for several reasons, three of which I want to underline. The first one is that New Testament scholarship would suggest that it is difficult to access the actual day-to-day life and teaching of Jesus in that our primary resource, the New Testament, comes to us many years after the life of Jesus, has been modified by the preunderstanding of the authors of the Gospels, and represents a patterned tradition and, in most cases, not an eyewitness account. The second challenge is not unlike the first one, that our reading and understanding is also influenced by our own preunderstanding; though careful in our study, we still have the tendency to impose our assumptions about the life and teaching of Jesus onto our reading about him in the New Testament. Third, the advice to go to a quiet place to read and reflect has merit and gets us part way there, but it too has

---

7. He had previously written a thoughtful book on spirituality titled *Celebration of Discipline*.

8. Foster, *Streams of Living Water*, 1–22.

9. See Thomas à Kempis, *Imitation of Christ*.

limitations as we bring our culture and its understanding of reality to our reflections, even in quiet and beautiful settings.

As one who has traveled this path, I want to affirm that it is still possible to gain access to the life and teaching of Jesus, but it is demanding and is both a spiritual and scholarly endeavor. This observation is confirmed by the fact that there are hundreds of descriptions of Jesus in our libraries, not all agreeing on who he was, what he did, and what he taught. Most have traces of the author's background. Yet I have found in my lifelong search that we do have a body of knowledge about Jesus that we can essentially trust, but it is somewhat difficult to access it directly. It does require using thoughtful New Testament research that is very helpful to us and then to combine it with other research that deals with his historical setting and the specific place and period of time in which he lived and the language which he spoke.

Given the nature of the subject, we move toward a better understanding when we have a knowledge about his setting and an open heart and an attitude of quiet prayer. In my judgment, it is possible to at least partially access the life, the heart, and the spirit of Jesus sufficiently for us to follow him and make his life and teaching a solid foundation for our way of life. Even the most critical scholars now acknowledge that we have enough historical information to have a relatively accurate and good understanding, and they do grant that personal understanding with empathy is an important dimension of the place Jesus has in our devotional practices.[10]

The second "stream of living water" suggested by Richard Foster is "The Contemplative Tradition,"[11] a way of nurturing our spirituality by discovering the prayer-filled life. I have found this model increasingly helpful as I move through the years in my quest to become more spiritual. What is taught in the Christian tradition, and is also present in many other religious traditions, is that prayer is more than the occasional request of what is needed, but essentially a way of consciously being in the presence of the divine as one goes through the day. There will be special moments to rekindle one's spirit. Increasingly, the invitation to engage in centering prayer is being accepted as a way of being with God and sense the divine presence. In centering prayer, one is able to move beyond words to contemplation and even meditation, the quiet inner calm of being in the presence of God.[12]

---

10. It is true that in the early 1900s there were reputable scholars (e.g., Rudolph Bultmann) who questioned whether there were sufficient historical records to know much more than Jesus lived in Israel/Palestine in the first century.

11. Foster, *Streams of Living Water*, 23–58.

12. Thomas Keating, a Catholic priest, has led what is now a better-understood spiritual practice and it is has become central to the lives of many people. There are

A third stream of living water from which one may cultivate the spiritual life in the Christian tradition is "The Holiness Tradition: Discovering the Virtuous Life."[13] He refers to the noted Christian scholar in the early twentieth century Walter Rauschenbusch who said that our holiness is goodness on fire. The quote suggests that spirituality is more than just being ethical in one's behavior, but with deep commitment and dedicated energy, one pursues a way of living that has "the same mind . . . that was in Christ Jesus" (Phil 2:5). Within the larger Christian family, there are denominations and movements that have stressed that faith has a strong emotional dimension, one that inspires and empowers one to live a holy life. By holy, this tradition puts the emphasis on what they consider to be God's uniqueness, and that as one is committed to God and living faithfully, one lives in a holy and righteous way. In the Christian faith, the way one lives the holy life is to follow the example of Christ in that his life and teaching reflect the holiness of God.

Frequently in this tradition there is the encouragement to be sanctified, one who is dedicated to the will and way of God. In some cases, this occurs by another act of commitment in which one is transformed by God. As one who was initially exposed to the Christian faith, I was encouraged to live an ethical life, and I was taught that the basic values of faith, hope, and love were the way of understanding and practicing the Christian life. There was an emphasis on honesty, kindness, helping others, and, in many cases, to care about creating a more just and humane world. I was introduced to the notion that it was possible to have God's presence in my life, and that God would provide the guidance and empowerment to lead a Christian life. Along the way, I began to live what was described as a Christian way, being honest, loving those around me, and helping others. I thought it was enough to just believe and follow what Jesus did and said; I was told to follow his example.

I did, however, because of a close friend, get invited to a church in the great Methodist tradition, although one that had broken away from the mainline denomination. They noted and were pleased that I was "justified by faith" as I was taught, but suggested that I needed another "work of grace." There was justification, but I also need to be sanctified, or filled with the Spirit.[14] The life of John Wesley was mentioned, and they explained that

several descriptions and guidance; one online resource which has a basic description of centering prayer and how to practice it is The Contemplative Society, "Centering Prayer." The book by Cynthia Bourgeault, *Centered Prayer and Inner Awakening*, is most helpful.

13. Foster, *Streams of Living Water*, 59–96.
14. See Levison, *Filled with the Spirit*.

there were three works of grace: justification, sanctification, and glorification. I thought it wise to postpone the last one, but they urged me to become sanctified, or filled with the Spirit and empowered to live in the Christian way. I was also taught, in this early exposure to the life of faith, that one needed the experience of being sanctified, expressed by going forward to the alter in the church and receiving the full presence of the Holy Spirit. In some cases, in this larger tradition, there was the confirming experience of "speaking in tongues," one that was viewed as a gift of the Holy Spirit and one that gave the believer a profound sense of God's presence and the resulting peace.[15]

I did explore that path, but sensed that while it might be important to have an experience of the power of the Holy Spirit for those in that tradition, I remained more of a "dignified" Presbyterian who fused the two works of grace, justification and sanctification, into one life of faithful dedication. But I got the larger point, that it is integral to the Christian way to stay in touch with the divine through prayer, study, and service. To be holy is be set apart in the way of dedication to God and the love of all people. Richard Foster lists how the holy person lives:[16]

1. Holiness is not following rules and regulations, but is rather a commitment to follow one's heart, the source of all godly action.

2. Holiness is not other worldliness, but world affirming in terms of caring about justice and peace.

3. Holiness is not consuming asceticism, but a deep spirituality that enriches all aspects of life.

4. Holiness is not "works of righteousness" or perfectionism, but divinely nurtured progress in purity and sanctity.

5. Holiness is not absorption into God, but living in unity with God.

There is a fourth related stream of living water called "The Charismatic Tradition"[17] that differs in some ways from the Holiness tradition. It too places a strong emphasis on experiencing the presence of God and emphasizes that the *experience* of the presence of God empowers one to be transformed to live in a truly spiritual way. This movement is careful to emphasize that God's presence empowers one to serve the will and way of

---

15. There are some distinctives in the different denominations within the larger tradition of Holiness, even a sensitivity about the distinctive of one part of the larger Holiness movement.

16. Foster, *Streams of Living Water*, 83–84.

17. Foster, *Streams of Living Water*, 97–134.

God in the world and places an emphasis on continuing to have a charismatic experience that sustains one in the spiritual journey. The Greek word *charisma* means "gift of grace," and the charismatic movement stresses that one may be truly transformed by the presence of God and then empowered by receiving the gift of grace from God to live in a spiritual way. There is often a reference to the third person of the Trinity called the Holy Spirit. This movement, drawing upon the description of the day of Pentecost (Acts 2:1–4) emphasizes that such empowerment from God did not cease at the close of the age of the apostles, but continues across history and in all the corners of the earth. The Pentecostal movement is one of the fastest growing branches of the Christian church and has a large and remarkable presence in Latin America.

It is important to note that the Holiness movement and the charismatic movement within the Christian church have separate identities, although there are some similarities. Richard Foster writes, "While the Holiness Tradition centers on the power *to be*, the Charismatic Tradition centers on the power *to do*."[18] I find this distinction quite helpful, although such a statement has exceptions, and individual churches which are related by denomination and spiritual practices vary greatly.

As I have visited congregations within these traditions, I noted that those more in the Holiness tradition, such as the Methodist denomination, with its historical linkage with the Church of England, preserves a sense of order in their worship and places a strong emphasis on the cultivation of the spiritual life, nurtured and sustained by the power of the Holy Spirit. The services are part of long tradition and even have a slightly formal structure that is often expressive of the Anglican tradition from which they came.

I also want to emphasize that this tradition does have a keen sense of service and does not ignore the "to do" component of Christian mission, but would want to fulfill this obligation of service with those who are deeply committed to the Christian way. They would say, "We are transformed to serve."

The Pentecostal churches affirm that the Holy Spirit is God's immediate presence and that one experiences God, often through glossolalia or speaking in tongues, and then feels a deep sense of inner peace and joy. Those in the tradition sense that it is the experience of God's blessing and empowerment, and they are now called to serve. Sensing that they are gifted by God, those in this tradition do reach out to those around them, encouraging them to endorse the Christian faith.[19] They are quite evangelical, in

---

18. Foster, *Streams of Living Water*, 99.
19. Evangelistic practices can be helpful for those who find a peaceful way by

the best sense of sharing the good news (the evangel) and being those who serve to help create a world that reduces suffering and works diligently in the causes of peace and justice.

If there is a possible concern about the active presence of God in these traditions, and indeed nearly all the Christian denominations and other religions, it is that they too easily become a somewhat closed community, express exclusive behavior, and inadvertently become sectarian, even a bit judgmental and tribal. Not infrequently, because they are so sure that they are right, they do not easily support and share ministry with Christians in other spiritual traditions. God's family is inclusive and spacious; God speaks all the languages of the human family.

A fifth stream of living water or way of living the Christian life mentioned by Richard Foster is "The Social Justice Tradition: Discovering the Compassionate Life."[20] It is that dimension of Christian faithfulness that stresses that Christians should be deeply caring about those who are victims of an unjust society and a dangerous world. Those in this stream engage in addressing poverty, helping those who lack access to high quality education and good health care, and those who do not have the benefits of the good life. Like many others in the Christian family, they take their guidance on how to live faithfully by following the pattern of the life of Jesus who was full of compassion for all those who are victims of neglect and injustice.

One thinks, of course, in American history, of Martin Luther King Jr., who devoted his years of service to challenging unjust social structures that prevented black people from having full access to the wide range of benefits in American society. Drawing upon his Christian understanding of life, he surveyed the range of laws that were unjust and the prevailing culture of prejudice against the black community. He began his life work to emancipate black citizens from the prevailing attitude that all people are not created equal nor do they have equal opportunity, but are limited by the injustice that exists in nearly all parts of the United States, and especially in the South.

What is especially noteworthy and admirable is the he was committed to challenging these unjust social structures in a nonviolent way, even though those whom he was challenging were likely to resort to violence to preserve their privileged status. Rooted in his Christian faith and commitment to follow the example of Jesus, he found nonviolent ways to challenge injustice and lead those in positions of power to begin the process of

---

endorsing a way of faith, but there are some evangelistic practices that can be harmful and controlling. Christians share their faith in love.

20. Foster, *Streams of Living Water*, 135–84.

making the necessary changes in social structures so that those who have been the victims of injustice might join him in saying, "Free at last. Thank God almighty, we are free at last."[21] He saw the work of seeking justice for all is never done, and those who have understood the Christian teaching of love and justice continue, not only in the United States, but all around the world, to be prophets of change, using a variety of means.

One may have great admiration for the work done in the name of love and justice by Gandhi, Mother Teresa, Dorothy Day, and hundreds of others, seeking justice in the personal arena of their own lives, the settings in which they live in towns and cities, the arena of our nation that makes and changes laws to ensure justice, and in the international arena where there are pockets of suffering and aggressive actions by dictatorial leaders, and whole nations suffering from poverty with few resources with which to make change. God loves the world and invites those who follow the loving example of Jesus to create a better world, one in which people can live without fear and have equal opportunity to have a safe and fulfilling life.

Richard Foster identifies and describes two other traditions and ways to express one's faith and pursue a spiritual life within the worldwide Christian faith. A sixth stream of living water flowing into the larger ocean of the Christian church is "The Evangelical Tradition,"[22] what Dr. Foster calls "The Word-Centered Life." The word *evangelical* means that one needs to embrace and believe the "good news" that Jesus came to redeem and save all people. It is through believing (having faith in the life, death, and resurrection of Jesus) that one is saved. This belief, articulated in the inspired Bible, identifies a certain part of the Christian population that understands their beliefs and goals as the true way to encounter and serve God.

At times, this segment of the Christian family tends to be exclusive and very active in promoting their views, even to other Christians. For example, one part of the evangelical tradition is maintaining that their faith understanding was integral to the founding of the United States and should be continued as not only a spiritual way but also a political way, often called Christian nationalism. I am somewhat disconcerted that parts of this movement have nearly taken over the meaning of the words *Christian* and *evangelical*, at least in the popular press. The word *Christian*, of course, describes a worldwide community that has great diversity, and in many cases disdains Christian nationalism. It also claims the word *evangelical*, or *evangel*, which means "good news," is not really very good news in this tradition in that those who do not fully affirm the faith may be eternally condemned.

---

21. King, "I Have a Dream," para. 28.
22. Foster, *Streams of Living Water*, 185–234.

The best expression of the evangelical movement within the larger Christian family has emphasized that there is a saving word or way of becoming and being Christian that is loving, and then sharing the loving news with others in respectful ways. It is very risky to claim that its views should be central to our government, which might lead to the exclusion of civil rights for much of our country's population. It is much better to stay with the good news, the Logos,[23] the ground of being that was expressed to the human family as Jesus. As John the apostle writes, "In the beginning was the Word, and the Word was with God, and the Word was God. He was in the beginning with God. All things came into being through him, and without him not one thing came into being. What has come into being in him was life, and the life was the light of all people. The light shines in the darkness, and the darkness did not overcome it" (John 1:1–5). It is this understanding that best expresses the identity of the evangelical tradition within the larger Christian family, although the word *evangelical* now points to the more conservative and exclusive side of the Christian church.

Richard Foster identifies one further branch of the Christian church that seeks a spiritual way with practices and service. He calls it "The Incarnational Tradition"[24] and its identity is expressed in finding the presence of the divine in creation and in the best expressions of our humanity and our common life. God is present and incarnate in the person of Jesus Christ, and we are able to understand God and follow the way of God by learning and following the life and teaching of Jesus. It was Jesus who had within him the fullness of God and who followed God faithfully to the dramatic end of his life. This same godly presence, the Holy Spirit, is available to followers of Jesus, who sense the presence of God in their own being and see the presence of God in all of life and the beauty of creation. Where there is suffering, harmful ways that hurt others, the lack of responsible behavior, and policies and actions that harm people and destroy the good creation, we need to bring the ways of love and light, expressed in (incarnate) the life and teaching of Jesus, to heal the human family and preserve the good earth. It is a theme present to some extent in all of the branches of the Christian faith, but especially so in the Orthodox tradition and in many of the great and creative minds of humankind. God was in the life of Bach and Milton, Mahatma Gandhi and Abraham Joshua Heschel, Saint Clare and her partner, Saint Francis.

---

23. Logos, a Greek word, may mean good news and points to the order, goodness, and meaning that is inherent in all creation.

24. Foster, *Streams of Living Water*, 235–72.

We turn now to exploring the ways that our journey has a profound ethical dimension.

Questions for Reflection and Discussion

1. What are some ways that you have found to cultivate your spiritual life?
2. Do you think the cultivation of the spiritual life is possible to pursue in different ways within the Christian faith? Is it possible to be find resources for spiritual growth in and through the ways and resources of other religions?
3. Have you found a church or a religious community in which you are comfortable and find ways to learn and grow in a spiritual way?
4. Do you have people who are present in your life who have guided and inspired you by their way of life and their guidance?
5. What next steps might you take to become a kinder and more spiritual person?

Key Terms and Concepts

1. Evangelical: A word meaning "good news" used in reference to the coming of Jesus. The tradition affirms that Jesus died for our sins in order for us to be "saved" and that believers should follow the dictates of the Bible, which is a divinely inspired document.
2. Incarnation: In the Christian faith, it is the belief that God has entered into human history in Jesus and that the divine is fully present in him.
3. Reflection: Careful thought about a decision or subject, using reason to better understand a subject or way of life.
4. Contemplation: A deep, thoughtful, and personal way of thinking about a subject of importance, such as values, a way of life, and how to act, often in a philosophical or spiritual way.
5. Meditation: Related to contemplation, but more of a quiet pause, openness, and way of receiving insight and guidance.

Suggestions for Reference and Reading

1. *The Cloud of Unknowing and the Book of Privy Counseling* by William Johnston
2. *Contemplation in a World of Action* by Thomas Merton
3. *Filled with the Spirit* by John R. Levison
4. *The Imitation of Christ* by Thomas à Kempis
5. *The Naked Now: Learning to See as the Mystics See* by Richard Rohr

CHAPTER SIX

On Being Reformed
Emphasizing Those Practices That Encourage Strength of Character and Guide the Ethical Life

> If then there is any encouragement in Christ, any consolation from love, any sharing in the Spirit, any compassion and sympathy, make my joy complete: be of the same mind, having the same love, being in full accord and of one mind. Do nothing from selfish ambition or conceit, but in humility regard others as better than yourselves. Let each of you look not to your own interests, but to the interests of others. Let the same mind be in you that was in Christ Jesus.
>
> Philippians 2:1–5

THOSE SEEKING A DEEPER spiritual life have cultivated it across the years in a variety of ways with people in the several religious traditions of humankind.[1] Even in a particular religion there is diversity in part because the religion has been practiced for centuries and in many different cultures and countries. Religious devotion reflects the historical setting in which it is nurtured. For example, in the Christian faith there are several streams

---

1. There are several excellent books that provide an introduction to the world's religions. Among them is the classic *The World's Religions* by Huston Smith, now needing an update but still a good introduction. My book *Exploring the Spirituality of the World Religions* addresses the subject directly. There are many books that serve the need for a textbook in a class on world religions.

of living water, as Richard Foster names them, describing how the human family has sought a deep and integrating way to become whole and connect with God or ultimate truth. Most often, there is both a religious orientation (attitude and spirit) and then a description of practices and ways that enable believers to sustain their faith in a life-giving way and to practice it in an ethical way of life.

In chapter 5, we explored the variety of ways that Christians have sought to be a truly spiritual person who lives an ethical life. Our emphasis was on the practices in which one engages in order to cultivate a spiritual way of being and ethical way of living. I often spoke of this behavior as the journey of the soul.

I want to draw upon this framework and give more detailed attention to what has already been implied and partially explained—that is, how a spiritual way transforms the person, giving one a center and identity, one that is congruent, authentic, and which manifests itself in a life of love and service.

Paul's Teaching About the Mind of Christ

This theme is presented in a tangible way in Paul's letter to the church in Philippi. In this letter he seeks to guide these new Christians and help them understand how this spiritual transformation takes place. This letter describes a pathway to the spiritual life: because you are being transformed in your new faith in Jesus, (becoming a spiritual person), your life will manifest behavior that is an expression of your very being, what you were created to be and are becoming. You are in the process of becoming a person, transformed by faith and full of truth and love.

Paul's wording in his letter describes this transformation and, as we have noted, he begins his description with the following goal: "Let the same mind be in you that was in Christ Jesus" (Phil 2:5). He reminds them that many people observed the life of Jesus and understood his teaching, and we now have experienced what they saw, heard, and learned, summarized and called the mind of Christ. As we fully grasp and open our hearts to receive the mind of Christ, we begin to understand how we are to live as Christians. Paul speaks about how we are in the process of understanding the mind of Christ and in this process becoming more like Jesus, a person who was centered and congruent. He had internalized the ethical values that were the heartbeat of his teaching. We are being transformed and are now able to live in a way that is comparable to the way that Jesus lived.

Paul's comments on how this pattern works begin with "if" and move to "then"; *if* you have accepted the way of life that Jesus taught, *then* your life will be an expression of his understanding, attitude, and spirit, the very mind of Christ. *If* you have been encouraged by love and compassion, *then* practice it. Or, as Paul says, "be of the same mind, having the same love, being in full accord and of one mind" (Phil 2:2). Don't act out of selfish ambition or conceit, but be humble and regard others as having importance. Don't focus exclusively on your own interests, but focus on the concerns of others. To fully love is to treat others as we want to be treated; to "do to others as you would have them do to you" (Matt 7:12).

I take these comments to heart, especially as I observe what almost always happens in a conversation, that as a person shares their thoughts, concerns, and needs, the person listening quickly shifts the subject to his or her own interests, needs, and concerns. There is perpetual self-referencing; it is the norm for most people and in nearly every conversation. As this happens, the risk is that the one speaking does not feel heard or, in more serious conversations, does not feel worthy of being heard. As we study the ways that Jesus encountered and related to people and built life-giving relationships with them, we sense that he truly cared for them and listened well. It is possible to learn from him how to get to know and love another in a deep and true way. I learn how to love as I study his encounters with those whom he meets and speaks to.[2]

What follows is one way that we might interpret the New Testament's description of his relationships and put them into our categories of understanding. How did Jesus relate to others? The following is a list of what I sense was in the relationships Jesus had with those whom he lived, met, loved, and served. We note first that one feels a certain way when love is not present; Jesus met many people who did not feel loved and may have felt the following in their relationships:

- You do not really care about me. You are too busy or think of yourself as too important to take time for my concerns.
- You give me an answer to my problem before I have finished describing it, often with an illustration from your own life.
- You cut me off before I am finished speaking.
- You find me boring and you are only pretending to be listening.
- You may even feel critical of my feelings, although I cannot fully control my feelings.

2. See Oswald and Jacobson, *Emotional Intelligence of Jesus*.

- You tell me about your experiences before I have finished my comments and seem to find mine less important.
- You are often communicating with someone else while I am talking.
- You are somewhat insecure and have to control your "realities" by constantly speaking about them and putting them in categories, like putting the dishes out of the dishwasher in organized cupboards and drawers.

There are many good ways to listen when another person is sharing what may be very important to them. It is possible to have a good and life-giving exchange with others when the following qualities are present:

- Give full attention when the other person is speaking.
- Accept the other person as they are.
- Listen and withhold judgment.
- As time allows, communicate openly and honestly.
- Show appreciation of the other person and enjoy their distinctiveness.
- Overcome your own poor self-image, your ego needs, and fear of rejection; as you do, you will be enabled to listen and care about the other person.
- Extend yourself into the world of the other person.
- When you do speak, do so from your heart; have integrity in what you say.

It is possible to see these qualities in Jesus as we read about his conversations. Paul references Jesus as a model for human behavior. We are reminded of Paul's words: "Let this same mind be in you that was in Christ Jesus, who, though he was in the form of God, did not regard equality with God as something to be exploited, but emptied himself, taking the form of a [servant], being born in human likeness" (Phil 2:5–7).[3]

There may be times when we may feel quite different than the person with whom we are speaking, perhaps because the other person has a different background, is in a different generation, and may be from another culture. The other person then brings to the conversation different norms of communication. It then may be difficult to engage in a thoughtful conversation. If this happens:

---

3. The word translated as "servant" is often translated as "slave."

- It is important that you attempt to learn about the person's culture. What are the reasons this person speaks about an important subject in a particular way?
- You may even need to find a way to put yourself in the person's context and culture and ask for help in understanding what is being said in a more empathic way.
- You then may be able to identify with the other person, especially those who may have been mistreated and need our attention and care.
- You discern as far as possible what is truly being said, what feelings might be behind the words, and reflect this understanding with compassion, not advice.
- It is okay to make some mistakes; simply smile and apologize.
- Hang in there when the going gets tough. Do not rudely withdraw; stay in the conversation and ask for clarification.

And if there are deep differences or even conflict, there are good ways to continue engaging with the other person, ones that have understanding love at the core.

- Begin by attempting to understand the other person's point of view. Why do they say what they say? Come with a spirit of openness to listen rather than judge and speak.
- In general, do not confront the other person harshly if you want to continue in the relationship, although you may want to offer your views in a careful and thoughtful way.
- Be aware of your own need to address the difference or the conflict, and do so in a sensitive way without making an unfair judgment or an accusation.
- Keep your eye on the greater good, to gain understanding and restore the relationship and show love.
- Be open to accepting your negative feelings and those of the other person, and demonstrate understanding, empathy, timing, and the nature of the relationship.
- Listen carefully, ask if your understanding is correct, and be willing to adjust your judgment to reflect reality, overcoming the misunderstanding.

In short, if these behaviors are present, we and they will likely feel understood. Then we will be able to show respect and, perhaps in time, a good measure of love. The following will then likely be present in the communication:

- We will be able to come quietly and carefully into each other's world, and we will let each one be who we are.
- We will need to let go of our need to correct them and win the argument, an attitude and action that only deepens the separation.
- We will be able to invite the other person into a genuine effort to understand us, not judge us in the midst of a difference of opinion or a conflict. We do not get defensive and then push back with anger or advice, but help with ways of mutual understanding and honor the other person.
- We accept the other person even if there are differences, some of which may be a bit difficult to accept because we may not like their behavior and disagree with them. We recognize that they are a child of God who needs love and acceptance, even if we sense there is a need for some transformation.
- As possible, we express gratitude to the other person for the learning that has occurred. They are who they are in large part because of their past; we accept them and learn from the encounter about the journey of their soul.

Strengths of Character and Ethical Formation

The behavior we express in our relationships with others grows out of who we are. Of course, there are some exchanges that are just a way of getting through the day, and our pattern for these is to be polite. However, our long-term relationships have within them more than just routine actions and words we express because we are following a list of expected and preferred behaviors that are the norm in our setting. When Paul urges the Philippian Christians to love one another, he speaks not as one just giving routine guidelines, but one who senses that loving behavior is the result of being mature. One kind of maturity may be present because we have begun to live a life filled with love, understanding, and nurture. This kind of respect and polite behavior is a foundational starting point. Yet Paul speaks of another kind of maturity, one that is the result of a transformation, a fundamental change that has occurred in our character. He writes: "Let this same mind be in you that was in Christ Jesus, who, though he was in the form of God, did not regard equality with God as something to be exploited, but emptied himself, taking the form of a [servant], being born in human likeness. And being found in human form, he humbled himself and became obedient to the point of death—even death on a cross" (Phil 2:5–8). Paul uses this example of Jesus to make the point that loving and truthful behavior grows out of a change in character, not just a shift in becoming more polite, although to be polite may be appropriate as well. Yet to have the mind of Christ is to be transformed into a new person, to have one's identity and character changed, enabling and empowering one to live in a loving and truthful way.

We read this passage sensing that it is an invitation to a profound change, not to just rearrange a few guidelines for getting through the day. It is rather to give oneself to the God of truth and light and become a new person with changes in one's character that manifests in a way of being and living.

One of the challenges of using this biblical guidance in order to express ways of growing and becoming more mature is that the Bible often lists those qualities that are present in the truly mature person in the language of the time in which the passage was written. These expressions have great value, although to learn from them, we may need to do some very careful study of the culture and language in which they were written. We do need to be sensitive to the hermeneutical challenge of gaining wisdom and guidance from the literature of the past and bringing it forward into the present. There is the risk, if we ignore the need for careful interpretation, that we will make it say what we want it to say rather that what it does say. It is often difficult to do this work of translation from one time and culture to another time and culture—and language! I am suggesting that it is worth the effort if we want to truly learn from Jesus.

There is perhaps no greater model of what it means to be a mature and good human being than the one we have of Jesus in the New Testament. Yet we are not always given, in contemporary language, the stories of how Jesus encountered others and how he became who he was, what he taught, and what he did.[4] Yet we do have some very good information. We are told that Mary and Joseph were likely good parents, although Joseph may have passed away as Jesus moved toward becoming an adult. There is a sense that the parents of Jesus gave him love and guidance. We know that he was likely exposed to the values inherent in the Hebrew Bible as the family most likely attended a small synagogue in Nazareth. He learned the spiritual practices of the time from those who surrounded him. Although we have few specific records, we sense that he was especially loved by his mother, following his

---

4. I have well over a hundred books about Jesus in my personal library, and as I read them, I discover that there are many ways to understand Jesus and interpret what he says and does.

father's death. And as a Jewish family, there may have been prayer, reflection, and contemplation in the context of this family.

What is partially lacking, even though numerous efforts have been made and many of them are very well done and helpful, is the full description of his growth and development in the categories of current psychological understanding. Our accounts of his life move almost directly from his childhood to his adulthood. Our task, then, has some complications as we try to understand and then teach the story of Jesus. With careful study, we do learn that he likely had good models in his parents, some exposure to the Hebrew Bible, and the occasional connection with a rabbi or an elder in the Judaism of his time. In addition to the limited accounts in the Gospels, we can surmise that he had mature people in his life, those who guided him in the study of the Hebrew Bible, attendance in religious services, and encouragement to pray.

By understanding this process and pattern in the life of Jesus, we learn that his culture was present in his teaching, yet we also learn that his life and teaching have within them what is universal, rising above his culture, language, and the limitations of his time in history. He is and has been the world's teacher. We can be grateful for what he said and did because of this universal character; it speaks to all of us regardless of our time in history, our different culture, and our variety of languages. With good hermeneutical practices, we learn a great deal about that which is good and true from Jesus.

Fortunately, when this is the case, we are then able to have his life and teaching cross over into the contemporary study of human growth and development and the extensive literature in the field of ethics. This wealth of information, coupled with our understanding of biblical history and of Jesus, can guide us as we seek to find our way into the good and fulfilling life. Then, with some care, it may be wise and acceptable to expand our understanding of the life and teaching of Jesus within the categories of contemporary research and study. If we do it wisely and well, not in a narrow, cultic way just to prove a theological point or defend a cultic practice, we are able to find a profoundly informed and healthy way to mature and to live.

Character Strengths and Maturity

In order to inform our understanding about how spiritual maturity leads to character strengths and the ethical life, I would like to turn to a brief review of character strengths as understood by The Positivity Project, a curriculum based on a three-year study of character strengths by Dr. Chris Peterson, one of the founders of positive psychology.[5] The Project's model provides us with a frame of reference to review the values that Jesus lived and taught, put them in contemporary language, and apply them to our lives and our social context. The Project expresses its goal of enhancing our youths' "self-awareness and self-confidence, understanding and appreciation of others, and interpersonal relationships—which will positively influence our youth (individually and collectively) across their lifespans. Ranging from bravery and creativity to integrity and gratitude, positive psychology's 24 character strengths are the foundation of The Positivity Project's model."[6]

The Project begins with a definition of character, suggesting that it is not "simply individual achievement. It's the intersection of our thoughts, our feelings, and our behaviors."[7] This assumption matches our assumption that it is the whole person who is in the process of becoming in Christian formation, not just one part of the person such as the spiritual component of the person often called the soul. As Paul reminds us, "the fruit of the Spirit is love, joy, peace, patience, kindness, generosity, faithfulness, gentleness, and self-control" (Gal 5:22–23). In this affirmation, Paul is saying that our relationship with God, having the presence of God's spirit within us, will inform and empower our total transformation, leaving behind sexual exploitation, idolatry, strife and jealousy, quarrels and dissensions, envy, drunkenness, etc., behaviors that do not reflect being filled with the presence and power of God (Gal 5:16–21).

The Model of Character Strengths

As stated above, the goal of the Project's model is to provide self-confidence, grounded in self-awareness, and to have clear goals for self-improvement, ones that will lead to better interpersonal relationships. Or to put it in our context of Christian understanding and growth, we might say to empower us to cultivate a life filled with unconditional love that is expressed in our relationships and is applied to the larger task of creating a more just and humane society and world. We are underlining that character matters.

The model we are referencing speaks of character as an integrated center of the person filled with one's thoughts, feelings, and behaviors. It is to speak of one's identity as a person who is in the process of becoming, not

---

5. The Positivity Project notes that the material has not undergone full academic validation. The focus of the Project is on assisting youth in the school setting in the cultivation of character strengths. We will reference this study as "Project."

6. Project, "Character Strengths: Overview," paras. 4–5.

7. Project, "Character Strengths: What Is Character?," para. 1.

yet fully whole, but one on the way, seeking guidance and empowerment. As one speaks of this process, there is a distinction between one's identity, our center, and the values and goals within the person, our way of living. There is a person who has character strengths, and as the person matures, these values are able to be expressed in consistent ways. We say in a Christian context that as the person develops and becomes whole, the person is enabled and empowered by God's grace to express the deepest values of Christian understanding: truth, love, and justice. We are on the right track (truth), expressing the central value of love, and giving ourselves to the goal of creating a more just and compassionate society and world. We are transformed, love those whom we encounter daily, care deeply, and do our part in reducing human suffering. We join with others in making our context and the world settings in which all people can flourish.

Positive psychology, a branch of the larger discipline of psychology that we are following, maintains that for us to be a positive force for good, we need to cultivate and express six virtues. The model also articulates how each of the six virtues has within it three to five dimensions or character strengths, which are the way the virtue takes form in behavior. There are a total of twenty-four character strengths on the list.[8]

- Wisdom and Knowledge: We really must know what we are doing in order to nurture and express the character strengths. For example, to truly love in a wise, healing, and intelligent way, we must have experience and be informed. To be sure, there is an innocent and spontaneous expression of love, but to help one another and make our love healing and life giving, we need to know what we are doing. There is the need to have the character strengths of creativity, curiosity, open-mindedness, perspective, and the love of learning about the nature and skills required to express selfless and nurturing love.

- Humanity: There are times when we may find in our life situation that there is a lack of deep concern for another; we may be preoccupied with our needs and challenges or find the other person unattractive. But to truly care for others, the ones whom we serve must sense our unconditional acceptance and deep concern for their well-being. The character strength list includes love, kindness, and social intelligence.

- Justice: In many cases in our interaction with others, we respond only to their feelings and thoughts and neglect that they may be suffering because they are in a context and social environment which is unjust and may not provide the basic necessities of the good life. We help

8. Project, "Character Strengths: Six Virtues," paras. 2–7.

them find solutions to their social condition, and the resources and how to access them in order to be sure that they are treated fairly. The character strength list includes teamwork, fairness, and leadership.

- Courage: In order to manage the context and thrive in a world filled with danger and neglect, we must have the courage to challenge injustice, neglect, and social conditions that may feel overwhelming. There may be times when we, and the people we love and serve, want to give up and say, in essence, it is not worth the effort, I am tired, and I don't want to try any longer. But we need to resist these attitudes, be brave, have integrity with our deepest values, and move forward with enthusiasm. The character strength list includes bravery, perseverance, integrity, and enthusiasm.

- Temperance: It is not uncommon for those whom we serve to live in a setting that has a measure of positive social circumstances and components which are harmful in the infrastructure of the environment. It is in these settings that we need to have a measure of moderation and some restraint in the ways we seek to improve our social context. We know it is complex, perhaps even dangerous, and we need to be thoughtful and careful. The character strengths we need to express this virtue are forgiveness, humility, self-control, and a spirit of facing and dealing with reality in an accurate and prudent way.

- Transcendence: In our secular world, it may be difficult to discern that there may be deeper realities best described in a religious and spiritual way. We may not easily recognize them because the assumptions in our understanding do not reflect the possibility of transcendence, another level of reality. And when we are hurt and angry because of the particular circumstances of our life, we are inclined to focus exclusively on that which makes us suffer. Yet, in most cases, there may be a deep reality below the surface that is present and that will help us see more accurately and understand our suffering. We manage and grow, even in the midst of suffering, as we call upon the wisdom and power of a transcendent outlook. The list of character strengths related to transcendence include purpose, optimism, humor, gratitude, and an appreciation of beauty and excellence.

The Spiritual Virtues

The list of virtues, six in number, and their respective character strengths (twenty-four in number) provide us with a practical and informative model of how we might understand the goals of a healthy and ethical life that guides us toward becoming a mature and responsible person. The Project's main venue for expressing these definitions of character and the values of a healthy and responsible life is the school system. It is an informed and practical way to understand education as a way of developing the whole person. Education should enable students to learn knowledge about the external world, but also to become mature people who know how to use knowledge for the good of the human family and the health of our threatened world.

Ways to the Center in the Religions of the Human Family

There is some continuity and similarity between the list of virtues and character strengths in the Positivity Project and the teaching of ethical behaviors in the spiritual model of most religions. The great religious traditions of the human family, with some idiosyncratic exceptions, attempt to help their adherents to grow in knowledge and understanding of foundational virtues and their expression of mature and ethical behavior; almost all of them are dedicated to helping their adherents become healthy and mature individuals. The difference between the two models, the Positivity Project and the religious/spiritual model, may be that the character strength of transcendence becomes more visible and central in the religious outlook. We turn now to explore in more depth the soul's journey of being transformed and how this transformation leads to a life dedicated to addressing the profound needs present in our perilous world.

Questions for Reflection and Discussion

1. How is possible for us to get outside of our beliefs and values and have empathy for and identify with those taught within a different religion and culture?
2. How would you answer the question, What is the heart of Christian ethics?
3. How does a deep spirituality manifest itself in empowering a person to become one with high ethical standards?

4. In what ways do the values of our culture match and interact with the values of a religious orientation?
5. What steps do you think you should take in order to become a more ethical person?

Key Terms and Concepts

1. Spirituality: That quality and experience in our lives that reflects the attitude and spirit of one who is in tune with God or other forms of transcendence. In Christian thought, spirituality is to have the spirit of God within one's life and to cultivate and practice a way of life devoted to the will of God.
2. Transformation: To be transformed is to be fundamental changed in terms of your outlook and way of life; in Christian thought, it is to invite the spirit of God to be the foundation of your life, a commitment that empowers you to become a person with a commitment to truth, the practice of love, and the pursuit of justice.
3. Mind of Christ: It is a term used by the apostle Paul in his writing which means that our center, our identity, our values, and our way of life are guided and patterned by the life and teaching of Jesus.
4. Hermeneutics: That scholarly practice of interpreting the literature of the past and bringing it forward into the present in a careful way and applying it to contemporary life. It is central to the study of the Bible.
5. Virtues and character strengths: In the Positivity Project there is the attempt to identify the best ethical behavior. Virtue is a general term covering a vast area of behavior, and character strength is a behavioral pattern within a particular virtue.

Suggestions for Reference and Reading

1. *Agape and Eros: A Study of the Christian Idea of Love* by Anders Nygren
2. *Ethics: A Complete Method for Moral Choice* by Daniel C. Maguire
3. *Kingdom Ethics: Following Jesus in Contemporary Context* by David P. Gushee and Glen H. Stassen
4. *The Nature of Love* by Irving Singer

5. *Unlimited Love: Altruism, Compassion, and Service* by Stephen G. Post

SECTION THREE

The Soul's Journey of Being Transformed

Engaging in Mission in a Troubled World

He has told you, O mortal, what is good; and what does the Lord require of you but to do justice, and to love kindness, and to walk humbly with your God?

Micah 6:8

You have heard that it was said, "You shall love your neighbor and hate your enemy." But I say to you, Love your enemies and pray for those who persecute you.

Matthew 5:43–44

God is love, and those who abide in love abide in God, and God abides in them. . . .
There is no fear in love, but perfect love casts out fear. . . . .
The commandment we have from him is this: those who love
God must love their brothers and sisters also.

1 John 4:16, 18, 21

> Love is reckless and carefree, small, trifling minds seek profit, but true lovers lavish everything on love and never expect benefits in return.
>
> *Rumi, Day by Day*

There is the continual challenge for the world's religions to invite each new generation of those whom they serve to place their faith in a loving God, to engage in the process of becoming transformed by the loving God in this act of faith, and then to take the difficult path of faith by committing to the responsible life of discipleship, loving service, and joining in the cause of creating a more compassionate, just, and peaceful world.

CHAPTER SEVEN

On Being Transformed
Understanding and Endorsing the Divine Presence as Love

> In everything do to others as you would have them do to you; for this is the law and the prophets. Enter through the narrow gate; for the gate is wide and the road is easy that leads to destruction, and there are many who take it. For the gate is narrow and the road is hard that leads to life, and there are few who find it.
>
> Matthew 7:12–14

JESUS TEACHES THAT GOD'S love is available and immediately present for all people. This blessing was illustrated by the reality that God makes the sun rise on both those who do evil and those who do good, and that God also sends rain on the righteous and on the unrighteous. As Jesus teaches his followers and encounters those from different cultures and religious traditions, he reassures them of God's love and invites them to endorse the invitation of God, to take the narrow gate, and to walk the road that leads to personal renewal, inner peace, and the life of love and service.

There is one quite vivid and illustrative story about Jesus speaking with a Samaritan woman, a minority person who struggled in life. As he traveled with his disciples from the region of the Galilee south to Jerusalem, he met people with different backgrounds such as the woman at the well in the region called Samaria in the town of Sychar (John 4:1–30). Jesus and his disciples pause there, and his disciples leave him briefly, perhaps to find food for the next meal. Jesus remained at the well.

It was a sacred place, one for rest and renewal and that honored their ancestor, Jacob, who got water from this common well. It was called and continues to be called Jacob's well. A Samaritan woman comes to draw water, and Jesus, across the boundaries of social class and cultural differences, asks her for a drink of water. The woman was surprised that this Jewish man would even speak with her, a Samaritan woman, let alone ask her for water. They have a conversation in which Jesus learns about her difficulties in life, that she is now on her sixth husband. He speaks with her about "living water" by which he means the forgiving, accepting, and guiding love of God. She grasps this great truth, is remarkably transformed by it, and returns to her village and tells the story of her encounter with Jesus and her transformation. The people in her village are deeply moved by her story and want living water, which Jesus was eager to give to all people. It wasn't long before the people in the village began a new life. We, too, need to receive God's love, open the gate, and walk the pathway of love and service. We, too, need living water.

The apostle John, in telling the story, remarks that the people of Samaria had a different pattern of worship and slightly different beliefs than those in traditional Judaism. But they nevertheless longed to encounter and learn from the God about whom Jesus taught. Jesus adds to the story and says that the time is coming when these people, and indeed all people, "will worship the Father in spirit and truth" (John 4:23).[1] The Samaritans sense that he is the Messiah, and "many Samaritans from that city believed in him because of the woman's testimony" (John 4:39).

This story, and indeed many of the other accounts and stories about Jesus, have been interpreted in many ways, passing through an oral stage initially and then later being put into writing. Perhaps the most common and least complex interpretation of this passage of Scripture about Jesus at Jacob's well is that the Samaritans believed in a coming Messiah who would emancipate them from their minority status and their suffering and bring them a life full of personal peace and life in a more just society. They sense that Jesus is that one to bring this new way of life, and he is called in this account in the Gospel of John, "the Savior of the world" (John 4:42).

The story, written by the writer of John's Gospel several years after the event, although preserved in an oral tradition, is inclusive rather than sectarian. It is not suggesting a tribal set of beliefs and cultic practices. In

1. This may be a statement suggesting an inclusive outlook, although it is not explicitly said in the text, and it is wise not to have it say more than was meant by the author of John's Gospel.

its current form, it is a promise to all people of God's love, expressed in the actions and teaching of Jesus in a particular setting that was not an integral part of Jewish life and mainline Judaism. The invitation is inclusive, not limited to Jewish people and the majority culture of Judaism.

The story is a wonderful invitation to all people that God's love, expressed in the life and teaching of Jesus, is available to the entire human family, not just the Jewish leadership in Jerusalem, for example. In fact, later in his ministry, Jesus challenges some of the beliefs and practices of the scribes, Pharisees, and Sadducees, in part because their beliefs and practices did not fully take into account the nature of God's unconditional love for all people, even for Samaritans and, as we read in the Gospels, also for Roman soldiers.

I want to take this story and several like it in other parts of the New Testament and say that God speaks all the languages of the human family and meets any and all people as they gather at their well and drink the living water of life and love. He gives this water to all, not just to the insiders of a particular and exclusive community with elements of a tribal and cultic religious orientation. Yes, I know that the majority of people, deeply rooted in a religious faith, often believe that their understanding of religious belief and practice is the right one. It may be, especially for them, but it is also true that God's love gives nurturing sun and rain to all people, even to those who do not always acknowledge it and drink from one particular well. The author in 1 John says to all of us that "God is love, and those who abide in love abide in God" (4:16). God's love is universal, not dependent upon exclusive idiosyncratic beliefs and practices.

Ways of Accepting and Endorsing the Divine Presence of Love

It is beyond the scope of this book to describe in detail the many ways that the human family has sought living water, ways of encountering the divine (God), and then following a prescribed pattern of belief and practice. Our goal is rather to discern and suggest four broad expressions of the human quest to encounter God and live an authentic spiritual life, even in perilous times.[2]

---

2. Of course, there are some risks in limiting these ways of encountering God to these four broad spiritual pathways. There may be many forms of these pathways, ideal for each individual. And each spiritual quest is by a unique person, making their journey ideal for them. I address some of these issues in my book *Exploring the Spirituality of the World Religions*.

1. One common way for many is to find a pathway of belief and spirituality in nature.
2. A second way is to discern the presence of God in powerful social and political realities, and even political leaders.
3. A third way, expressed in Abrahamic monotheism, understands the divine as other, the creator and sustainer of the universe, and one who invites a thoughtful faith based on the message of great teachers and the literature of a traditional religion.
4. A fourth way is expressed in the belief in one overarching profound truth, inherent in the universe. In deep meditation, one connects with this truth and finds personal peace and meaning. This orientation is often called transcendental monism.

As we study these traditions, we will discover that those who have followed a particular religious orientation have generally believed that their religious pathway is the true one, and it may be for them. In some cases, those with a particular faith orientation have believed that other religious pathways do not always teach what is essentially true, although perhaps their way may contain elements of truth. Not infrequently, these families of religious belief and practice assume and maintain that they have the truth, know what to believe, and how to follow the will of God.

As I have journeyed, I have begun to question the tendency to be exclusive and maintain that there is only one right way to believe and practice one's religion. It has certainly been tempting for me to affirm and make universal a way that appears to be credible, well informed, and life giving. Such an outlook is attractive and reassuring, giving confidence to those believing it is the way to encounter God, to be spiritual, and to be empowered to live a purposeful and ethical life.

I certainly understand why people endorse such views and understand them as the way. In fact, I had traces of this orientation early in my spiritual odyssey. I was introduced to a relatively exclusive religious outlook in my teenage years, a time when I was relatively uninformed about religion. Those who introduced this point of view to me were kind and sincere, and I had no reason not to trust them. As one growing up in the context of the mid-twentieth century in California, I observed their beliefs and practices that seemed to work for them and other teenagers. I reasoned that they should work for me as well, not fully understanding that these views grew out of a particular time in history and middle-class American culture in the 1950s.

Leaders of these more exclusive religious outlooks witness to those seeking a pathway of faith and say that what they teach is the truth and that one becomes a true believer by affirming the beliefs, practices, and ethical teaching of this orientation. It was quite easy in such a context for me to accept this way of understanding of the life of faith. It was a good and healthy path, although I was unable in my innocent youth to fully grasp that this way was somewhat limited by history, language, and culture. It took a while for me to understand that all religious traditions and their believers have historical and cultural backgrounds and a given preunderstanding as they come to the questions of religion and the practice of faith.[3] They come with a language, a culture, values, and a point of view, along with some questions, insecurities, and fears.

I am still guided by an expanded and better-developed form of faith related to the earlier one that I was introduced to in high school. But I now know it is wise, given the complexity of what we are describing, to say with some humility that my view is as accurate and truthful as I can make it. Yet I know that it contains the elements of my history, language, and culture that may not be universal. In fact, the human family has many religions and spiritual pathways and even deep differences within a particular religious orientation.

I have found it very helpful to have exchanges with others within the larger Christian community and those with a different faith tradition. In these conversations, I have tried to honor their sincerity and to find ways to collaborate in areas of common belief, often in spiritual practices such as meditation, the quest to reduce human suffering, and with the commitment to seek a more just society and compassionate world. There is much common ground.

In a somewhat limited way, with doctoral studies in the field, professional responsibility to teach world religions in higher education, and the privilege of traveling to the many settings where other religions are practiced, I have discovered and had confirmed that what humans believe about God is expressed in the language, history, culture, and the personal experiences of their time and place. For the most part, their religious orientation has generally given them a better life.

This understanding may sound acceptable to those who are open to other cultures and look at a particular religion as a cultural phenomenon, not always a full expression of universal truth but perhaps pointing to it. This more inclusive and accepting orientation may often be overlooked when we

---

3. I write about the place of preunderstanding in my book *Biblical Hermeneutics: An Introduction*.

assume that our own understanding is "the" truth. I accept that my views are limited, and then take this awareness and place it alongside the words of Matthew's Gospel, that God's love makes the "sun rise on the evil and on the good, and sends rain on the righteous and on the unrighteous" (5:45). This affirmation in the Gospel of Matthew is a way of saying that God does speak to and enter into all the languages and cultures of the human family, honors the many ways that these people grasp the divine presence, and invites the human family to make the connection with God and follow the divine will and way within the context of their history and the challenges in their lives.[4] We are not totally unlike the woman from Samaria who spoke with Jesus at the well.

Ways of Understanding the Divine and Following Divine Guidance

There are several ways of classifying religions and the pathways of spirituality. What I have generally used in explaining these many views in my teaching and writing is to identify the major starting point of the various religious outlooks, not always an easy task.[5] Yet it is a way to begin to understand how human beings have discovered and articulated the ways the divine takes expression in human life. We then begin to understand a religious orientation and how the spiritual journey flows from this understanding.

A careful study and reflection on the nature and character of a particular religious orientation will reveal how it may offer a healthy and life-giving spiritual pathway. It may also reveal to us whether, as we study it carefully, it is credible and prescribes a healthy way; religion can often be dangerous and be based on a flawed foundation.

I am suggesting that the human family has found at least these four broad ways of understanding the divine and pursuing a spiritual pathway described in the chapters below. As I briefly describe them, I will offer some

---

4. I have many wonderful and lifelong friends who sincerely believe that their way is God's way, and who wonder why I have "lost my faith" because I am open to the authentic nature of many religious traditions. I can only say in response that I believe in a God who loves the human family, and indeed all of reality in marvelous ways, and that I can learn from others in different religious traditions, even if they are not Scottish Presbyterians. The sun shines and it rains on all of us to sustain life, especially with the rain in Edinburgh! I learn from the Buddha, although I follow the life and teaching of Jesus, and I am not surprised that they both spoke about love. Many important questions are centered on whether a religious outlook is credible and helps, heals, and leads to a life of love.

5. Ferguson, *Exploring*.

guidance on whether these religious outlooks are credible (truthful,) and whether they offer guidance for spiritual practice that is based on a mature and healthy spiritual pathway that leads to a responsible and fulfilling life.[6]

- The divine is viewed as present in the power of human feelings and thought, often present in prophets, political leaders, and even government structures.
- The divine is viewed as being present in the grandeur of nature, and that the natural order of the universe guides us to a spiritual pathway.
- The divine is other, and is revealed to us as it is described in Abrahamic monotheism: there is one God who created all that exists and guides followers in the several modes of God's revelation, identified in Judaism, Christianity, Islam, and in other less well-known religious traditions.
- The divine is ultimate reality, or the center of the pattern of energy undergirding and moving all of reality described in cosmic evolution. Humans find a responsible spiritual pathway through reflection and meditation on ways the universe is functioning and then living in the suggested patterns of this great universal truth. It is a journey of awakening and the realization of a higher consciousness.

It is generally assumed in each of these views that the divine (God) does reveal a personal or nurturing presence, has extraordinary power, and gives guidance to the human family about how to live. There is ample historical evidence that suggests and supports that there are at least these four types of human understanding of the divine presence and divine wisdom, with each one filled with somewhat complex characteristics. They all affirm in their own way that the divine or truth is the positive energy undergirding the cosmos.[7]

I want to illustrate briefly these views of the divine, beginning with the first two views: first, that the divine is incarnated in the midst of the human drama in political power and cultural norms and second, the divine is expressed in the domain of nature and in the order and structure of the universe.

---

6. Other categories are often used to describe how humans have sought to connect with the divine; these four may not be fully inclusive. Yet this inquiry about the four ways is at least a place to start.

7. There may be other ways of describing the divine, and there is certainly diversity within the ones mentioned.

Spiritual Pathways Rooted in Culture and Nature

It was common in ancient civilizations to project the divine presence in the cultural patterns of an empire and the vast power residing in a tribal chief or king or emperor. The pharaohs in ancient Egypt (ca. 3500–1000 BC) were seen as divine, and their identity was linked to both nature and their political power. The divine was clearly present in many aspects of their common life. There was an awareness that the seasons were related to the majestic sun and the steady flow of the Nile River; this natural order was viewed as an expression of the divine, and it gave the Egyptians a measure of security and a pattern of life. This belief granted the pharaohs absolute control, and the wise pharaohs governed within the natural rhythms of nature, given special expression in the seasonal flow of the Nile.

In ancient Greek and Roman religion, there was the belief in a variety of gods, often projections of human emotions and expressions of the power of nature and government control. There were the primary gods: Zeus (the chief deity and related to the sky and weather), Apollo (the god related to human experience), and Dionysus (the god who gave freedom to the expression of human feelings and made them aware of their emotions, often leading them into ecstatic dance). There was a whole pantheon of gods, originating in Greece and adopted by the Romans who were inclined to change some of the names of the gods:

- Hera, the jealous wife of Zeus, was the goddess of women, children, and childbirth;
- Apollo, the son of Zeus, was the god of archery, prophecy, and music;
- Hermes was the god of highways and the marketplace;
- Poseidon was the god of the sea;
- Artemis was the goddess of wisdom;
- Demeter was the goddess of vegetation and grain;
- Ares was the god of war;
- Aphrodite was the goddess of love and beauty;
- Hephaestus was the god of fire; and
- Hestia was the goddess of the hearth.

The divine, as one observes from the names of the gods of ancient Greece and Rome, was clearly defined and identified in the leaders, the culture, political realities, and in nature.

This notion of discovering the divine in nature is basic in the native traditions of the human family. There was a strong sense that wisdom could be found within nature's ways. In American history, there was this sense of understanding the divine within the ebb and flow of nature by its first people. It was challenged by the more "civilized" people who attempted to take their land away from them. Many of the native tribes resisted when their land was taken from them and they were relocated on reservations. The way of life of American Indians was seen as primitive by many in the mainline culture of an earlier period in American life.

Yet the native people pushed back and continued to live within their beliefs and learn about the divine and how to be spiritual from the patterns of nature. Chief Seattle writes in 1854, "The President in Washington sends word that he wishes to buy our land. But how can you buy or sell the sky? The land? The idea is strange to us. If we do not own the freshness of the air and the sparkle of the water, how can you buy them?"[8]

I value learning about how early humans understood the presence of the divine in their daily lives, in government affairs, cultural life, and in nature. It was a way for them to understand the complexity of life and discern wisdom about how to live in a safe and healthy way. These ancient and premodern cultures gave divine names to human behavior and nature's ways, suggesting how they might live in harmony with and in reference to what surrounded them. They felt invited to follow a more natural pattern of life.

Even the invading "civilized" people had a good measure of humility in the presence of the power and beauty of the natural world. The disciplines of science and historical study were not yet sufficiently sophisticated to explain fully the many and profound expressions of nature's influence on individual life or the emperor's or the chief's power. Nature and tribal leadership remained awesome and powerful.

As human knowledge has developed and advanced, many of the human explanations of the divine, based on nature and culture, were nearly forced off the chart. We do live in a quite secular culture with little inclination to see the presence of the divine in nature or cultural expressions of political leadership. Yet it remains true that not all of reality has been fully explained by the natural sciences, the social sciences, historical study, and the insightful character of the liberal arts. We should honor the results of these scholarly inquiries as essentially describing and defining our environment, our understanding of what is, and its meaning for us; the resulting way of life need not have a reference to the divine. Yet many people still find guidance and grounds for religious belief in nature and the vast diversity of

---

8. Hardy, "Chief Seattle's Letter," para. 1.

human activity. There may still be questions that science, history, philosophy, and religious thought have not fully answered, and among them are some of life's most pressing questions such as the origins of cosmic evolution, quantum theory, global ethics, universal values, and the ground for hope in a world that seems to have lost its way.

It is certainly the case that many humans have attempted to describe and understand the divine by looking directly at their experience in the natural world. Humans know that nature is powerful, the foundation on which much of human life is based and an essential source of their well-being. Many ancient cultures sensed the divine presence in the natural world; its power caused them to tremble and be humble before it. Nature brought humans the food to sustain them and the rain and sun for the growth of the crops; its vastness and beauty created a sense of awe and wonder. They saw the divine presence in that which sustained them, contributed to their health and happiness, and caused them to feel humble before nature's power.

Nearly all of the human expressions of belief in the divine have many of these elements, although they are not always assumed to be sacred. It was more common in the ancient world to sense the incarnational presence of the divine in their immediate settings and circumstances, and there is still a semblance of this kind of belief in various forms in the modern world although the line between the sacred and secular may have shifted.

Those cultures that see the divine in nature and culture have spoken about it and continue to speak about it in a variety of ways. It is common to hear people speak about sacred powers that have changed their lives, often in reference to healing and the mysteries or unknown aspects of the cosmos. It is not uncommon to hear people speak about sacred stories that teach ethics, and then point to sacred actions that influence and reveal the divine presence and power.[9] There continues to be the belief in the presence of the divine in nature as one looks carefully and in depth at the marvelous world and beyond to the entire cosmos.

I found this to be the case as I had the extraordinary privilege of living in Anchorage, Alaska, for five years. I was especially interested in learning about the religious orientation of Alaska natives and gaining a deeper understanding of how the divine was often believed to be present in this vast, beautiful, and diverse natural setting. As I taught students about native religious belief, many of the Alaska native students confirmed that this sense of the divine in nature was part of their experience. In many ways, they taught me as they spoke about their religious understanding.

---

9. Ferguson, *Exploring*, 25–40.

I was especially encouraged when the students in Alaska noted that I had begun to understand their belief reasonably well. My categories of religious thought helped them understand their world, and their experience of nature taught me. It was a privilege to be invited to be a part of this religious orientation and see it and experience it directly.

As I taught, I began to put this experience into an orderly pattern, using some of the language and categories of religious studies. For example, I taught about animism, the belief that spirits and even souls inhabit and animate the mountains, the lakes, and the rivers, and that one should live with great respect for this essential natural order that kept humans alive and thriving. I also was led by devout Alaska natives to their grave sites and heard them speak about the influence and continuing presence of the life of their ancestors. Stories were told, becoming over time the central myths that guided those who now faced the same challenges as the ancestors. They gained an understanding of how to live within the destructive power of a storm, knowing that it was part of the abundant resources of nature.

As these stories were told, there were taboos or guidance on what one should not do in that it might be dangerous and invoke the anger of the gods. There were shamans, wise ones, accepted within the community and who would instruct the tribe about how to live in the wild and wonderful world of nature, huge and powerful, and sense within it the presence of the divine.

There were similar experiences of native peoples in other parts of North America, Australia, and indeed many other parts of the world. As a summary of this grand tradition, I want to underline five continuing contributions of this tradition to the human family, noting its value in this threatening time of climate change, and its capacity to inspire a deep spirituality.

1. These native people had great respect for nature and invited humans to integrate their lives within the natural patterns of nature rather than just exploiting nature for personal or social gain. Their church was outside in the grandeur of nature, and they learned from nature how to live in a spiritual way. The larger environment was vast in rural Alaska, and in many ways, nature became the church of the native people.

2. The indigenous wisdom traditions also gave the native peoples a centered life, not one that was driven by the quest for power, possessions, and prestige, although there were traces of this behavior in their lives. The native people were less likely to have competing values and conflicts that led to violence and the loss of human life. Yes, there was conflict in order to protect and preserve their land and a way of life, sometimes caused by the infusion of Anglo-Saxon people. Modest

conflicts were present among the tribes as well, and they were partially caused by the quest for power and control of a region where there were sources of food. These native peoples cultivated a sense of the divine rooted in preserving their way of life and it was a deeply spiritual odyssey for many of them.

3. In terms of religious belief, their way of life was in many respects their religion in that the divine was omnipresent in nature and integral to all of life; their life, in its original form, was rooted in nature. These people believed that they lived within the divine world order and understood nature and all of nature's creatures as containing and revealing the divine and suggesting a way of life. They lived with great integrity, especially in the rural areas where patterns of modern life were less intrusive.

4. There were the seasons—fall, winter, spring, and summer—each suggesting a pattern of life and a way of surviving. Nature suggested clear roles and taught a way of knowing and a way of acting to sustain their way of life. Nature's ways empowered them to survive and thrive, and taught them that there are ethical ways of treating others and the creatures of the world. Indeed, it was nature, the power and the structure and the order of nature, that taught them how to collaborate with other tribes in order to survive and experience the richness and joy of living in a marvelous world.[10]

The Current Challenge

There continues to be a wise and informed expression of finding a spiritual pathway in the natural order, although less prominent in contemporary life as people have moved away from their natural surroundings. We now live in cities with all the resources for survival given to us in grocery stores or in print or electronic forms. We learn if there will be rain by looking at the weather report on television and on our phones and computers, not as we might if we lived in less developed and rural regions.

We may look at the clouds in the sky that suggest possibilities for coming weather, but we get trustworthy information differently, living in the

---

10. Ferguson, *Exploring*, 23–40. These points suggest the need for an expanded definition and explanation, and there are valuable study resources. Thomas Berry's *The Dream of the Earth* has taken this pattern of understanding and suggested that the whole human family might benefit from living with nature, not being its competitor, caring for Mother Earth. See also Berry, *Sacred Universe*; and Christopher, *Holy Universe*.

realm of postmodernity, a context of advanced technology, global economic structures, and a cultural and political life that is pretty much removed from the natural world; we just go to the natural world on vacations. Our spiritual perspectives and practices have moved beyond and away from the more indigenous wisdom that comes from the native peoples of the world.

Yet there continues to be a strong belief that we humans are still very dependent on the natural world. We know that it is basic to our way of life, and so we now teach our children about caring for the environment and encourage ways of living that do not harm our natural environment. We are driven by the extraordinary threat of climate change.

The indigenous traditions of the native people had wisdom about how to live in and with the natural order, and this way of life pointed them to ways of expressing their religious ideas and values. They were present in the structure of the tribe, the place of wise leaders who taught care for natural resources, and the importance of maintaining cooperation and communication between tribes in order to preserve a way of life.

Yet mistakes were made as these cultures began to be integrated with the city life and the larger world order. Their way of life and their culture were forced to make an adjustment to modernity with all of its complexity and challenge. Increasingly, the need for this adjustment became a threat to the patterns of understanding inherent in their traditional way of life.[11]

Their threatened environment was complex and had many dimensions, and there is much for us to learn as we study the impact of modernity on native cultures. I want to mention one in particular that has a long history and reappears in political leaders who were thought to be endowed and empowered to lead because they had the divine presence within them. This understanding has a long history, and its presence was very visible in many ancient cultures and regions. It has surfaced again, ironically, in what is called Christian nationalism, a movement that in many ways has distorted the beliefs and values inherent in the Christian faith.

I want to suggest a few ways to counter trends that have contributed to the crisis related to climate change. The first is to understand that caring for the earth is an integral component of the of the spiritual life. We read in the story of creation in Genesis that we are to be responsible stewards of nature and to honor the earth (Gen 1:26–27). There is the risk that the nations of the world now function as asocial tribes, threatening the natural order of the earth. Studies and books address this challenge of a deteriorating natural order and its impact on the climate. They tell us that what we

---

11. This adjustment has been studied extensively; our reference is to just one aspect of this profound adjustment to the modern and postmodern realities.

are currently experiencing has been the impact of our abuse of the natural world; we have not been faithful stewards of the earth. Our neglect is right in front of us, and our cultural patterns of responding, while on target, are not sufficient. I want to underline just a few consequences of the way we have abused nature as a reminder of our current situation and underline how difficult it is for our current social structures to respond.

1. There are endless distortions about the severity of the climate change, often defending practices that increase wealth for companies or meet the severe needs of a nation or region. Mis- and disinformation abound, although these distortions are increasingly being proved wrong. We are waking up and returning to a spiritual outlook that honors human life and cares about the good earth that sustains us.

2. There are the extraordinary defenses among companies, regions, and nations, and it is exceedingly difficult to make the necessary changes to sustain natural resources and preserve the environment on which we depend. There are some challenges to the power of global wealth, its abuse of the environment, and its disregard for human welfare, but they may not be sufficient.

3. Around the world in different countries and regions, there are differences of opinion about the problem and the level of immediate threat among the tribes and nations of the world. There are international organizations, such as the United Nations, that are using strategies and resources to solve our climate problems, but these problems are outpacing many of the more responsible and admirable efforts to care for the earth.

4. Almost daily, we either experience this threat or read about another part of the world which is experiencing it. Climate change has arrived; it is no longer just a subject we read about and it will be a part of our future. The hottest day ever recorded occurred just a few days ago as I write, and the floods, the fires, and the destructive weather patterns continue to occur in nearly every corner of the earth.

Finding Spiritual Inspiration and Direction

One resource for our threatened world is to call upon the great religious traditions of the world to join together in the common cause to save our world. We might need to review our sacred literature as we face our great crisis. In Genesis, we read:

God spoke: "Let us make human beings in our image, making them reflect our nature, so that they can be responsible for the fish of the sea, the birds of the air, the cattle, and yes, Earth itself, and every animal that moves on the face of the Earth." God created human beings, he created them godlike, reflecting God's nature. God created them male and female. God blessed them: "Prosper! Fill the Earth! Take charge! Be responsible for fish of the sea and the birds of the air, for every living thing that moves on the Earth." (1:26–28 MSG)[12]

This passage, and many others found in the literature of the world's religions, underline human responsibility for the care of the earth. Indeed, because of the enormous threat, this passage and the values it and its counterparts contain should form the inspiration and motivation to change the direction of how we treat the earth, our home. It is our spiritual challenge and our spirituality must guide us. It contains our responsibility to be good stewards and to care for the earth. We need to find our inspiration and direction to care for the earth from our deepest spiritual values.

Awareness and Gratitude

One way to motivate us to be good stewards of the earth is to increase our awareness of our dependence on the resources of nature and let this awareness cultivate a profound sense of gratitude. Humans are responsible for the resources that sustain human life and nature's creatures, and we have to find ways to live wisely and well. We cannot just take these resources for granted. We need to let the current threat to the environment motivate us and then inspire and empower us to care for the earth, making it a foundational spiritual value and priority. There is an abundance of material that has this aim, and I have learned from the scientific research and by observing threatened regions in different parts of the world. In particular, I have listened carefully to those who have found peace and purpose by being grateful for the earth's beauty and its capacity to nurture us. My wife and I have changed some of the patterns of our lives by being grateful and more responsible in the way we care for nature, our environment, and its many blessings.

---

12. Modest changes were made by me.

An Informed Outlook: The Stewardship of the Earth

Given my background in the study of religion, I have given some attention to the spiritual component of wisely caring for the earth. I have been influenced and informed by several scholars who have sought to integrate their theology with the scientific literature. The literature in this domain is extensive and would require a book-length manuscript just to describe it. The general direction of this literature is to suggest that one way of being faithful to God is to revise our theology and to suggest the use of spiritual practices in ways that are integrated with nature.

On a personal note, I want to point to one theologian-scientist that has transformed my thinking, the French scientist and theologian of the early to mid-twentieth century Pierre Teilhard de Chardin. He is occasionally placed in the theological movement known as process theology, a point of view that explores the concept of discerning the presence of God in the process of an evolving and developing universe. He is widely thought of as one who articulated in a profound way the need for a study of the fundamental unity between science and theology.[13]

Father Teilhard was a priest, a missionary, and a scientist. Following his training to become a priest, he continued his education and received his doctorate in paleontology from the Sorbonne in Paris. After a brief time serving as a stretcher-bearer in the First World War, he traveled to China where he did extensive research and began his writing. He was especially interested in developing an evolutionary understanding of the earth, integrating theology and science, and maintaining a vision of the cosmos as a whole process, moving toward greater complexity. As much as nearly anybody in the early twentieth century, he found ways of overcoming what was thought of as a conflict between science and religion. His work, now somewhat dated, still gives thoughtful scientists and scholars in the field of religion a way of understanding the union of the Creator and the creation. He truly sang for all of us in his book *Hymn of the Universe*, inviting us to unify our views of science and our understanding of the guiding hand of God in cosmic evolution. It is a vision that must be continued in every generation, as the world faces perilous times.[14]

---

13. Among his several books are *The Divine Milieu*, *Hymn of the Universe*, and *The Phenomenon of Man*.

14. He has many followers of his views on the unity of science and theology, suggesting that they are two sides of one coin. See the extensive work of Ilia Delio, a scientist and theologian who has brought Teilhard's thought into the twenty-first century. See, for example, *Making All Things New*. See as well the brilliant work of Ken Wilbur; his *Integral Spirituality* is a good starting point for understanding his views.

Questions for Reflection and Discussion

1. How does one become better able to experience, understand, and endorse the presence of God in one's life? In nature? In human history?
2. Is it possible for God's love to be accepted and embraced outside of your religious orientation—for example, outside of the Christian tradition?
3. Do you have a sense God's power and presence when you are in nature?
4. Do you think that God is ever present in the governments of nations?
5. What might we learn from American Indians and other native peoples about the spiritual life?

Key Terms and Concepts

1. Samaria: A region between the Galilee and Jerusalem that in the time of Jesus had a population that was not exclusively Jewish and had some religious ideas different from Jewish views.
2. Cultic: An attitude and spirit that embraces the views and actions that are unique to them and thought to be true by a group that does not accept alternative views of belief and practice.
3. Tribal: The pattern of belief and practice in a group that believes it is correct in its views and has a particular location and tends to be exclusive and protective.
4. Transcendental monism: The view that there is one true way to the truth and spiritual understanding, often referring to ultimate truth.
5. Cosmic evolution: The view that all that exists in the cosmos has evolved, not just what exists on earth.

Suggestions for Reference and Reading

1. *Hymn of the Universe* by Pierre Teilhard de Chardin
2. *Integral Spirituality: A Startling New Role for Religion in the Modern and Postmodern World* by Ken Wilbur
3. *Making All Things New: Catholicity, Cosmology, Consciousness* by Ilia Delio

4. *The Phenomenon of Man* by Pierre Teilhard de Chardin
5. *The Sacred Universe: Earth, Spirituality, and Religion in the Twenty-First Century* by Thomas Berry

CHAPTER EIGHT

On Being Transformed

Discerning and Cultivating One's Values, Responsibilities, and Spiritual Gifts for the Divine Mission in the World

> So God created humankind in his image, in the image of God he created them; male and female he created them. God blessed them.
>
> Genesis 1:27–28

> By contrast, the fruit of the Spirit is love, joy, peace, patience, kindness, generosity, faithfulness, gentleness, and self-control. There is no law against such things.
>
> Galatians 5:22–23

The Role of Humankind

WE AFFIRMED IN THE previous chapter that God is the creator of all there is, and that the divine hand continues to create, sustain, and guide what has been created. We attribute to God not only the creation of the cosmos and speak about it in the language of cosmic evolution, but also the special creation of humankind, often thought of as the final climax of the divine creation within the context of the evolutionary process. To humankind God gave the major responsibility for sustaining the goodness of the creation of our earth and forming and managing a just and humane social order.[1]

The role of humankind, then, is twofold: to care for the natural world in all of it richness and diversity ensuring that it continues to have the capacity to remain stable and healthy; and the responsibility to create a social order based on love and justice, one that empowers humans to have resilience and to live with peace and purpose. It is a total system in which humans care for creation and create social systems that nurture those who live carefully and wisely within the systems of nature. Humans flourish on a healthy earth and in a social system based on love and justice.

Caring for the Garden

The first human responsibility is to care for the earth and make it an environment that sustains the life of all of its parts and living beings. Only then will the earth be a place of beauty and a setting for human growth and development. It must be a healthy garden. We are to care for the creation for its own sake; it has inherent value. Yet it is also the setting for the welfare of the human family. If the creation is healthy, then we are ensured that basic human needs have the capacity to be met. We learn how to care for nature, one part of our home, and have the responsibility to create a peaceful world and a just social order, the other part of our home.

God is present in the natural world, and we celebrate this divine presence as we walk in the forest and look at the sea. We then undertake our task, knowing that it will be challenging to care for the created order in all of its vastness, beauty, and power. Grateful, although somewhat overwhelmed, we do it even though we do not always understand the totality and continuing development of the created order. As we affirm this special responsibility of humankind to be good stewards of the earth, we know we must have some humility about understanding the vastness and continuation of God's creative activity. We need to remind ourselves that we may not know all that the eternal and loving God has created elsewhere in the cosmos or might continue to be creating in our earth domain. We are wise, then, to be grateful for our special place in creation and undertake our task to honor the

---

1. We humans have generally affirmed that humankind was the peak of creation with humans having consciousness and the capacity to think, feel, and connect with God. Of course, there are many who think that the presence of God as integral part of the explanation for creation is unnecessary; cosmic evolution is what happened and is happening. There is no need for another layer of explanation.

Divine One who has created the vast cosmos. We are a bit overwhelmed as we learn that we are but a grain of sand on a vast beach and we give thanks and humbly assume our special role in cosmic evolution.

Managing the Garden

As we begin to understand and feel attracted to our assigned role in the created order, given to us by God, we cautiously say yes. We know that there is a profound need to study the sciences that inform us and the worldwide movement of ecology that addresses the severe problem of climate change. We also know that we must come to the problem well informed or we will just get in the way.

Our goal in this volume is to look at the concern more from a spiritual perspective than a scientific perspective, keeping a scientific understanding as our starting point. We soon learn that we must engage in an extensive study in order to grasp our particular mission and responsibilities. It may not be immediately apparent how to bring religious values and sensitivity to the problem of climate change.

We do this research about a spiritual perspective on the problem in a variety of ways, as did many of those who lived before us. Those in the Judeo-Christian tradition look first to the doctrine of creation and explore the divine intention for what exists. We turn to the early chapters of Genesis, carefully examine the life of Moses, and read with care the teaching of the great prophets. We systematically study the life and teaching of Jesus for guidance. We honor this accumulated wisdom, and then study and consult with other religious traditions in order to understand how to care for the earth, how to be responsible in the comprehensive system, how to love one's neighbor wisely and in an informed way in every corner of the earth. Traditional do-gooders may help, but might also get in the way if they deny the reality of the problem and perhaps project their dated beliefs about the age and the evolutionary development of the earth or their beliefs about the end of time, discounting science.

As we begin our preparation, we study the theology of creation, our mixed history of caring for the earth, and how to be wise and helpful in our dedication to care for the world and all that dwells in it. It is no small task, but the God of compassion has given us major responsibility. "Then God said, 'Let us make humankind in our image, according to our likeness; and let them have dominion over the fish of the sea, and over the birds of the air, and over the cattle, and over all the wild animals of the earth, and over every creeping thing that creeps upon the earth.' So God created humankind in [the divine image]" (Gen 1:26–27).[2] We are here to care for Mother Earth.

There is an interesting account in the Gospels about a lawyer who asks Jesus which commandment in the law is the greatest. Jesus replies, "'You shall love the Lord your God with all your heart, and with all your soul, and with all your mind.' This is the greatest and first commandment. And a second is like it: 'You shall love your neighbor as yourself.' On these two commandments hang all the law and the prophets" (Matt 22:37–40).

As Jesus gives this answer, he is assuming that human beings have the capacity to be in relationship with a personal God and to love their neighbor. To love our neighbor is to care about the garden in which our neighbor lives. Jesus learned from his faith and spiritual practices that human beings were created to love God and one's neighbor. Although he assumed that his listeners had this capacity, he knew firsthand that it was not easy to be consistent in following the dictates of the commandment. So, part of his mission was to help human beings put love at the center of their life, love for others of course, but also be concerned about the setting in which they lived. In fact, this may be one way of speaking about his life purpose, to help humans to understand how to love their neighbor and how to be empowered to love in a wise and constructive way, which includes being good stewards of creation.

I am somewhat taken by Dr. Caleb J. Lines's comment about the place of love in religious teaching: "The goal is not to bring people to Christianity; the goal is to bring people to love. If that's through Christianity, fine. If it's another religion or no religion at all, fine. What the world needs is love, not more people professing right belief."[3] God becomes present for us in loving relationships, and with divine guidance we join with our neighbors in caring for the creation, and help them to create just and humane social systems that value our earth home. Jesus may have given a bit more credit to religion than Dr. Lines, although he made some fairly harsh judgments about hypocritical religion.

The Priority of Love and the Capacity to Love

Love is a fairly broad term used in a variety of ways in many cultures and languages. One can love one's neighbor, love great music, and love to hike in a beautiful setting. We especially love our pets! In the time of Jesus, the word *love* had different nuances depending on the language spoken and the

2. I try to avoid understanding God in a masculine way.
3. Lines, "The goal is not."

different settings where Jesus had conversations. Jesus, likely influenced by the Hebrew of his religious upbringing, would have learned that love meant that we should care about and have compassion for one another. As he spoke about love, he may have spoken in Aramaic, which was the common language of his setting. Love would have had a similar meaning in Aramaic as it did in Hebrew, the language of the Jewish Bible. Greek also was used as the language of commerce in his time, and love, as it was spoken, would have had the influence of the three classical meanings of love in the Greek language, *agape* as unconditional love, *philia* as the love in friendships, and *eros* or the love of beauty and physical attraction. The word *eros* would not likely have been used in the Jewish communities, but would have been part of the larger worldview expressed in loving the beauty of creation.[4]

As Jesus spoke about God's love, it would have had the meaning of unconditional acceptance with caring and compassionate action on behalf of others. It certainly had some traces of *philia* or friendship, but it would have meant primarily *agape* or unconditional love. As we look at our capacities for love and the priority we give it, we need to be careful about what we mean as we use the word *love*, and then to ask how we cultivate the capacity to love. As those with deep spiritual convictions, we give love as unconditional acceptance a high priority in our behavior and assume that this true love goes beyond just mere acceptance of others, and engages in making life better for those whom we love. It is often our most important value, and if we truly care for others, we want them to have good home, Mother Earth, and have special compassion for those who suffer, and ease their suffering by forming just and humane social systems that draw the resources of a healthy earth environment.

Yet when we say that we ought to love others in these ways, we often find ourselves wondering where we gain the motivation and the capacity to love in such wise and healing ways. Our libraries and bookstores are full of books that suggest answers to these questions, and our faith traditions guide us as well. As I have reviewed these resources, I begin to find guidance about how, at least partially, to answer both of these questions: how should we care about creation, and how do we cultivate the capacity to truly love others by improving the settings in which they live?[5]

As one rooted in the Christian faith, I attempt to answer these questions daily in my experience and more systematically in my study and research. Increasingly across the years, my conviction that love is the essential ingredient in caring for our earth home, creating healthy and healing

---

4. See the entry on love in Patte, *Cambridge Dictionary of Christianity*, 739.
5. Ferguson, *Lovescapes*.

relationships, and in forming just and peaceful social settings has expanded and deepened. I also find it reassuring that Jesus gave love the highest priority in speaking about our earth home, a just society, and caring for human welfare. The answer, then, to question one about the nature of love is to understand it as *agape*, which means loving others unconditionally and caring for their well-being. To care for their well-being is to engage in at least four different concerns and tasks.

The first is to make sure that their basic needs for good health are present. Jesus consistently put this goal at the front of his concern for those that he met. He fed them when they were hungry, and he healed them when they were sick. On at least one occasion, as Jesus was teaching the multitudes, the people were vitally interested and remained listening beyond the meal time. The disciples suggested that Jesus let them go and seek food in the surrounding area.

> But he answered them, "You give them something to eat." They said to him, "Are we to go and buy two hundred denarii worth of bread, and give it to them to eat?" And he said to them, "How many loaves have you? Go and see." When they had found out, they said, "Five, and two fish." Then he ordered them to get all the people to sit down in groups on the green grass. So, they sat down in groups of hundreds and of fifties. Taking the five loaves and the two fish, he looked up to heaven, and blessed and broke the loaves, and gave them to his disciples to set before the people; and he divided the two fish among them all. And all ate and were filled; and they took up twelve baskets full of broken pieces and of the fish. Those who had eaten the loaves numbered five thousand men. (Mark 6:37–44)

There is another story about healing:

> When they had crossed over, they came to land at Gennesaret and moored the boat. When they got out of the boat, people at once recognized him, and rushed about that whole region and began to bring the sick on mats to wherever they heard he was. And wherever he went, into villages or cities or farms, they laid the sick in the marketplaces, and begged him that they might touch even the fringe of his cloak; and all who touched it were healed. (Mark 6:53–56)

In addition, he cared for their safety and security. Many whom he encountered were threatened by the political environment in the setting of first century Israel/Palestine. Roman soldiers were often present, as was the case toward the end of the ministry of Jesus:

> When Herod saw Jesus, he was very glad, for he had been wanting to see him for a long time, because he had heard about him and was hoping to see him perform some sign. He questioned him at some length, but Jesus gave him no answer. The chief priests and the scribes stood by, vehemently accusing him. (Luke 23:8–10)

Third, he cared deeply about the emotional and spiritual well-being of those whom he encountered. There are several stories in the Gospels that describe Jesus as a caring pastor, nurturing those near him. A dramatic one is recorded in chapter 8 of the Gospel of John:[6]

> Early in the morning [Jesus] came again to the temple. All the people came to him and he sat down and began to teach them. The scribes and the Pharisees brought a woman who had been caught in adultery; and making her stand before all of them, they said to him, "Teacher, this woman was caught in the very act of committing adultery. Now in the law Moses commanded us to stone such women. Now what do you say?" (vv. 2–5)

After some discussion, Jesus turns to them and says,

> "Let anyone among you who is without sin be the first to throw the stone at her." And once again he bent down and wrote on the ground. When they heard it, they went away, one by one, beginning with the elders; and Jesus was left alone with the woman standing before him. Jesus straightened up and said to her, "Woman, where are they? Has no one condemned you?" She said, "No one, sir." And Jesus said, "Neither do I condemn you. Go your way, and from now on do not sin again." (vv. 7–11)

It appears that Jesus did resist the objective of the religious leaders to catch him making a mistake about the teaching of the Torah on human sexuality. Jesus, rather that engaging in a long discussion about the law and its interpretation, appealed to the higher value of caring for a troubled woman, one who may have even been violated by one of the accusers. He places her welfare, with great sensitivity, above an argument about the interpretation of the law, and treats the woman, who may have even been violated by one of them, as worthy of love and healing care, a priority that rises above an argument about the hermeneutics of the law.

Fourth, he expressed a deep concern for all of those in the region of his travels, knowing that their well-being was dependent upon living in a

---

6. I am aware that this story has been questioned as authentic, perhaps made up at a later time. It is a complex question, but it certainly does reflect the loving spirit of Jesus.

setting of justice and peace. As a brilliant and thoughtful interpreter of the Jewish law, he again and again had conversations about the value of the law and its purpose to make life better for the citizens, not abusing the law by interpreting it as a means to discriminate against a foreign visitor or one of their own who had a need for help and healing. One question that came up on more than one occasion was the essential purpose of the Sabbath, understood by most as a day of rest. In the time of Jesus, and even in our time, among Jewish rabbis there is the question of what constitutes work on the Sabbath. What is it that really might violate the teaching of the law that the Sabbath is to be a day of rest? Again, there are several stories in the Gospels that illustrate the way that Jesus understood the meaning of the Sabbath as a day of rest. In most of these cases, Jesus says that the well-being of a person, or perhaps even an animal, may require some energy and time on a particular Sabbath day. One story that involved Jesus and his disciples quite directly has to do with feeding his disciples on the Sabbath day. Luke records the story (6:1–9), and the setting is a Sabbath Day on which Jesus and the disciples were walking through a grainfield and some of the disciples plucked some heads of grain to feed themselves. Jesus was questioned by some Pharisees who said, "Why are you doing what is not lawful on the Sabbath?" Jesus answered, using the authority of Jewish history and law, by saying, "Have you not read what David did when he and his companions were hungry? He entered the house of God and took and ate the bread of the Presence, which it is not lawful for any but the priests to eat, and gave some to his companions?" For Jesus, it was a matter of priorities, that the health of human beings is the priority, a foundational truth in the law, and to eat the grain and the bread that was to be used in a religious ceremony, representing the Divine Presence, is not an offence. It is to place the welfare of human beings as the highest priority, which, by the way, is the primary intention of the law. The law is for human good and the welfare of all, providing guidance to the human family. In cases where there may be a possible conflict, such as working on the Sabbath, rescuing a dying animal or enabling a person to see should be given the priority. Jesus affirms that this is the best interpretation of the law and says to the Pharisees, "The Son of Man is lord of the sabbath." This last sentence gives Jesus a title of authority, The Son of Man, and records the story about the intention of the law to serve the welfare of all people, not to be a legalistic catch to prevent humans from the need to eat, or on another occasion, preventing a human from being healed.[7]

7. Matthew 12:9–14 tells the story of Jesus healing a man with a withered hand on the Sabbath and suggests that it is all right to help a sheep that has fallen into a ditch and needs to be rescued.

Jesus knew that providing some tangible help and encouraging personal growth and development in the immediate situation where there was need was a high priority, even on the Sabbath. He healed, fed, nurtured, and counseled. He valued creation's gift of food and cared about the kind of life they would have after he left. He knew the situation could be changed so people could manage their personal lives with a sense of security about having basic needs met from creation and practicing caring love. He knew that the hungry person needed to be fed at that particular moment or day, but he was also concerned about transforming the setting so that there would be food for the family daily and without excessive worry.

The Quest for Social Justice: The Challenges of Our Ethical Mandate

Our underlying question in studying these accounts of Jesus caring for those in his life is how we might get our priorities straight and gain the capacity to care for those whom we encounter in our setting. How is it that we may live a life full of peace and purpose, one that makes a constructive contribution to the formation of a social setting which ensures that others are healthy and live in a just society? How do we find the right balance between using the law to ensure human welfare while not adopting a legalistic interpretation that often nearly neglects the purpose of the law by its legalism? The teaching of both the Testaments, Jewish and Christian, and the third cousin, Islam, is to make life better for humankind. The key ingredient and purpose of the law in the three Abrahamic monotheistic religions is to care for basic human needs and create a just society, one in which all people are treated fairly and have equal access to pursue a good life.

There will be those in each of the three Abrahamic monotheistic religions who will continue to stress obedience to the law over and above a deep spirituality that transforms the believers and empowers them to live a healthy life and engage in ministries of social justice. Yet the deeper teaching in all three monotheistic religions is to personally encounter God, be transformed in a pattern of community life, and in the process become a faithful disciple of God, whether named Yahweh, Lord, or Allah. Each of these great religious traditions teach their followers to engage in a life that seeks to follow the will of God and a commitment to serving the causes of love and justice for all of humankind.

In fact, each of these great monotheistic religions has a comprehensive ethical system, one connected to care for Mother Earth and to create a just and humane culture. These goals touch politics, economics, health care, ecology, violent war, peacemaking, sexuality, and ways of facing the end of life. The faithful leaders in these religious systems are concerned about the issues of sexism, racism, poverty, classism, and militarism. Acknowledging this belief system and infrastructure in these religions is not to imply that they are always consistent in their views nor dedicated to justice for all. In fact, it is often the case that these ethical systems and values may be ignored as they are controlled by militant leaders and self-seeking quests for power and money. Yet these systems do exist, have some influence, and need to be recognized as integral to the well-being of most of the human family. Occasionally hidden in the founding documents is the guidance given in nearly all countries to have the goals of providing ample resources for good health and peace and justice for their people.

These documents, such as our Bill of Rights in the United States, are based on the belief that there are values that have a universal character, and as far as possible, should guide the policies of the nation. The complexity of our world, with increasing populations, climate change, world hunger, deep divisions about government structures and ideology, and conflicting moral and religious values, makes the question of ethics central to the welfare of the world. Behind the scenes in the discussion of what is ethical are a range of fundamental questions, each having a spiritual component.[8]

One is whether there are really universal moral truths, ones just below the surface in nearly all of the social conflicts and political battles that exist within countries and between countries. These governments, especially those in countries with large populations, must constantly juggle their values in reference to threats to the welfare of their people. Ethical choices may have a profound impact on the welfare of the people of the country, and decision makers often have to choose between what feels like a moral truth and a practical action that may cause great suffering for the people of another country or the people of part of their own country. Ecological choices often fall in this category; yes, we must honor Mother Earth in all ways for the future of humankind, but right now we must support an army that is resisting an invasion of a foreign power in a country that is part of our financial system and in an alliance such as NATO, an action that will damage nature's capacity to provide.

A second challenge is that our ethical systems may appeal to universal ethical norms in our founding documents, but are now a bit obsolete in the new world that is being born almost daily. We may discover that one foundational principal made sense when the nation was somewhat isolated,

---

8. See the helpful, although partially dated, work of Daniel Maguire, *Ethics: A Complete Method for Moral Choice*.

but now in strange ways can't be defended, even on ethical grounds. This may happen because the value of supporting one part of our country now clashes with the destiny of a small country that needs our food resources.

As one nation and its government are committed to the ethics within its founding documents, it may need to begin to face whole new questions, ones that didn't exist prior to universal travel, the threat of climate change, the emancipation of women, the complex electronic systems of communication, and what some have called the invasion of artificial intelligence. The ethical system must be adaptable as it faces new questions and therefore must be modified to determine what is the just and right response; older principles now hinder the movement of food across national and even continental boundaries. What then is justice? Is it supporting the local farmers or aiding a country that is not able to provide food for its population?

It is no longer easy to find answers just by careful reasoning, although reason is essential. Yet not infrequently there is commitment to a dated value system that may not be sufficiently universal for the need and complexity of contemporary global welfare. As we go back to our values, seeking to understand the moral principles that undergird decision making at several different levels, we may need to engage in a new form of moral reasoning. We may have to give credence to the new demands and complex decisions that must be made in our new world. So, we draw upon the moral values that have guided decisions on the previous challenges, yet use tough-minded reason to find a consistent pattern of decision making, and assess the outcomes, whether they justify a change of priorities from the interpretation of similar decisions in the past. There will be the inevitable contradictions, asking that in this case we must go in one direction, and that the last time we faced this issue, it was wise to go in another direction. There are few decisions, as one moves up the scale of responsibility, that come with simple clarity about the best decision based on our abstract ethical norms. We know that even partial myths about our founding principles have a tug on us, although class, race, and gender biases may be present. New ways of finding an ethical way of solving a problem may take different forms among those gathered to make the decisions. Often, we must decide and go forward, facing some discomfort in our moral consciousness, and do the best we can, given the range of well-reasoned arguments. Such a condition is part of the reality of our new world, calling on decision makers to do their careful work of extensive study and systematic reasoning, but not infrequently deciding before all this work is done because the concern has given us a timeline.

Going Forward

We go forward as individuals by following the double commandment to love God and to love our neighbor as we love ourselves.

1. We are saying that to love God is the foundational principle and implies that we seek to be transformed by God's love and to follow God's will in all aspects of our lives. We continually ask for divine guidance and empowerment in order to understand and fulfill the call to love.
2. We love our neighbor in a thousand ways, yet especially so caring for the earth, the home of all living things and the human family.
3. Our love for God and our neighbor is expressed in palpable ways, by tangibly caring for all who come into our circle of nearness, reducing their suffering and helping them to live lives of peace and purpose.
4. In short, we love God and our neighbor as we seek to create a more just and humane world.

Questions for Reflection and Discussion

1. How might I change some of the habits and patterns of my life in order to become a more loving person?
2. What makes a loving relationship? What are its essential features?
3. What is the best way to make changes in an organization or group of people in order to make it more sensitive to the needs of those in the group?
4. What are some of the best ways to speak with others who have different views than you have?
5. What are the best ways to empower a group to make changes that will enable them to be more efficient in achieving goals?

Key Terms and Concepts

1. **Empower:** A term that suggests that there may be a way to help to change or improve a pattern of life by an external source such as a close friend or an insight or a powerful idea. It is often used in describing

the change that God makes in a person's life to improve their life and expand their ability.

2. Divine image: The notion that if human beings are created by God, then they may have some of the characteristics of God, such as concern for the truth and the capacity to love.

3. Transcendental monism: The idea of there being just one God who is above and beyond our immediate setting, such as the God of Judaism, Islam, and Christianity.

4. Nature: The patterns, order, and energy that exist in creation, sometimes without the addition of intervention by humans and other times as humans are involved.

5. Double Commandment: The two primary commands of God are to love God with one's whole being, and to love one's neighbor as one loves oneself.

Suggestions for Reference and Reading

1. *Eager to Love: The Alternative Way of Francis of Assisi* by Richard Rohr
2. *How to Expand Love: Widening the Circle of Loving Relationships* by the Dalai Lama
3. *Justice: What's the Right Thing to Do?* by Michael J. Sandel
4. *Love in the Western World* by Denis de Rougemont
5. *Teachings on Love* by Thich Nhat Hanh

CHAPTER NINE

On Being Transformed

Finding Peace in a Troubled World Through Spiritual Awakening and Wisdom

> The fear of the Lord is the beginning of knowledge;
> fools despise wisdom and instruction.
>
> Proverbs 1:7

> Peace I leave with you; my peace I give to you. I do not give to you as the world gives. Do not let your let your hearts be troubled, and do not let them be afraid.
>
> John 14:27

Pain is inevitable. Suffering is not. Suffering arises from grasping. Release grasping and be free of suffering.[1]

Yes, I think happiness can be achieved through training the mind.[2]

To arrive at clear water, one must first shovel through mud.[3]

---

1. Kornfield, *Wise Heart*, 241.
2. Dalai Lama, *Art of Happiness*, 14.
3. Mafi, *Rumi, Day by Day*, 14.

The Current State of Human Health and Peace of Mind

It does appear that these perilous times in which we live are causing deep discouragement and anxiety in the human family. Writing at a time in which there is a national election, I find myself listening to many who are running for office; they often start with the observation that there are serious problems causing great distress, and that if we vote for them, they will reduce some of our fear and help solve the problems we face. I suspect that much of what they observe about our perilous times is accurate and that occasionally one of their suggested actions, if they are elected, will help to overcome the deep divide in our country and prevent what is almost thought of as another civil war. Our candidates, on occasion, have conflicting ideas about how to address our problems, and even about what might be a positive outcome, with one almost encouraging discord and another hoping to manage this serious division, reduce human suffering, and lower our anxiety. Yet the situation in which we live, whether in the busy and demanding city life or the worrisome and poverty-stricken settings of rural areas, probably won't change in any dramatic way in the near future. Some small problems may be solved, but it is difficult to imagine how many of our global, national, and even regional problems can be solved.

Though we may find solutions for occasional regional problems and have programs aimed at national and global threat, these efforts do not seem to remove the deep-seated challenges. As one problem is addressed, another one goes on the list. On many levels and locations, there is weariness, dissatisfaction, and fear. There seems to be a high degree of discouragement, severe in a direct way for those in poverty who are threatened by violence or face discrimination. While less apparent among those with adequate wealth and education, the peril is nevertheless very real, even if it is occasionally and partially disguised and sometimes ignored or forgotten by our high standard of living, our possessions, and our status.[4] Mass media will continue to inform, and at times misinform us, but won't deliver constructive ideas for social change.

The list of problems varies some from one generation to the next as do the solutions which are proposed. There continues to be several global, national, and regional problematic conditions that remain on all the lists. There is the ever-present problem of climate change with temperatures in some settings higher than any time since there have been records. My friend from Bangladesh informs me about the rising coastal water level impacting coastal areas in his country. Many have lost their homes. There is the

---

4. Young men, in particular, seem to be filled with unrest, as their traditional roles are slipping away. Patriarchy is on the decline if not gone.

concern about the increasing population and the inability in several regions of the world to meet even the basic needs of their people. There is the challenge of the distribution of food causing world hunger. There is the rise of autocratic governments, the decline of democracy, infectious diseases such as COVID, unjust laws that underline differences about the rights of women to care for their bodies, the abuse of drugs, the lack of gun control, migration that threatens regional boundaries, and in the background is the ever-present threat of nuclear warfare.

These external threats and challenges don't exist just out there or over there, but have come to rest on the front porch of millions of people. Worry, by people sitting on the rocking chairs on front porches, will not create a safe environment, improve health, and bring happiness. In fact, the awareness of the severity of the problems without solutions has had a negative impact on the human psyche; there is a dramatic increase of mental illness, and there is fear in one form or another in each of us. The global context and the regional situations at this point in human history appear to have problems that are nearly out of control. As we seek solutions, we are often faced with mis- and disinformation, and especially in America when we are in the time of national elections. Finding the truth about our situation and then pursing answers is difficult and challenging.

Searching for Answers

There is no shortage of proposed ways to solve many of our problems, and some of these suggested ways are working; some gains have been made. Yet these accomplishments have not reduced our fear and anxiety. There are still the continuing threats of climate change, world hunger, and the resort to violence in those areas where there are serious conflicts; they continue in Ukraine, Gaza, and the vast and conflicted region of the Middle East.

As we continue to search for ways to manage our distress, we do need to stay focused on the serious problems and their solutions and not be distracted by less important concerns. In addition, we must work very hard to keep a semblance of peace and justice in the countries of the world with diplomacy and the management of trade and commerce, and then give extensive attention to regions where there is deep conflict and where resorting to violent war has already occurred. The problems will not just go away with our limited attention; in fact, as one problem diminishes, new ones emerge, and they need to be carefully addressed in ways that prevent violence and regional war.

In many cases, alongside the many specific and tangible ways of finding solutions to global, national, and regional problems is the modest concurrent movement to change the spirit and attitudes of people in threatened regions. A change to the very negative narrative of threatening conditions needs to occur. The current set of serious problems can be managed although not fully eliminated. There is a broad range of both public and private initiatives designed to deal directly with these problems, yet there is still the need for reassurance that wise and collaborative efforts to address the problems are underway. Fear and anguish need not win the day.

The leaders of governments in threatened areas must reduce their warring and threats and explore collaborative and compassionate solutions to aid and bring hope to those who are threatened. There are positive examples of this strategy in our history. For example, the Civil War in America did not cease just because the Northern states had more power and won on the battlefield. Most historians suggest that part of the journey toward peace was a change in attitude about the evil of slavery. Yes, there were many who did not change their attitude, but a majority of those with power did so. There was still the use of some force, but the spirit of "malice toward none"[5] helped to create a change of attitude about slavery. For many there was a values shift, influenced in part by being informed and also by calling for a transformation of attitudes, and even a spiritual center and an ethical shift toward compassion. To a large extent, Hitler was defeated by a powerful military coalition formed by Europe and the United States. Yet behind and motivating this action was a philosophical and to some extent a religious outlook that gave a vision for overcoming evil and doing what is right for the people of the world. This outlook fostered a deep desire for world peace, created courage, and provided the motivation to find peaceful solutions for global, national, regional, and local conflicts. It produced resilience and the motivation to find nonviolent solutions to a wide range of problematic issues. It was a matter of education and controlling the narrative, offsetting the tendency to get even and turn to guns and bombs. Fortunately, many of the nations' leaders used the strategy of advancing the vision of a just and peaceful society and world.

Behind the peaceful solutions were these motivated leaders, many of whom had a worldview that gave precedence to the value of human life. Our purpose in this writing is to add one more voice that suggests the need for accepting and cultivating universal values and spiritual practices, ones that stand against violence as a solution to human problems. We do this by participating in problem solving in local communities and by encouraging

---

5. Lincoln, "Second Inaugural Address," para. 5.

our elected leaders to support life-affirming values and engage in ways to reduce human suffering. We then join with others in the creation of a more just and humane society and world.

Along the way, we can help by articulating and cultivating a healthy vision, carefully describing the goals for justice and peace and advancing them regionally and nationally in tangible ways. Those in power will need to be converted to this positive strategy and be willing to become full participants in creating a more compassionate world, starting with their positive spirit, embracing the values of justice and peace, and the way they remain positive in managing the problems that exist in their own situation.

I want to stress that these leaders must catch the vision about the wisdom of creating a more just and compassionate social order. This vision must be explained in a way that demonstrates that there are positive gains for everyone. Of course, the leaders must avoid the temptation to just talk about it; actions need to be taken, some of which must have symbolic value as well as the value of improving the lives of the people in their setting. The leaders, as they journey toward awakening and cultivating a transformed consciousness, have the special responsibility to articulate the vision and design specific plans for constructive change. To some extent, it becomes a way of being, not just implementing a few surface changes. It is a spiritual journey of enlightenment and an expanded consciousness for all those who share the responsibility for change. It is creating a context for change, one that empowers people to care about those who suffer and then join with others in order to sustain the motivation and find the means and power to facilitate change.

The Journey of Enlightenment

I begin on a personal note and share how I began to make some progress in my spiritual journey, one that guided me toward becoming more responsible and led me to be concerned about human suffering and the need for change. As I look back, I sense that it wasn't so much by taking an academic class or following a clear and systematic set of instructions; these were available and I took advantage of them. In fact, I valued them very much. I became better informed and a lifelong reader, which took me deeply into my faith and my responsibilities. I have found a measure of peace, even in our troubled world, through having a sense of God's empowering presence, a spiritual awakening, and an increase of wisdom about the journey and task. It took decades to arrive at an informed and positive outlook and now requires daily attention in order to cease being a part of the problem and become a part of the solution.

I was exposed in the beginning of my spiritual life to a thoughtful though traditional faith orientation with a relatively healthy evangelical edge; it was not fundamentalism, but rooted in the traditional views. Later, I was exposed to a much broader understanding of faith and began to discard some of those elements that were a bit narrow, bordering on being somewhat cultic, tribal, and exclusive. It was a relatively healthy process of growth, not a dramatic conversion, and I found that I was gradually making progress in becoming an informed and responsible Christian, one that was more spiritual.[6] I found ways to be with God, day by day, and to learn about faith in a more advanced and nuanced way that gave me a foundation for staying on course across the several decades of my life.

The first component of this journey was a different narrative, a new way of thinking about life and a new way of being. What began to disappear was competition with others for attention and achievement, a challenge for many as they move into adulthood. I did have some leadership skills, although they were not sufficiently refined to participate fully in creating a new narrative. I discovered that some of these natural tendencies and impulses were driven by deep needs to be accepted and worthy in the eyes of others. I began to realize that I had some insecurities about how I was viewed by my peers and how to deal with some low self-esteem. These carryovers from my childhood were to some extent driving my behavior. In time, I began to discover that I was loved by God and by many adults and peers for the real and authentic me rather than what I was working so hard to project. Over time, with this affirmation, I began to accept myself and celebrate who I am rather than projecting what I thought was the worthy person. I discovered that I was okay and could relax, be myself, and learn how to move toward full adulthood by natural growth and development. What was added to my personal understanding in the community of faith was the sense that it was God who had accepted and gifted me, and there was the presence of dear friends in the community of faith to guide me in

---

6. I have gradually learned over the last fifty years about what it means to be spiritual. I had some growth in deepening my spiritual life in the early years of faith, although this sense of development was more personal growth in attitude and spirit, not so much the motivation to engage in tangible help to reduce human suffering and care about social justice. These dimensions emerged as I found myself in settings where human need and suffering were right in front of me. I learned that becoming more spiritual is not only about internal change, but also the motivation to engage in tangible action by loving wisely and helping to create a more just and peaceful environment.

healthy directions.[7] I began to sense that there may be something spiritual about this natural process of growth and becoming more mature.

By gradually overcoming many of my insecurities rooted in my childhood experiences and family life, I began to enjoy being in a community of good friends, finding my niche to make a contribution, yet not driven by the deep insecurity of feeling unattractive and the need to compensate for it. In fact, as I participated in the various youth groups and with teams of leaders, I began to find my natural place in and with them. I could help by using my interests in sports, my desire to learn, and my inclination toward giving some leadership. I sensed that perhaps I might be able to make a modest contribution in the groups that I joined. I was even given a sense that there were gifts and abilities given to all people, and that cultivating these gifts and abilities gave me a place in the community, a way to be an integral part of a community, and make a positive contribution. I began to relax, be fully present and genuine in relationships, find my natural role, and be other-oriented rather than me-oriented.

It also helped to be invited to learn, both in my formal education and also by my natural attraction to relevant books which addressed the patterns of spiritual growth and responsible service. There were some small support groups that met on a regular schedule that had some Bible study and guided prayer, and I was invited to be a participant in some of them.

There were endless suggestions for books I should read.[8] There were a few classics such as John Bunyan's *Pilgrim's Progress*, Thomas à Kempis's *The Imitation of Christ*, and Charles Sheldon's *In His Steps*. There were a few by Scottish authors that were put on the list when I had mentioned my Scottish heritage. I read John Baillie's *A Diary of Private Prayer*, and later, in my graduate studies at the University of Edinburgh, I was exposed to the Scottish Reformation and the writing of John Knox and the many fine Bible scholars and theologians such as Thomas Torrance who followed and contributed to this tradition. A bit later, I read the books of C. S. Lewis and J. B. Phillips, which were quite popular. Many of these books had a scholarly edge, suggesting that the Christian faith could be and needed to be understood in a more thoughtful way.

Further, those in my community of faith stressed the need to be engaged in some form of ministry and care for others, and it wasn't long before I was helping a local church with their youth program. I continued to be

---

7. The notion of being a part of the body of Christ was helpful and comforting.

8. Books, almost more than films and electronic programs, guided me in the early years of growth, and they have been my close companions for years.

involved in many forms of Christian nurture and teaching, making good use of my university education, a wonderful gift in many ways.

During my university days, and especially as a graduate student, I moved more boldly into the books of such people as Reinhold Niebuhr, Paul Tillich, and Pierre Teilhard de Chardin, and found good ways to use what I learned in my campus ministry programs. There were several stimulating works by women authors such as Mary Daly and Rosemary Radford Ruether. These authors invited me to make a major shift in my outlook, and I developed a profound appreciation for the insightful and sensitive perspective of women. Later, I was given invaluable guidance in my faith journey by the British scholar Karen Armstrong and the books by Diana Butler Bass, both of whom provided insight on how to understand faith in a secular world.

I was not spoon-fed, but invited to engage in thinking through the foundations of the Christian faith, and I was exposed to the outlook of many different schools of thought. For example, I began to sense when and where Western theology was somewhat colonial in tone. I learned that it was wise to read widely, and that I didn't need to feel threatened by my exposure to different views. I was, as were many in my generation, challenged and motivated by liberation theology. It guided my interest and provided a foundation for challenging racism and social injustice. Once again, my heart and mind were transformed and enlightened. I read the pivotal work of such authors as the Peruvian Gustavo Gutierrez whose book *Theology of Liberation* was foundational.

I continued to sense I could make an informed, although modest, contribution in the life of the Christian church. I was especially grateful for my graduate study at the University of Edinburgh as it gave me a perspective that was somewhat different from what I was exposed to in the United States. On returning to the United States, I continued my work in higher education, serving as a chaplain, faculty member, and senior level administrator in university settings. I was privileged to serve in four church-related universities and in the national offices of the Presbyterian Church (USA) with responsibilities for the church's mission and ministries in higher education.

Across these years of learning and teaching, I continued to learn about the journey of faith. I still had questions about this journey; they were not a threat but a challenge. Some of the questions of that time in my life have been answered, but were often replaced with other questions. Questions, I learned, were a positive part of life and the drivers of personal growth and deeper understanding.

Now in retirement, I look back across these years and sense that I have found a good measure of inner peace and have been on the path of awakening and gaining wisdom. I was experiencing what was promised. The range of experiences have helped me to cope, rethink my views, and to serve more wisely and boldly in our perilous world. I sense that I have been able to find meaning both through a natural pattern of growth and also by receiving a good education. There were the early years of being exposed to and embracing a new narrative that was not a part of my childhood. It gave me a direction, a sense of meaning, and a path to follow. A second phase of this life narrative was finding a community in which to serve, one that had the capacity to keep me on track, give me support, and point me to a good future. I did find that community within the Presbyterian Church (USA), a mainline denomination with all of their problems, yet a home filled with wisdom and guidance.

I still had to deal with many challenges, but I was better prepared to manage them, had a foundational home, and felt guided by my education to serve in a new world that was being born almost yearly, one filled with unrest and profound change. I sense that I have been blessed to have the opportunity to grow and to serve those causes that have led to a mature faith, a commitment to justice, and an enduring peace. In short, I learned how to express agape love.

I do need to add that as I engaged in the global dimension of ministry, I was invited to learn about the spirituality of other religious traditions.[9] I soon discovered that the quest for a deeper spirituality should not be limited to exploring the spiritual practices and outlooks in my corner of the United States. Neither Buddha nor Jesus lived in New York or Los Angeles. I sensed that my spiritual journey should be more inclusive, stretch across time, and include visits to many parts of the world. I needed to be emancipated from a regional perspective and to gain an understanding of other outlooks in different parts of the world, especially in the world's several religious outlooks. I traveled extensively in my work and was exposed to the many ways of spiritual formation and the spiritual pathways of those in Asia, Latin America, and Africa. It was liberating, and I discovered a richness of spiritual understanding in other countries and other faith traditions.

In addition, I read the books and teachings of the founders and followers of the other religious traditions and began to think about the kinship of

---

9. A few years later, after a careful reading of the literature and several visits to Asia, Africa, and Latin America, I sensed that I needed to do some integrating of what I was learning. I pulled a lot of it together in the book *Exploring the Spirituality of the World Religions: the Quest for Personal, Spiritual and Social Transformation*.

faiths.[10] I read the writing of the such people as the Dalai Lama and Thich Nhat Hanh as this literature found an audience in many parts of the West. Buddhism arrived in Europe and the Americas and received a warm welcome. Several of my friends eagerly read Alan Watts's book *The Way of Zen*, as I did. So too did we read the literature of Hinduism, and I identified with the special influence of Gandhi as I spent many weeks in India. On returning home, I was exposed to many teachers in North America who drew upon the teachers in Asia and were teaching a form of this literature that was called New Age, and books by such authors as Eckhart Tolle were on the shelves of the super markets and drug stores, not just in specialized book stores.[11] The Islamic poet Rumi was translated and became a book of readings, *Rumi, Day by Day*, and many Americans welcomed this literature and its teaching as I did.

The Contours of Spirituality

From my exposure to this vast array of religious life and literature, I began to move toward being more open to the teachings and practices of the world's religions and began the process of integrating the life-giving literature of other religious traditions with what I had received and developed within the Christian faith. I began to think in terms of finding some coherence in the several points of view, noting in particular the many shared practices and the common commitment to work for justice and peace contained in this worldwide revolution in spirituality.[12] I continued to ground my faith in the insights and inspiration from the vast literature and thoughtful voices within the Christian tradition. I did not just leave one family of faith and join another, but began to see that there were some universal truths, insights, and practices that these traditions had in common. For example, it was relatively easy to see how the insights of the Buddha were much like those of Jesus, although each were distinctive in their own way.[13]

The classic three-volume work of Mircea Eliade, *A History of Religious Ideas*, invited me to grasp the common themes in the finest expressions of

---

10. I read with great interest the book by the Dalai Lama *Toward a True Kinship of Faiths: How the World's Religions Can Come Together*.

11. See *Power of Now* and *New Earth*.

12. There really was a revolution in the quest for finding inner peace and a life direction in last quarter of the twentieth century and well into the current century.

13. I read, for example, the Dalai Lama's books *The Art of Happiness* and *Toward a True Kinship of Faiths*. I read with interest Thich Nhat Hanh's book *Living Buddha, Living Christ*.

religious thought in the several religions of the human family. I gave particular attention to the spiritual guidance of the world religions and attempted more fully to understand their starting points. I felt the need to explore the foundations on which they based their beliefs and practices. Joining with others, I grouped these religions into three large families, based on their approach to religious understanding: (1) Pathways rooted in nature and culture; (2) Pathways rooted in transcendental monism; and (3) Pathways rooted in the Abrahamic monotheistic religions.[14] I also kept in mind my own categories and beliefs, largely rooted in Abrahamic monotheism, and they invited me to understand and to integrate the many dimensions of these religions with my foundational beliefs. I used the following categories in the comparative endeavor: (1) creed or beliefs; (2) code or the essential ethical teachings; (3) cultic practices that were distinctive to each of these religions; and (4) the sense of community based on the ways that their adherents joined together for mutual nurture and service.

Patterns of Religious Life and Thought: The Way in Alaska

I want now to provide an example of what we have been describing as the spiritual pathways of religion. It will help us move from the general observations of belief and practice to a way in which these more general observations take tangible form in one expression of faith. A brief picture of religious life, belief, and spiritual practice in one setting will help to illustrate what we have suggested in the various descriptive categories. I have selected to use my experience of religious practice where I lived for five years, Alaska. I select this experience for illustration, in part because it was in a transition mode, adjusting to the influx of the people and culture from the Lower 48. It was also possible to observe and experience this expression of faith in a relatively self-contained community of people.[15] It will allow us to provide a tangible example that illustrates one pattern of the belief and practice of a spiritual way of life.

I began to understand one part of the religious life in Alaska by becoming an active participant in the life of a local congregation in Anchorage and by serving on the Presbytery committee, called The Committee on Ministry, which had the responsibility to assist the churches in the region

---

14. See my book *Exploring the Spirituality of the World Religions*.

15. It is important to note that the Alaska native religious beliefs and practices are shared by many other native traditions and not altogether unique in Alaska.

to sustain and improve their ministries.[16] The members of the Committee visited every congregation in their region, which did not include the lower coastal region of Alaska. The Committee's mission was to help the congregations to refine their beliefs and improve the practices in which they engaged for the cultivation of their spiritual life.

As we did our work, we found that there was a range of different situations and challenges in the churches, many just needing basic assistance and others asking for ways to change their approach. The sort of big picture of these congregations is that they had one of three patterns in their relationship to their settings: (1) Many of the Alaskans, including just a few of the Alaska natives, accommodated to the new culture and worldview and passively accepted some of the new expressions of values and a way of life comparable to their counterparts in other regions of the United States.[17] It was go-with-the-flow strategy, one without much stress. (2) There were some who saw the need to embrace a new and God-given calling, and they engaged in trying to transform the values and beliefs of their culture. They saw a new way of life emerging from the profound changes occurring in their culture and wanted to be responsive to a new world that was being born, one quite different than what they had experienced earlier. (3) There were others who wanted to preserve the way of life that had been present for generations, and they retreated from the new culture in order to preserve their unique identity and purity. Many of the native people remained within their tribal structure, preserved their language, and continued to live in the vast rural regions of the state. One of these people commented to me, "Alaska is about fifty miles outside of Anchorage."

As I thought about the native religion in the tribal areas of Alaska, with a fairly close look and even personal experience, I gave attention to how their values, beliefs, and some practices had changed unintentionally. Change happens. I also compared the Alaska pattern with my experience and observations about the practices and values in other regions of the United States and in the several religious traditions in other regions of the world. These same three major patterns seem to be present in Alaska: (1) There continues to be the traditional pattern of understanding values in reference to reaching upward to the universal God as in the Abrahamic monotheistic traditions. Judaism, Christianity, and Islam believe that values are God given. This understanding is certainly present in Alaska, although it is not universal. (2) What was also present for many of the Alaska natives

---

16. Nearly every denomination has committees who serve in this way, but in the Presbyterian system, these committees essentially take the place of a bishop.

17. The churches which served primarily Alaska natives had a different ethos.

was their deep belief that their values came to them by opening inward to the presence of the divine as it is expressed in nature. (3) There was also the strong sense of expressing the values of care and compassion by expanding outward in service.[18] Many people in Alaska lived a long way from cities with hospitals and without easy transportation to these cities. In the vast rural regions, one finds a profound sense of belonging to others and the need to care for each other. The region is vast, about one-fifth of the geography of the United States, and, while there are airplanes and small airports, travel can still be difficult, especially with emergencies needing immediate attention, but also just normal care that was often hard to receive locally, and the harsh weather made travel very difficult.

What Religion in Alaska May Teach Us About Spirituality

The several categories we have used have suggested a way of understanding and assessing the way their religion is practiced, how it has an influence on the believers, and how it shapes the settings and cultures where it is practiced. It is beyond our scope to describe and assess the many religions of the human family, but a few more examples from what I observed in Alaska may help us understand the spiritual dimensions of life in a particular setting. Perhaps, as we do this work, we may be able to find ways to be awakened to deeper realities that surround us, gain wisdom by this learning, and hopefully to find a spiritual way that brings us peace of mind as we move through life in our troubled world. We can often learn about religious thought and spiritual practices by observing and studying the religion of people in different settings and cultures.

From the beginning of the human quest to discover categories that encompassed and identified the patterns of order in the world they inhabited, humans started from what they could see and experience directly. They lived in nature which had the resources for survival as well as the threat of dangerous storms. They began to put these realities into a pattern of living, ensuring that they could live comfortably and without threat by preserving food and having enough to survive in the winter months. In time, these adjustments were organized into a whole culture, based on nature, and filled with values and patterns of organization that guided their way of life in reference to their surroundings. It involved more than just having food; it involved them in expected behavior and a range beliefs and practices that were designed to make life safe and worth living.

---

18. "Christian Forms of Spirituality," in Patte, *Cambridge Dictionary of Christianity*, 1182–89.

Many of the world's religions began with the human experience in nature, the ways they found to live together in safety, and a social structure in tribes that had a way of communicating and functioning that preserved order. A culture emerged from their setting and daily challenges. Many of the world's religions were based on the powerful and unpredictable natural setting, and then they advanced in terms of the languages and values that enabled them to survive and relate to other groups.[19]

These indigenous wisdom traditions gradually began to develop a more inclusive view of the world, giving categories to what they experienced. As they lived within a weather pattern, one that they could not control, they began to name and give categories to what they were experiencing. For example, they saw the power of nature, both its way of sustaining them and also its way of threatening them, and named what they experienced as *sacred powers*, ones beyond what they could control. In addition, they began to personalize these powers and told stories about how they were formed and their impact on behavior. In order to survive, they tried to anticipate what might happen in nature and find some order for the sacred actions that function within sacred space and time. The stories expanded to more universal myths, giving them a sense of basic ethics. There were, of course, many taboos and ethical norms, and the wise ones within the tribe, the shamans, guided people on how to survive and even thrive. An initial worldview, made up of these elements, was born and guided them.

It was within this pattern of development and view of life that many of the human religions developed. For example, the religious beliefs and practices of the other North American indigenous peoples had the elements of the Alaska natives, linked to nature and with a pattern of belief and a set of values and practices that became a definable culture. I had the mixed blessing to live in Alaska for an extended period of time and was exposed to what was left of the wisdom traditions of Alaskan natives that still existed in rural regions.

There were many needs and challenges for these several tribes as the mainline culture of the United States became a dominant way of life for many of the native tribes. What I discovered, even in the midst of this major transition of cultures, was a semblance of the original culture that had several positive features. Although mixed and not universal, the following were values that were still present and had a positive role in sustaining their

---

19. A good introduction to this development of religions is the classic work of Mircea Eliade *From Primitives to Zen*. Another introductory book on the formation of religion, *Ways to the Center* by Carmody and Carmody, provides a list of twenty-five key dates and events stretching from 100,000 years ago. See as well my introductory book *Exploring the Spirituality of the World Religions*.

original culture. They provided a partial foundation in the midst of major change that occurred in the early to mid-twentieth century.

- Their culture, of course, had a deep respect for nature and they understood their way of life as living in an integrated way with nature, using rather than exploiting the natural resources of their beautiful world.[20] In time, with the influx of the petroleum industry, the resources of nature provided them with wealth and some power, and their life began to change, resembling the patterns of life in what they called the Lower 48, which also caused profound social problems.

- Their way of life was centered rather than fragmented. Nature gave them a unified view of life, patterns that followed the seasons of the year, and ethical and social structures that provided order. They hunted and fished within the changing climate and the pattern of accommodating to nature's way. This pattern of life has been challenged by the many changes that have occurred with the opening of Alaska, and especially by the discovery of oil and the exploitative patterns of major corporations.

- They saw the divine as omnipresent and integral to all of life. They attempted to live in harmony with what they understood as the divine in nature's patterns. Once again, this understanding was challenged when nature began to be understood more as the resource for wealth than for providing a pattern of life. Almost immediately, as big corporations moved in, there was the temptation to exploit the resources of nature. The presence of oil in Alaska invited many Alaskans to change their way of life and to seek wealth. Nature lost some of its divine qualities, and the native people were especially challenged.

- They also believed that the patterns of nature provided wisdom and the way to know what one needed to know in order to live wisely and well. Nature was their teacher, and Alaska natives sought inner peace in following the sacred ways of nature. The rhythms of the seasons gave order to their way of life. This pattern has been sustained by many people in Alaska, but except in the very remote areas, the population has had to accommodate to new realities.

- And, of course, as they studied the ways of nature, they learned an ethical way of life, and that one was living ethically as one followed the ways of nature. One thrived and was good to others, as nature, if treated with care, gave back the resources for life. But the new realities

---

20. Ferguson, *Exploring the Spirituality*, 36–37.

of gaining wealth from the natural resources changed the way of life for many of the native people. Old patterns of life changed quickly and those in leadership had to create a new social order and patterns of life in order to keep up with the change. Unfortunately, there was an increase of the abuse of alcohol, drugs, and the quest for wealth became very normative for most Alaskans. Nature was no longer the primary teacher of many Alaskans.

The religion of the native peoples of Alaska, prior to the dramatic shifts and changes across the mid-twentieth century, had the dimensions of understanding nature's ways and finding within these patterns some guidance for life. It was a spiritual way to live. One saw the divine in the power of nature, saw nature as the giver of life, and it had many of the lessons that taught native people how to live in a way that not only nurtured a single person or family, but had within it the lessons of wisdom for the tribes to survive and live with a measure of care and harmony with other tribes. Yet much of that earlier way of life has disappeared with only a few tribes, now somewhat isolated, still maintaining the traditional way of life.

Questions for Reflection and Discussion

1. In what ways does our environment, both natural and sociological, invite and inform us about how to form and embrace religious ideas and practices?

2. In what ways are religious beliefs and practices helpful to people, guiding them to live in constructive and fulfilling ways?

3. In what ways does religion, if it is not carefully expressed and based on positive values, tend to create conflict and be harmful?

4. What are some of the ways that the indigenous wisdom traditions differ in their views about religion from those that are monotheistic such as Judaism, Christianity, and Islam? Is there any common ground?

5. In what ways does our understanding of the natural world teach us about how to live wisely, well, and enable us to flourish?

Key Terms and Concepts

1. Spiritual: The way we seek to live in the presence of God and by incorporating the elements of our religious traditions in a way that provides

guidance in life and growth toward wholeness, purpose, and inner peace.

2. Culture: The socially transmitted behavioral patterns, values, and beliefs of a community or population.

3. Myth: A sacred story that captures a profound or sacred truth; or one that may mislead and cause confusion about the best way to live.

4. Shaman: A person who is sanctioned by the community to exercise powers to guide others in belief and practice, often thought to have some influence on what are thought to be spirits that influence our lives.

5. Taboo: A prohibition against a certain behavior or action that is thought to be harmful or violates a sacred rule or behavior expected by the divine.

Suggestions for Reference and Reading

1. *Bury My Heart at Wounded Knee: An Indian History of the American West* by Dee Brown

2. *Creation Spirituality: Liberating Gifts for the Peoples of the Earth* by Matthew Fox

3. *The Golden Bough: The Roots of Religion and Folklore* by James G. Frazer

4. *The Mastery of Love: A Practical Guide to the Art of Relationship* by Don Miguel Ruiz

5. *The Wisdom of the Native Americans* by Kent Nerburn

CONCLUSION

The Soul's Journey of Being Conformed
Following Jesus

> I therefore, the prisoner in the Lord, beg you to lead a life worthy of the calling to which you have been called, with all humility and gentleness, with patience, bearing with one another in love, making every effort to maintain the unity of the Spirit in the bond of peace. There is one body and one Spirit, just as you were called to the one hope of your calling, one Lord, one faith, one baptism, one God and [Parent] of all, who is above all and through all and in all. But each of us was given grace according to the measure of Christ's gift.
>
> Ephesians 4:1–7

> If then there is any encouragement in Christ, any consolation from love, any sharing in the Spirit, any compassion and sympathy, make my joy complete: be of the same mind, having the same love, being in full accord and of one mind. Do nothing from selfish ambition or conceit, but in humility regard others as better than yourselves.
>
> Philippians 2:1–3

THE APOSTLE PAUL, AS he writes, seeks to help those whom he has visited, wanting them to have a good life, one that is truly spiritual and more than just managing the challenges of living in the first century. He has a strategy in his letter to help them, beginning with a description that summarizes his teaching. It contains a pattern of belief that will sustain them. He then describes the spiritual principles which, if faithfully practiced, will empower his readers and guide them in their new way of life. As we look closely at his writing, we see a rhythm and pattern that will sustain them, even in troublesome times.

He generally starts with a greeting and then invites the readers to remember what he taught them about the life, teaching, and final days of Jesus. He often expresses joy that the members of the new church have made great progress. He then urges them to stay with it and continue this new life of faith. He tells them not to forget the foundations of their new Christian faith. He then moves to particular issues that need attention, reminding them that their new faith is not just a theological outlook, but a way of life filled with specific concerns, ones that are interwoven with how to live the life of faith in their setting. He closes with a warm affirmation.

CHAPTER TEN

On Being Conformed
The Way of Jesus

Let each of you look not to your own interests, but to the interests of others.
Let this same mind be in you that was in Christ Jesus.

Philippians 2:4–5

PAUL, IN NEARLY ALL of his letters, is concerned that his readers, mostly new Christians, stay on course, change their way of life, and conform to the Way that Jesus taught and lived. I have used the word *conform* because it underlines that their new life should be guided by the example and values of Jesus. The perfect model is there, and he urges them to change their lives and bring them into harmony and accord with the life and teachings of Jesus. He wants them to walk in his steps. While their lives were not identical with the life of Jesus, Paul nevertheless wants them to modify their way of living so that it conforms to the pattern of the life of Jesus and the values that he taught. For this to happen, Paul writes, these new Christians must open their hearts and minds to the spirit of God.

Paul, in his teaching, maintains that this way involves having deep faith in God and a commitment to living as Jesus did. Paul, wisely in many cases in his teaching, speaks about the true nature of God, knowing that his readers will have a variety of views about who God or the gods are. The risk for them, as it is for us, is that this new Christians will frequently create God in their own image and out of their limited understanding. They would have been exposed to several different definitions of God and examples where the explanation of an event points to the presence of God or the divine. Forms of polytheism were present in their culture. These new disciples of Jesus would bring these ideas to the conversations with Paul and other Christian leaders. They would have to modify their understanding of God as they listened to Paul, and assess whether their present efforts to understand the divine were still valid. The same questions emerged as they reviewed the variety of practices associated with their beliefs. Paul maintains that these new Christians needed to change their beliefs and practices, modifying them and, in many cases, rejecting them. What Paul does is give another way as he describes the God of Jesus, the God of the Jewish tradition, anchored in a profound monotheism. The shift for many of his listeners would be difficult.

These new Christians did not come to their new faith with a blank slate or an empty mind. They came with an understanding that was rooted in the worldview of their culture, one filled with many definitions of God. Paul teaches that they would have to adjust to a monotheistic view, one that affirmed that God was cosmic and universal, the very ground of being. Paul would also teach them about spiritual practices, that God was present and personal as they prayed, and as they shared their new faith, they should understand that all conscious beings are able to relate to God in faith, a faith that would give them hope and teach them to love.

These first-century Christians had much to discard and much to learn. The teachers of this new orientation would want the new Christians to begin the long journey of understanding the nature of God, and the way their new faith in God would give them a life of meaning, purpose, and peace. While the discussions about God may have been lengthy, Paul in his teaching would want to make sure that the new Christians would understand God through the lens of his Jewish faith, a monotheistic view epitomized and advanced by Jesus.

Paul often taught from his own life and circumstances, knowing he was in a comparable culture yet able to move to a more profound faith. He could be an example of how these new Christians could easily grasp the notion of one God and a new way of life expressed in the life and teaching of Jesus. He sensed that his listeners could almost immediately apply this new understanding of God and the example of Jesus to their lives. It becomes clearer as Paul teaches how this understanding of God is directly connected to the life and teaching of Jesus. Paul explains that it was Jesus who was sent by God to give humankind a true understanding of God and a full description of how to live in an ethical way. Jesus, his life, his teachings, and his death and resurrection, provide the essential components of the new faith and way of life. This new way of life, based on the life, the teachings, and the redemptive events of Jesus, are expressed in Paul's teaching and have become the center of the beliefs, practices, and writings of the early church. We learn, as we review the historical accounts, that:

1. "God is love," a description that is assumed by Paul, although used more directly by the author of the first letter of John. The author writes, "God is love, and those who abide in love abide in God, and God abides in them" (1 John 4:16). The love about which they speak is unconditional, agape love.

2. "God is light" or truth. Again, the author of 1 John writes, "This is the message we have heard from him and proclaim to you, that God is light and in him there is no darkness at all" (1 John 1:5). Light, in this writing, refers to the capacity to see clearly and understand. The reference to God as light means that we have been informed that God is the ground and source of all that is true.

3. "God is spirit, and those who worship him must worship in spirit and truth" (John 4:24). By Spirit, the author is referring to the omnipresence of God, not unlike the wind that is always with us. It is a wind that is gentle and healing, nurturing and guiding, enlightening us in the journey of life.

There are other passages of Scripture that describe, explain, or refer to the identity and character of God, but these three are essential, love, light, and spirit. As Jesus taught, we are profoundly loved by the personal God, who is ultimate truth, and we are empowered to see and understand the essence and meaning of life. We are surrounded and filled with the presence of God who is love and truth, and this God will never forsake us and always be with us, even as God was in the life of Jesus.

The Church's Response to the God of Love, Truth, and Presence

The new Christians, many of whom were taught by Paul, had much to learn. In fact, many of them had to learn a whole new narrative, although those who brought their Jewish faith with them could at least partially see that the life, teaching, and actions of Jesus were an extension of the Jewish faith. There were some communities in the first few decades following the life, teaching, and redeeming events of Jesus who saw themselves as a new expression of Judaism. Even Paul initially had this tendency, and James, the brother of Jesus, established a community church in Jerusalem that understood and taught about a direct connection of their Jewish faith with the new expression of faith based on the life, teachings, and final redeeming events of Jesus. This new faith community, calling itself "the church," saw in the teaching of Paul and several others with a Jewish heritage, that the church was a new expression of Jewish faith. Initially it was Paul who saw that Jesus had expressed in his life and teaching a reformed view of Jewish faith.

Yet it wasn't long before even Paul became aware that what he proclaimed was seen as a genuine break from Judaism. It was in part the radical teaching of Jesus and later the understanding of the redemptive events of Jesus, which invited a new direction for the community of faith. In time, the understanding of Jesus as divine would be contrary to Jewish monotheism. Jesus was viewed as too radical, and the understanding of the redemptive events in the life of Jesus were not a part of the Jewish tradition of redemption.

Paul, then, felt that he must be sanctioned to be the one to lead the mission to reach out to the gentile communities, a movement that did make a distinction between the Jewish faith and practice and the new faith in Jesus. His writing and letters in the New Testament, both to the Romans and also to the Galatians, provided a way to understand the new expression of faith. In time, Jesus began to be understood as one with a Jewish heritage and close connection to Judaism, but with a divine identity that was not easy to integrate into mainline Judaism.

Paul's new mission was primarily to non-Jewish people, although he encountered many who were Jewish. With some resistance, he was sanctioned by what was then a developing community structure led by the apostle Peter, and this group approved his mission and ministry in the gentile world. It is probable that Paul, right after his conversion, took time to retreat and formulate his understanding of the mission of Jesus. He then began his new ministry as a missionary, which was extensive. He traveled nearly across the expanse of the Roman Empire, proclaimed the new Christian faith, gave the new churches a theological foundation for their faith, and essentially led one part of the mission of the church to a vast region. His ministry ended in a prison in Rome, although he had hoped to extend the mission to Spain.

From his several letters, the book of Acts, and the Gospel of Luke, we are able to piece together his mission and teaching. Paul's message regarding Jesus, the long awaited one who was Messiah, was received by many communities of faith and even by those who stood outside of the Jewish faith tradition. His work was extensive, crossing many cultures, languages, and belief systems. It would be hard to overstate the influence of Paul in the formation of the church. In time, his influence would be felt around the world.

His teaching and ministry had several dimensions and goals. In the beginning, as Paul himself was gradually developed his understanding of the life and ministry of Jesus, he traveled and taught in many parts of the middle East, founding communities of faith, and they were soon called churches. The notion of church, *ekklesia* in Greek, meant a congregation, and what he founded continues with us in the twenty-first century. This ministry and teaching had both the proclamation dimension, inviting people to become Christians, and the practical side of nurturing and sustaining their new faith. In time, his teaching became a central way of understanding what was to become known as Christianity.

From the oral traditions about Jesus, some written fragments, and then from the teaching and writing of Paul, the Christian church began to develop a written account, later to be called The New Testament. As it matured beyond a few local congregations into movement, with new churches in many parts of the Roman Empire, Christianity was born as a religion that extended far beyond one location and culture.

The letters of Paul were important for these new churches. A generation later, there were additional written documents that were based on the oral tradition and fragments of writings, and this collection was the beginning of what became the New Testament. In time, there were other writings that guided the church, ones that we know as the Gospels, with Mark's Gospel being written first and available in the sixties.[1] The Gospels of Matthew and Luke come later, with Matthew being quite dependent upon Mark's Gospel. Luke, a gentile, appeared to have several sources in addition to Mark for his Gospel, as he explains: "Since many have undertaken to set down an orderly account of the events that have been fulfilled among us, just as they were handed on to us by those who from the beginning were eyewitnesses and servants of the word, I too decided, after investigating everything carefully from the very first, to write an orderly account for you, most excellent Theophilus, so that you may know the truth concerning the things about which you have been instructed" (Luke 1:1–4). The Gospel of John is often placed as late as the nineties, and it is more theological in character, reflecting how the new faith was developing its theology.

From the oral tradition alive in the heart and mind of regional leaders, some fragments of writing, the letters of Paul, and the writings called the Gospels, the new church now had a foundational collection of writing that provided a more theological framework and foundation. Soon, the new religion, now with congregations, was present in several town/cities, with

---

1. Most scholars place the Gospel of Mark coming in the late sixties, followed by Luke and Matthew a few years later, and the Gospel of John almost in the end of what we call the first century.

a base in Jerusalem. As we study this complex and quite dramatic development, we see how the church took the responsibility of implementing the mission, understood as reflecting the life, teaching, and redemptive events of Jesus. It was still developing, although by the end of the first century, it had four major components, with idiosyncratic ministries emerging in the several regions where there were Christians.

1. The first ministry was *koinonia*, a Greek term often translated as "fellowship." Small groups of Christians came together, shared their needs and good news, and sought ways to support one another. It was a nurturing and supportive community.

2. The second ministry, designed to help new Christians, was teaching (*didaktikos*) the faith, its history, foundational beliefs, and its mission. The English word *didactic* comes from the Greek word.

3. Ministry number three was *diakonia*, or reaching out to those in need, assisting individuals who were struggling to survive given the social conditions in which they lived. The ministry was to work for a more just and humane society.

4. A fourth ministry, basic to the first century Christians, was *kerygma*, the ministry of proclaiming the gospel message and inviting people to embrace the good news. This ministry was foundational, and soon the church began to grow.

The Contemporary Response to the Way of Jesus

We have used the word *conform* in reference to our responsibility as Christians. It is based on the earlier word we used in this section, *transformed*, understanding it as the experience of profound renewal, based on our encounter and presence with God; it is an experience that begins the process of us moving from a self-oriented person to an other-oriented person, a process of conforming to the model of the life of Jesus. It is a shift of our values and goals, one that empowers us to seek and to live with guidance and grace, giving us the capacity to understand and follow the will of God. This new direction does not mean that we no longer think about ourselves, but that we begin to be less preoccupied with our personal desires and needs and more focused on using our gifts and talents in expanding the reign of God, loving all who come our way, and caring for the many whose circumstances have patterns of injustice blocking their way to the good and abundant life.

Flowing from this frame of reference is the awareness of the several values that enhance the positive growth and development of those who are close to us and those whose environment has dimensions that block the journey toward wholeness and mature living. It is when we hear the words of Jesus and internalize them that we begin to care for others in an unconditional way—that is, "In everything do to others as you would have them do to you" (Matt 7:12). The point of this verse is to care for others in sensitive and tangible ways.

I want to share the words and concepts that have come to me as I have had to find the way and fully understand the dictates of the Golden Rule. The pattern of life and the values that fill the God-centered life will be familiar; I found them so, but restating them for others and viewing my life from the lens of the Golden Rule have given me fresh insights, a deeper awareness of what motivates me, and then inspired me to make the Golden Rule my model, fresh each day. The charge "to do unto others as I would have them do unto me" has been central to my understanding.

The Golden Rule is quite tangible and relatively free from all of the "buts" and the sentences which make it just another piece of empty advise. It is now an integral part of my inner life. I continue to be inspired to live by the Golden Rule.

I want to suggest six values that illustrate the daily presence of the Golden Rule, the day-by-day sense of God's presence, empowering me to live by this wise and profound teaching. The first value, one that is foundational in character, is that I should *honor life*. It is, of course, human life where I focus, but I also care deeply about other life that surrounds us and is given to us by the loving God. It does appear in postmodern world that this other life is only partially valued; there are other wants and needs that often take precedence. For example, we only care for nature in ways that suit us and further our goals. We tend to neglect the way we have abused nature and exploited it. We have done so in many irresponsible ways that the world we know is profoundly threatened. Even human life is viewed as dispensable, as, for example, when Prime Minister Netanyahu used violent warfare to achieve the legitimate goal of preserving the safety of Israeli people, but killing thousands of innocent Palestinians. I do not have any sympathy for Putin and the Russian attack on Ukraine or the current suffering of so many Palestinians. We must always value life, even in the midst of political disputes.

The second value comes to the surface as we watch the violent warfare in Ukraine and Gaza, with each side justifying the case for violence. Lies are used again and again to justify killing. Living with the accusation of being naïve, I still believe that we must live by truth, speak truthfully, and be persons of integrity, living and speaking in authentic ways. Our recent presidential election underlined for me that the direct telling of lies was an integral part of promoting candidates for offices. Donald Trump lies so easily that I often wonder if he has a conscience. What I do know is that he wants power and to be treated with honor, perhaps sensing that he will not be in the place of power if he does not consistently be dishonest. The office of the president of the United States of America desperately needs a person with integrity; the position will only be respected if those who hold the office speak truthfully (not that everything needs to said). But Donald Trump uses dishonesty as a way of exercising power, making it nearly impossible to believe anything he says. Benjamin Netanyahu, the prime minister of Israel, gets his way in advancing his goals of controlling all the land of Israel by the utter destruction of innocent people whose home was in Gaza. He justifies his dishonesty by being untruthful about his need to get even with Hamas, a militant group seeking power. A clear statement and wise resistance may have been the best response to the militant Hamas, but the government of Israel did not judge it to be enough. Instead, there was the near destruction of a vast region, and claiming in his Zionist ideology that it is the rightful home of Jewish Israel.

One value that undergirds nearly all the other values needed for a peaceful world order and a good life is *love* and its twin, *compassion*. The Sermon on the Mount, recorded in the Gospel of Matthew, quotes Jesus as saying, "You have heard that it was said, 'You shall love your neighbor and hate your enemy.' But I say to you, Love your enemies and pray for those who persecute you'" (Matt 5:43–44). He is also quoted as saying in answer to the question, "'Teacher, which commandment in the law is the greatest?' He said to him, '"You shall love the Lord your God with all your heart, and with all your soul, and with all your mind." This is the greatest and first commandment. And a second is like it: "You shall love your neighbor as yourself." On these two commandments hang all the law and the prophets.'" (Matt 22:36–40). The word Jesus uses for *love* has the meaning of selfless and unconditional acceptance, a love that accepts those in our circle of nearness, cares for those in desperate and dangerous settings, and suggests another word in English with a comparable meaning, *compassion*.

Still another word that is on our list of needed values in our strange and confused world is *peace*. The world in which we live is filled with national governments, often with controversies about land, resources, and values. Even the smaller regions with governments such as states, counties, and cities often have conflicts. In many ways, these levels of government have policies and gifted leaders who are able to prevent harmful conflict, making peace between those with deep differences and empowering them to pursue their goals. Yet conflicts seem to be universally present, and fortunately for us, most of these levels of government do manage to govern wisely and well. We are so grateful when the appointed or elected leadership manage their domain of power with wisdom and grace. We long for settings where there is peace rather than discord.

Jesus, sensitive as he was to this reality, is quoted as saying in his final words to his disciples who were afraid, "Peace I leave with you; my peace I give to you. I do not give to you as the world gives. Do not let your hearts be troubled, and do not let them be afraid" (John 14:27). The disciples were in fact afraid because they knew that the time with Jesus was coming to a close. They sensed that he would soon be arrested; they were afraid and had worry in their hearts, not peace. As Jesus speaks, he is likely referencing the differences between groups that cause conflict. He may also be speaking to his disciples who are deeply afraid because Jesus may soon be arrested. He may be comforting them, speaking about the deep inner peace that comes from the quiet rest in the love and wisdom of God.

Jesus, rooted deeply in his faith, likely used the Hebrew word *shalom*, a Hebrew word full of deep meaning that included both the reconciliation between groups with differences and the deep inner peace that comes to us as we move away from worry and rest in the wisdom and love of God. He would desire that their total setting would be free from troublesome conflict—conflict that is present between groups with differences—and also filled with peace that is present in an individual believer who trusts in God's providential care. He reminds them that this kind of peace is a different kind of peace than that which is given by the world.

The word *shalom* was often used in reference to peace of mind in an individual's life. Jesus says, regarding the peace that he brings, that it is not as the world gives, implying that the world's peace may be here today and gone tomorrow, as was certainly the case in the regions where Jesus and the disciples were located. As he was speaking, he was concerned about conflict between diverse groups of people and hopes for peace between the conflicted groups, but was more likely speaking about a peace that comes to an individual of faith. It is the peace that God gives as one places confidence and trust in the divine wisdom. It may easily be understood as a reference to the deeply spiritual person who trusts in the love of God, regardless of external conflicts.

In the passage in John's Gospel, Jesus is providing pastoral care to the disciples because he was at the end of his public ministry and the disciples were worried and afraid because they were viewed as a renegade group causing trouble on a very busy weekend. Violence was possible. The disciples did fear that they might be arrested as a trouble-making group. Jesus and his disciples were not free from fear, and were anxious about what might happen. In some ways, the reference to peace by Jesus may be about the conflict between groups with deep differences. But his comments, toward the end of his time with the disciples, are more likely targeted toward the deep inner peace that comes to individuals who have the reassurance that God is with them. Yet it may have had the secondary meaning for the disciples who might soon be in a setting that was untouched by violence or misfortune, one that allowed for full growth toward maturity in a harmonious community.

Another foundational value, related to peace, is *justice*. In some ways, it might be wise to reverse the word order, placing justice before peace in that peace comes when justice is present. Jesus was profoundly aware that the social structures of his time in the region of Israel/Palestine were strained because of the Roman occupation. There were Roman soldiers who were exercising power in a conquered region.

The Jewish community and its religious leaders had a forum for making and ensuring a modest level of justice. The Jewish community, with an approximation of a theocracy, had a forum for religious and public concerns called the Sanhedrin in which they resolved religious differences and conflicts between groups. On occasion, as was the case with Jesus, it dealt with government concerns about the law. Jesus is quoted in Matthew's Gospel as saying, "Woe to you, scribes and Pharisees, hypocrites! For you tithe mint, dill, and cumin, and have neglected the weightier matters of the law: justice and mercy and faith" (Matt 23:23). Jesus was not only concerned with the unjust way he was treated, but also concerned about the common people, who, with three levels of government, did not get treated justly. In fact, the arrest of Jesus was adjudicated by three levels of government: the Jewish Sanhedrin, the regional government of the Herodians, and the government of Rome; Jesus spoke directly with Pilate, the officer of Rome. The larger point in this discussion is that a stable society must have carefully crafted laws and a good system of enforcing the laws. Where there is no justice, all suffer, and there is unrest across the land. This was the final setting in the life of Jesus as he speaks about peace to his disciples.

It does lead us to the additional value that must be present for there to be a just and peaceful society. If there is injustice and suffering among the people, it will mean that the people must take action. To overcome injustice, the people may have to engage in seeking justice for the citizens of the region. For there to be peace, the citizens must be engaged in *service* and help to create a more just and humane society. To be a participant in the governance structure, even if it is in a minor role, gives one a sense of hope and creates a higher level of trust in the government. There will always be some levels of injustice, and it may be easier to trust the government structures if the citizens have the opportunity to participate is some way with the government system, even if it is just a vote.

Our question for this section is, What is the best way to respond to the mission and ministry of Jesus in the contemporary world? We have responded to this question by suggesting a set of values, drawn in large measure by our study of the life and teachings of Jesus. We settled on six values, present in the life and teachings of Jesus, and then asked how these values might jump forward across the centuries to help us understand how we must cultivate these values and express them in our daily lives.

1. We must respect all of life, given to us as stewards, with special attention to caring for human beings who are neglected and mistreated.
2. As we move into our divine calling and work, we must be people who honor the truth and have integrity in all aspects of our lives.
3. We must make love and compassion our way of life, caring for those in need and reaching out in compassion to those who are in need and neglected.
4. We must be committed to creating settings where there is peace and justice, creating settings for all people to live wisely and well.
5. There will be no peace without justice, and we must do our part in creating a more just and humane setting and world.
6. We do that by being willing to engage in service, using our skills and gifts to help create settings in which people flourish.

Questions for Reflection and Discussion

1. What were the government structures in Israel/Palestine during the time that Jesus was engaged in his mission?
2. In what ways did Jesus relate to the different levels of government that were present in his time?
3. What were the main components of the church's ministry in its early development?
4. How would you describe the contemporary response of the church to the issues of peace and justice? How involved should the church be in reference to these concerns?

5. What does nature in all of its beauty and power teach us about how to live? What would Jesus say about how we live on our home, the earth, and how might he suggest that we take care of our gift of the earth?

Key Terms and Concepts

1. Septuagint: The early translation of the Old Testament from the original Hebrew.
2. Kerygma: The original proclamation of the gospel message.
3. Diakonia: The mission of the church that addresses the needs of the people, often focused on issues of peace and justice.
4. Koinonia: The ministry of community life in the church; being together to help one another.
5. Shalom: Hebrew word for peace.

Suggestions for Reference and Reading

1. *Altruism and Christian Ethics* by Colin Grant
2. *Filled with the Spirit* by John R. Levison
3. *Journey of Awakening and Higher Consciousness* by Jane Kim Yu
4. *Reading the Bible Again for the First Time: Taking the Bible Seriously but Not Literally* by Marcus J. Borg
5. *Revolutionary Love: A Political Manifesto to Heal and Transform the World* by Michael Lerner

Bibliography

Achtemeier, Paul J., ed. *Harper's Bible Dictionary.* San Francisco: Harper & Row, 1985.
Alberta, Tim. *The Kingdom, the Power, and the Glory: American Evangelicals in an Age of Extremism.* New York: Harper, 2023.
Augustine. *The Confessions.* Translated by E. B. Pusey. London: Dent & Sons, 1913.
Baillie, John. *A Diary of Private Prayer.* London: Oxford University Press, 1954.
Bass, Diana Butler. *Christianity for the Rest of Us: How the Neighborhood Church Is Transforming the Faith.* New York: HarperOne, 2006.
Berry, Thomas. *The Dream of Earth.* San Francisco: Sierra Club, 1988.
———. *The Sacred Universe: Earth, Spirituality, and Religion in the Twenty-First Century.* Edited by Mary Evelyn Tucker. New York: Columbia University Press, 2009.
Borg, Marcus J. *Days of Awe and Wonder: How to Be a Christian in the Twenty-First Century.* New York: HarperOne, 2017.
———. *Jesus: Uncovering the Life, Teachings, and Relevance of a Religious Revolutionary.* San Francisco: HarperSanFrancisco, 1989.
———. *Reading the Bible Again for the First Time: Taking the Bible Seriously but Not Literally.* San Francisco: HarperSanFrancisco, 2001.
Bourgeault, Cynthia. *Centered Prayer and Inner Awakening.* Lanham, MD: Cowley, 2004.
Bunyan, John. *Pilgrim's Progress.* New York: Grosset & Dunlap, n.d.
Carmody, Denise L., and John T. Carmody. *Ways to the Center: An Introduction to World Religions.* Belmont, CA: Wadsworth, 1984.
Christopher, David. *The Holy Universe: A New Story of Creation for the Heart, Soul, and Spirit.* Santa Rosa, CA: New Story, 2014.
The Contemplative Society. "Centering Prayer." https://www.contemplative.org/contemplative-practice/centering-prayer/.
Dalai Lama [Tenzin Gyatso]. *The Good Heart: A Buddhist Perspective on The Teachings of Jesus.* Translated by Geshe Thupten Jinpa, edited by Robert Kiely. Somervillle, MA: Wisdom, 1998.
———. *How to Expand Love: Widening the Circle of Loving Relationships.* Translated and edited by Jeffrey Hopkins. New York: Atria, 2005.
———. *Toward a True Kinship of Faiths: How the World's Religions Can Come Together.* New York: Doubleday Religion, 2010.
Dalai Lama [Tenzin Gyatso], and Howard Cutler. *The Art of Happiness: A Handbook for Living.* New York: Riverhead, 1998.

Dawkins, Richard. *The Greatest Show on Earth: The Evidence for Evolution*. New York: Free Press, 2009.

Delio, Ilia. *Birth of a Dancing Star: From Cradle Catholic to Cyborg Christian*. Maryknoll, NY: Orbis, 2019.

———. *Making All Things New: Catholicity, Cosmology, Consciousness*. Maryknoll, NY: Orbis, 2015.

———. *The Unbearable Wholeness of Being: God, Evolution, and the Power of Love*. Maryknoll, NY: Orbis, 2015.

Doniger, Wendy, ed. *Merriam-Webster's Encyclopedia of World Religions*. Springfield, MA: Merriam-Webster, 1999.

Echegaray, Hugo. *The Practice of Jesus*. Translated by Matthew J. O'Connell. Maryknoll, NY: Orbis, 1984.

Eliade, Mircea. *From Primitives to Zen: A Thematic Sourcebook of the History of Religions*. San Francisco: Harper & Row, 1977.

———. *A History of Religious Ideas*. 3 vols. Chicago: University of Chicago Press, 1978–1985.

Ferguson, Duncan S. *Biblical Hermeneutics: An Introduction*. Eugene, OR: Wipf & Stock, 2016.

———. *Exploring the Spirituality of the World Religions: the Quest for Personal, Spiritual and Social Transformation*. New York: Continuum, 2010.

———. *Lovescapes: Mapping the Geography of Love; An Invitation to the Love-Centered Life*. Eugene, OR: Cascade, 2012.

———. *The Radical Invitation of Jesus: How Accepting the Invitation of Jesus Can Lead to a Living Faith and Fulfilling Life for Today*. Eugene, OR: Wipf & Stock, 2019.

———. *The Radical Teaching of Jesus: A Teacher Full of Grace and Truth; An Inquiry for Thoughtful Seekers*. Eugene, OR: Wipf & Stock, 2016.

Foster, Richard J. *Celebration of Discipline: The Path to Spiritual Growth*. San Francisco: HarperSanFrancisco, 2018.

———. *Streams of Living Water: Celebrating the Great Traditions of Christian Faith*. New York: HarperCollins, 1998.

Fowler, James W. *Becoming Adult, Becoming Christian: Adult Development and Christian Faith*. San Francisco: Harper & Row, 1984.

———. *Stages of Faith: The Psychology of Human Development and the Quest for Meaning*. San Francisco: HarperSanFrancisco, 1981.

Fox, Matthew. *Creation Spirituality: Liberating Gifts for the Peoples of the Earth*. New York: HarperCollins, 1991.

———. *Original Blessing*. Santa Fe: Bear, 1983.

Frazer, James G. *The Golden Bough: The Roots of Religion and Folklore*. New York: Avnel, 1981.

Grant, Colin. *Altruism and Christian Ethics*. New Studies in Christian Ethics 18. Cambridge: Cambridge University Press, 2001.

Gushee, David P., and Glen H. Stassen. *Kingdom Ethics: Following Jesus in Contemporary Context*. Grand Rapids: Eerdmans, 2003.

Gutierrez, Gustavo. *Theology of Liberation: History, Politics, and Salvation*. Translated and edited by Sister Caridad Inda and John Eagleson. Maryknoll, NY: Orbis, 2018.

Haidt, Jonathan. *The Anxious Generation: How the Great Rewiring of Childhood Is Causing an Epidemic of Mental Illness*. New York: Penguin, 2024.

Hardy, Donna Fitzroy. "Chief Seattle's Letter to All." California State University–Northridge. https://www.csun.edu/~vcpsyooh/seattle.htm.

Harris, Sam. *The End of Faith: Religion, Terror, and the Future of Reason*. New York: Norton, 2004.

Hawking, Stephen W. *A Brief History of Time: From the Big Bang to Black Holes*. New York: Bantam, 1988.

Hitchcock, Susan Tyler, and John L. Esposito. *Geography of Religion: Where God Lives, Where Pilgrims Walk*. Washington, DC: National Geographic, 2004.

Hitchens, Christopher. *God Is Not Great: How Religion Poisons Everything*. New York: Twelve, 2007.

Horsley, Richard A. *Jesus and the Politics of Roman Palestine*. Columbia, SC: University of South Carolina Press, 2014.

John XXIII, Pope. *Journal of a Soul: The Autobiography of Pope John XXIII*. Translated by Dorothy White. New York: Signet, 1966.

Johnston, William, trans. and ed. *The Cloud of Unknowing and the Book of Privy Counseling*. New York: Image, 1973.

Jones, Cheslyn, et al., eds. *The Study of Spirituality*. New York: Oxford University Press, 1986.

King, Martin Luther, Jr. "Read Martin Luther King Jr.'s 'I Have a Dream' Speech in Its Entirety." NPR, Jan. 16, 2023. https://www.npr.org/2010/01/18/122701268/i-have-a-dream-speech-in-its-entirety.

Kornfield, Jack. *The Wise Heart: A Guide to the Universal Teachings of Buddhist Psychology*. New York: Bantam, 2008.

Küng, Hans. *On Being a Christian*. Translated by Edwin Quinn. Garden City, NY: Doubleday, 1976.

Lerner, Michael. *Revolutionary Love: A Political Manifesto to Heal and Transform the World*. Oakland: University of California Press, 2019.

Levison, John R. *Filled with the Spirit*. Grand Rapids: Eerdmans, 2009.

Levitin, Daniel J. *Successful Aging: A Neuroscientist Explores the Power and Potential of our Lives*. New York: Dutton, 2020.

Lincoln, Abraham. "Lincoln's Second Inaugural Address." National Park Service, last updated Apr. 18, 2020. https://www.nps.gov/linc/learn/historyculture/lincoln-second-inaugural.htm.

Lines, Caleb J. "The goal is not to bring people to Christianity." Facebook, Sept. 23, 2023. https://www.facebook.com/revdrcalebjlines/posts/when-in-doubt-love/763857505751190/.

Mafi, Maryam, trans. *Rumi, Day by Day*. Charlottesville, VA: Hampton Roads, 2014.

Maguire, Daniel C. *Ethics: A Complete Method for Moral Choice*. Minneapolis: Fortress, 2010.

McGrath, Alister. *The Big Question: Why We Can't Stop Talking About Science, Faith, and God*. New York: St. Martin's, 2015.

McLaren, Brian D. *Do I Stay Christian? A Guide for the Doubters, the Disappointed, and the Disillusioned*. New York: St. Martin's Essentials, 2022.

———. *A New Kind of Christianity: Ten Questions That are Transforming the Faith*. New York: HarperOne, 2010.

Merton, Thomas. *Contemplation in a World of Action*. New York: Image, 1973.

———. *Contemplative Prayer*. Garden City, NY: Image, 1971.

———. *New Seeds of Contemplation*. New York: Image, 1973.

Miller, Lisa. *The Awakened Brain: The New Science of Spirituality and Our Quest for an Inspired Life*. New York: Random House, 2021.
Miller, Madeline. *Circe*. New York: Little, Brown, 2018.
———. *The Song of Achilles*. New York: Ecco, 2012.
Mott, Michael. *The Seven Mountains of Thomas Merton*. Boston: Houghton Mifflin, 1984.
Nerburn, Kent, ed. *The Wisdom of the Native Americans*. Novato, CA: New World Library, 1999.
Newell, J. Philip. *Listening for the Heartbeat of God: A Celtic Spirituality*. New York: Paulist, 1997.
Nhat Hahn, Thich. *Living Buddha, Living Christ*. New York: Riverhead, 1995.
———. *Teachings on Love*. Berkeley: Parallax, 1998.
Nygren, Anders. *Agape and Eros: A Study of the Christian Idea of Love*. Translated by Philip S. Watson. London: S.P.C.K. Westminster, 1953.
Oswald, Roy M., and Arland Jacobson. *The Emotional Intelligence of Jesus: Relational Smarts for Religious Leaders*. Lanham, MD: Rowman & Littlefield, 2015.
Patte, Daniel, ed. *The Cambridge Dictionary of Christianity*. New York: Cambridge University Press, 2010.
The Positivity Project. "Character Strengths." https://posproject.org/character-strengths/.
Post, Stephen G. *Unlimited Love: Altruism, Compassion, and Service*. Radnor, PA: Templeton Foundation, 2003.
Robinson, Marilynne. *Reading Genesis*. New York: Farrar, Straus, and Giroux, 2024.
Rohr, Richard. *Eager to Love: The Alternative Way of Francis of Assisi*. Cincinnati: Franciscan Media, 2014.
———. *Everything Belongs: The Gift of Contemplative Prayer*. New York: Crossroad, 1999.
———. *The Naked Now: Learning to See as the Mystics See*. New York: Crossroad, 2009.
———. *The Universal Christ: How a Forgotten Reality Can Change Everything We See, Hope For, and Believe*. New York: Convergent, 2019.
Rohr, Richard, and Friends. *Contemplation in Action*. New York: Crossroad, 2006.
Rougemont, Denis de. *Love in the Western World*. Translated by Montgomery Belgion. Princeton: Princeton University Press, 1956.
Ruiz, Don Miguel. *The Mastery of Love: A Practical Guide to the Art of Relationship*. Toltec Wisdom. San Rafael, CA: Amber-Allen, 1999.
Schleiermacher, Friedrich. *The Christian Faith*. Edited by H. R. Mackintosh and J. S. Stewart. 2 vols. New York: Harper Torchbooks, 1963.
Sheldon, Charles M. *In His Steps*. New York: Hurst, 1997.
Singer, Irving. *The Nature of Love*. 3 vols. Chicago: University of Chicago Press, 1984–1987.
Smith, Huston. *The Soul of Christianity: Restoring the Great Tradition*. San Francisco: HarperSanFrancisco, 2005.
———. *The World's Religions*. New York: HarperOne, 1991.
Suleyman, Mustafa. *The Coming Wave: Technology, Power, and the Twenty-First Century's Greatest Dilemma*. New York: Crown, 2023.
Taylor, Charles. *A Secular Age*. Cambridge: Belknap Press, 2007.
Teilhard de Chardin, Pierre. *The Divine Milieu*. New York: Harper Torchbooks, 1957.
———. *Hymn of the Universe*. New York: Harper & Row, 1965.

———. *The Phenomenon of Man*. London: Collins, 1959.
Teresa, Mother. *Life in the Spirit: Reflections, Meditations, Prayers*. Edited by Kathryn Spink. San Francisco: Harper & Row, 1983.
Thomas à Kempis. *The Imitation of Christ*. Revised translation by John C. Graham. Self-published, 2023.
Tolle, Eckhart. *A New Earth: Awakening to Your Life's Purpose*. New York: Dutton, 2005.
———. *The Power of Now: A Guide to Spiritual Enlightenment*. Novato, CA: Namaste and New World Library, 1999.
Watts, Alan. *The Way of Zen*. New York: Vintage, 1957.
Wilbur, Ken. *Integral Spirituality: A Startling New Role for Religion in the Modern and Postmodern World*. Boston: Integral, 2006.
———. *The Religion of Tomorrow: A Vision for the Future of the Great Traditions*. Boulder, CO: Shambhala, 2017.
———. *Sex, Ecology, Spirituality: The Spirit of Evolution*. Boston: Shambhala, 1995.
Wolsey, Roger. *Kissing Fish: Christianity for People Who Don't Like Christianity*. Self-Published, 2011.
Yu, Jane Kim. *Journey of Awakening and Higher Consciousness*. Absolute Author, 2023.

Index

Abrahamic monotheistic religions, 149–50, 164
adulterous woman at the well, 147
Agape and Eros (Nygren), 119
agape love, 84, 145–46
AI technology, 12n17
Alaska
　natives, the divine among, 132–33
　religion in, 166–69
　religious life and thought, 164–66, 164n15, 165nn16–17
Alberta, Tim, 44n11
Alexander the Great, 89
Altruism and Christian Ethics (Grant), 184
animism, term usage, 133
answers, searching for, 156–58
Aphrodite, 130
Apollo, 130
apologetics, term usage, 93n2
Apostles' Creed, 47
Ares, 130
Armstrong, Karen, 161
The Art of Happiness (Dalai Lama), 163n13
Artemis, 130
Assembly of God churches, 52
Augustine of Hippo, Saint, 9–11, 18
authority, of the apostles faith, 48–49
The Awakened Brain (Miller), 39n1, 55

Bach, Johann Sebastian, 104
Bailey, Kenneth E., 36
Baillie, John, 160
Baptist Church, 50–51

Bass, Diana Butler, 62n9, 69, 161
Becoming Adult, Becoming Christian (Fowler), 86
Berry, Thomas, 134n10, 140
biblical epigraphs
　1 John 4:16, 18, 21, 121
　Acts 9:1–9, 57
　Ephesians 4:1–7, 171
　Galatians 5:22–23, 141
　Galatians 5:22–26, 73
　Genesis 1:27–28, 141
　John 8:12, 19
　John 14:1, 21
　John 14:5–6, 37
　John 14:27, 154
　Mathew 5:43–44, 121
　Matthew 7:12–14, 123
　Micah 6:8, 121
　Philippians 2:1–3, 171
　Philippians 2:1–5, 107
　Philippians 2:4–5, 173
　Philippians 4:8–9, 88
　Proverbs 1:7, 154
Biblical Hermeneutics (Ferguson), 27n13, 125–26
biblical understanding of spiritual maturity, 41–43, 41nn5–7
Big Question (McGrath), 59n6
Bill of Rights, United States, 149
Birth of a Dancing Star (Delio), 69
Black Church, 53
Blood Brothers (Chacour), 36
Borg, Marcus J., 36, 184
Bornkamm, Günther, 86
Bourgeault, Cynthia, 99n12

Brethren Church, 51
Brown, Dee, 170
Buddhist/Buddhism, 96, 96n6, 163
Bultmann, Rudolph, 98n10
Bunyan, John, 18, 160
Bury My Heart at Wounded Knee (Brown), 170

Calvin, John, 49
Cambridge Dictionary of Christianity (Patte), 46n13
Carmody, Denise L., 167n19
Carmody, John T., 167n19
Celebration of Discipline (Foster), 97n7
Centered Prayer and Inner Awakening (Bourgeault), 99n12
centering prayer, 96, 98, 99n12
"Centering Prayer" (Keating), 99n12
Chacour, Abuna Elias, 31–32, 36
character strength
    maturity and, 114–15
    model of, 115–17
    in Positivity Project, 119
    practices, 112–14
Charismatic Tradition, 100–101
Chief Seattle (1854), 131
Christian churches
    Baptist Church, 50
    Black Church, 53
    Brethren Church, 51
    categories of, 54, 54n19
    first century ministries, 148
    fundamentalist movement, 52
    liberal and progressive, 53–54
    literal sense of Scripture, 52n17
    Orthodox tradition of, 48–49
    Puritans, 50
    Quakers (Friends Church), 51, 53
    Roman Catholic Church, 46nn12-13, 48–50
Christian communities in Paul's time, 175
The Christian Faith (Schleiermacher), 53n18, 55
Christian nationalism, 44n11, 103
Christianity for the Rest of Us (Bass), 62n9, 69

Christians/Christianity
    basic practices of, 92
    church, struggles living the faith, 64–67
    church beliefs, 63–64
    Jesus got it right, 62–63
    key terms and concepts, 69
    living with questions, 60n7, 61–62
    reflection questions, 68–69
    staying in the church, 67–68
    struggle with diversity, 58n1
Christopher, David, 134n10
Circe (Miller), 4n3
Civil War in America, 157
Clare, Saint, 104
climate change, 135–38, 155
Cloud of Unknowing (Johnston), 71, 95n5, 106
The Coming Wave (Suleyman), 12n17
commitment, need for, 58–60
common good, serving, 45
communications, 112
compassion, 180
Confessions (Augustine), 9, 18
conflicts
    dealing with, 111
    world-wide, 29–30
conform, term usage, 178
contemplation, term usage, 105
Contemplation in a World of Action (Merton), 94n4, 106
Contemplation in Action (Rohr), 95n5
contemplative experiences, 94–95
Contemplative Prayer (Merton), 55
context understanding, 43–44
conversion experiences, 91–92
Corinth, term usage, 86
cosmic evolution, 139, 142n1
Council of Trent (1545–1563), 46–47
courage, as character strength, 117
Creation Spirituality (Fox), 170
Crossan, John Dominic, 36, 86
Cultic, term usage, 139
culture
    in Alaska, 168
    term usage, 170
    understanding religion in, 164

Dalai Lama, 39, 94n3, 153, 163, 163n10, 163n13
Daly, Mary, 161
Darwin, Charles, 59
Dawkins, Richard, 59
Day, Dorothy, 103
Day by Day (Rumi), 121
Decalogue (Ten Commandments), 47
Delio, Ilia, 24n7, 69, 138n14, 139
Demeter, 130
destination, of our journey, 14–16
diakonia, term usage, 184
A Diary of Private Prayer (Baillie), 160
Dionysus, 130
disciples of Jesus
  pastoral care, 181–82
  selection, 91–92
divine, in nature's patterns, 168
divine image, 153
The Divine Milieu (Teilhard), 138n13
divine mission in the world, 141
divine presence as love
  accepting and endorsing, ways of, 125–28
  awareness and gratitude, 137
  current challenge, 134–36
  earth stewardship of, 138
  key terms and concepts, 139
  overview, 123–25
  reflection questions, 139
  spiritual inspiration/direction, 136–37
  spiritual pathways, 130–34
  understanding, ways of, 128–29
Do I Stay Christian? (McClaren), 59n2, 70
double commandment, term usage, 153
The Dream of the Earth (Berry), 134n10
dysfunctional families, 10–11

Eager to Love (Rohr), 153
earth, stewardship of, 138, 142–50
Eastern Orthodox church, 48
Echegaray, Hugo, 44n10
educational strategies, church mission in
  apostles, faith of, 48–49

faith, saved by, 49–50
Free Church, 50–53
key terms and concepts, 55
liberal and progressive, 53–54
overview, 45–46
reflection questions, 54–55
sacramental, 46–48
Egyptian's belief in the divine (BC era), 130
Einstein, Albert, 27n14
Eliade, Mircea, 163, 167n19
empower, term usage, 152–53
End of Faith (Harris), 59n6
enlightenment, journey of, 158–63
Ephesus, 30
Erickson, Erik, 34
eros love, 145
Esposito, John L., 39
ethical formation, 112–14
ethical life guide, 107, 168–69
ethical mandate, 149–52
Ethics: A Complete Method for Moral Choice (Maguire), 119, 150n8
evangelical
  practices, 101–2n19, 104
  term usage, 64n10, 69, 105
Evangelical Tradition, 103–4
Evans, Rachel Held, 87
Exploring the Spirituality of the World Religions (Ferguson), 107n1, 125n2, 134n10, 162n9

faith
  of apostles, 48–49
  pathway of, 57–68
  term usage, 55, 86
  understating content, 40–41
faith formation, spiritual practices in, 96–105
Ferguson, Duncan S.
  Biblical Hermeneutics, 27n13, 1227n3
  early months/years of pilgrimage, 92–94, 159–62, 159n6, 160nn7–8
  Exploring the Spirituality of the World Religions, 107n1, 125n2, 134n10, 162n9
  personal belief on religion, 128n4

Ferguson, Duncan S. *(continued)*
"Preunderstanding in Historical and Biblical Interpretation" (Ferguson), 26–27n13
The Radical Invitation of Jesus (Ferguson), 24n8
The Radical Teaching of Jesus (Ferguson), 24n8
Filled with the Spirit (Levison), 106, 184
flesh, works of, 75
formative journey of the soul
components of, 13–16
contours of, 1–3
key terms and concepts, 17–18
perilous odyssey, 6–13
reflection questions, 17
staying the course, 16–17
term usages, 3–6
Foster, Richard J., 97–98, 100–104, 108
foundational center, forms of, 14n19
Fowler, James, 34, 86
Fox, Matthew, 70, 170
Francis, Pope, 47n14
Francis, Saint, 104
Franciscan/Roman Catholic model, 34
Frankl, Viktor E., 18
Frazer, James G., 170
Freud, Sigmund, 33, 59
Freudian/Jungian model, 34
Friends Church (Quakers), 51, 53
From Primitives to Zen (Eliade), 167n19
fruits of the Holy Spirit, 75
fundamentalist movement, 52, 64n10

Gandhi, Mahatma, 103, 104, 163
Gaza, 1n1, 29–31, 59, 156, 179–80
gentiles, Paul's ministry, 73–74
God
"image of God," 39
light/truth, 175
as love, 41n7, 175
presence of, 179
spirit, 175
God Is Not Great (Hitchens), 59n6
The Golden Bough (Frazer), 170

Golden Rule, 28, 35, 179
Grant, Colin, 184
Greek's belief in the divine (BC era), 130
"ground of being," term usage, 5n8, 8n13
Gushee, David P., 119
Gutierrez, Gustavo, 161

Haidt, Jonathan, 6n9
Hamas, 30–31, 33, 180
happiness, 154
Harris, Sam, 59
Hawking, Stephen, 59
healing, 146
Hebrew Bible, teachings in, 43, 45
Henley, William Earnest, 1
Hephaestus, 130
Hera, 130
hermeneutics, term usage, 42n8, 119
Hermes, 130
Herodians, 182
Heschel, Abraham Joshua, 104
Hestia, 130
The Historical Jesus (Crossan), 36
A History of Religious Ideas (Eliade), 163
Hitchens, Christopher, 59, 59n6
Hitler, Adolf, 157
Holiness movement, 52, 100–101, 100n15
Holy Spirit
as divine, 5
early understanding of, 78n4
fruits of the Holy Spirit, 75, 115
Pentecostal movement, 51, 101
speaking in tongues, 52, 99
spiritual gifts of, 79
term usage, 86
Holy Universe (Christopher), 134n10
honoring life, 179
hope
life of, 80–82
term usage, 86
Horsley, Richard A., 36, 44n10
How to Expand Love (Dalai Lama), 153
human development, model of, 33–35
human health, 155–56

human suffering, 59, 62
humanity, as character strength, 116
humankind, role of, 141–42
Hymn of the Universe (Teilhard), 138

"image of God," 39
The Imitation of Christ (Thomas à Kempis), 18, 19n1, 97n7, 106, 160
In His Steps (Sheldon), 160
In Search of Paul (Crossan & Reed), 86
incarnation, term usage, 105
Incarnational Tradition, 6n9
Integral Spirituality (Wilbur), 138n14, 139
integration, term usage, 55
"Invictus" (Henley), 1
Israel
    Jewish community in, 30–31, 76–77
    term usage, 35

James, William, 34
Jesus
    adulterous woman at the well, 147
    challenges, 25–29, 65
    concern for humankind, 146–48
    contemporary response, 178–83
    disciples, pastoral care of, 181–82
    disciples, selection of, 91–92
    on eternal life, 7–8
    focus of, 66n12
    following life of, 97–98
    got it right, 62–63
    healing ministry of, 26n11
    as interpreter of law, 148–49
    Jewish heritage of, 176
    key terms and concepts, 184
    model of, 21–22n1, 21–25
    parents of, 113–14
    Paul, on mind of, 108–12
    peace from, 154, 181
    radical teachings, 61–63
    reflection questions, 183–84
    relationships with others, 109–10
    Samaritan woman and, 123–25
    Transfiguration of, 94–95
    way of, 171–83

Jesus and the Politics of Roman Palestine (Horsley), 36, 44n10
Jesus Through Middle Eastern Eyes (Bailey), 36
Jesus: Uncovering the Life (Borg), 36
Jewish community
    Christians in, 76–77, 78n3
    in modern day Israel, 30–31
John the Baptist, 22
Johnston, William, 71, 95n5, 106
Jones, Cheslyn, 6n9
"Joshua Fit the Battle of Jericho" (song), 42
Journey of Awakening and Higher Consciousness (Yu), 184
journey of the soul, term usage, 17–18
judgement, 37
Jung, Carl, 18, 34
justice, 116–17, 151, 182–83
Justice (Sandel), 153

Keating, Thomas, 98–99n12
kerygma, term usage, 184
key terms and concepts
    on being reformed, 105
    formative journey of the soul, 17–18
    perilous times, living wisely and well in, 21–36
    soul, journey of being reformed, 86, 119
    soul, journey of being transformed, 152–53, 169–70
    soul's journey of being informed, 35
    well-being, alternative ways, 55
King, Martin Luther, Jr., 102–3
Kingdom Ethics (Gushee and Stassen), 119
Kissing Fish (Wolsey), 70
knowledge
    character strength, 116
    search for, 84
Knox, John, 160
koinonia, term usage, 184
Kornfield, Jack, 96n6
Küng, Hans, 62n9, 86

law
   Jesus as interpreter of, 148–49
   legalistic interpretations, 149
Lerner, Michael, 184
Levison, John R., 106, 184
Lewis, C. S., 160
liberal, term usage, 69
life, honoring, 179
life of faith, hope, and love, 79–85
Lines, Caleb J., 144
listening, 110
Listening for the Heartbeat of God (Newell), 55
Living Buddha, Living Christ (Nhat Hanh), 163n13
living wisely and well in perilous times
   human development, model of, 33–35
   Jesus, challenges in perilous times, 25–29
   Jesus, model of, 21–22n1, 21–25
   key terms and concepts, 35
   our odyssey, beginning of, 29–30
   peace, bonds of, 30–33
   reflection questions, 35
   soul, journey of being informed, 21–36
   spiritual formation, model of, 33–35
logos, term usage, 104n23
Lord's Prayer, 47
love
   of God and neighbor/self, 144, 152
   life of, 82–85
   priority and capacity, 144–49
   relationships when not present, 109–10
   term usage, 86
   variety of ways, 144–45
Love in the Western World (Rougemont), 153
Luther, Martin, 49

Maguire, Danial C., 119, 150n8
Making All Things New (Delio), 138n14, 139
male population, unrest in, 155n4
Man's Search for Meaning (Frankl), 18

Mar Elias Educational Institutions (Galilee), 31
Marx, Karl, 59
The Mastery of Love (Ruiz), 170
maturity, term usage, 17
McClaren, Brian D., 70
McGrath, Alister, 59n6
McLaren, Brian, 59n2, 62n9
mediation, term usage, 105
meditative experience, 95–96
Merton, Thomas, 55, 94n4, 106
message to us from Paul, 74–77
Methodist Church, 52
Methodist tradition, 99–101
Miller, Lisa, 39n1, 55
Miller, Madeline, 4n3
Milton, John, 104
mind, term usage, 4, 6
mind of Christ, term usage, 119
mindfulness, term usage, 7n11
miracles, 59
mission in troubled world, 121
mission of empowering goals
   common good, serving of, 45
   context understanding, 43–44
   faith, understating content of, 40–41
   prophetic education, 44–45
Modern Man in Search of a Soul (Jung), 18
Monica, Saint, 10
Mother Teresa, 103
mysteries, of life, 84
myth, term usage, 170

The Naked Now (Rohr), 96n6, 106
native peoples, worldwide, 131–35
natural world
   caring for, 142–43
   managing, 143–49
nature
   Alaska spirituality and, 168
   the divine in, 131–34
   sacred meaning of, 38
   understanding religion in, 164
nature, term usage, 153
The Nature of Love (Singer), 119
Nazarene Church, 52
Nerburn, Kent, 170

Netanyahu, Benjamin, 179, 180
New Kind of Christianity (McLaren), 62n9
New Seeds of Contemplation (Merton), 94n4
New Testament
  formation of, 19n1
  Gospels chronology, 177n1
  interpretation of, 49–50
  literal sense of, 52n17
  Paul's letters, 176–77
  teachings in, 43
Newell, J. Philip, 55
Niebuhr, Reinhold, 161
Nietzsche, Friedrich, 59
Nygren, Anders, 119

odyssey
  beginning of, 29–30
  of life, 1–18
  term usage, 7n10
Old Testament, 43, 45
On Being a Christian (Küng), 62n9, 86
Original Blessing (Fox), 70
Orthodox, term usage, 69
Orthodox tradition, of Christian church, 48–49, 48n15, 104

Palestine, term usage, 35
Palestinian people, 30–33, 43, 59, 179
Patte, Daniel, 46n13
Paul (Bornkamm), 86
Paul of Tarsus (apostle)
  components of conversion, 79
  conversion of in Damascus, 77, 91
  faith, life of, 79–82
  imprisonment of, 92
  Jesus' Jewish heritage, 176
  love, life of, 82–85
  message to us, 74–77
  on mind of Christ, 108–12
  ministry in Corinth, 79–85, 82n5
  ministry in Philippi, 88–90
  ministry to gentiles, 73–74
  ministry to Roman Empire, 78
  mission of, 30–32, 77, 77n2, 173–75
  mission to the gentiles, 176
  physical disability, 83, 83n6

  trust, in God's presence, 79–82
  worldview, 90n1
peace
  bonds of, 30–33, 35
  from Jesus, 154, 181
  term usage, 18
  in troubled world, 154, 180–81
peace and justice causes, 96
peace of mind, 155–56
Pentecostal churches, 52
Pentecostal movement, 101–2
perilous odyssey, of our journey, 6–13
Peterson, Chris, 114
The Phenomenon of Man (Teilhard), 138n13, 140
philia love, 145
Philippi, city of, 89
Phillip II, king of Macedonia, 89
Phillips, J. B., 160
Pilate, 182
Pilgrim's Progress (Bunyan), 18, 160
polytheistic gods, 130
Poseidon, 130
positive psychology, 116
Positivity Project, 114–15, 115nn5–7, 118
Post, Stephen G., 120
postmodern, term usage, 69
The Practice of Jesus (Echegaray), 44n10
prayer, for soul journey of being reformed, 71
Presbyterian Church (USA), 162
"Preunderstanding in Historical and Biblical Interpretation" (Ferguson), 26–27n13
process theology, 138
prophetic, term usage, 55
prophetic education, 44–45
Protestant Reformation, 49–50
Puritans, 50
Putin, Valdimir, 179

Quakers (Friends Church), 51, 53

The Radical Invitation of Jesus (Ferguson), 24n8
The Radical Teaching of Jesus (Ferguson), 24n8

Rauschenbusch, Walter, 99
Reading Genesis (Robinson), 43n9
Reading the Bible Again for the First Time (Borg), 184
reconciliation, ministry of, 84
Reed, Jonathan L., 86
reflection, 93–94
reflection, term usage, 105
reflection questions
  on being reformed, 105
  Christianity, 68–69
  formative journey of the soul, 17
  soul, journey of being reformed, 85–86, 118–19
  in soul, journey of being transformed, 169
  soul, journey of being transformed, 152
  ways to well-being, 54–55
The Religion of Tomorrow (Wilbur), 39n1, 56
religions of human family, 118
religious life and thought, 164–66
religious models, 40n2
religious orientation, 3n2
Revolutionary Love (Lerner), 184
Robinson, Marilynne, 43n9
Rohr, Richard, 25n9, 95n5, 96n6, 106, 153
Roman Catholic Church
  Eastern Orthodox church versus, 48–49
  Protestant Reformation, 49–50
  sacraments/sacramentals, 46–48, 46nn12–13
Roman Empire, Paul's ministry, 78
Romans' belief in the divine (BC era), 130
Rougemont, Denis de, 153
Ruether, Rosemary Radford, 161
Ruiz, Don Miguel, 170
Rumi (Islamic poet), 121, 163
Rumi, Day by Day, 163
Russell, Bertrand, 59

Sabbath laws, 148–49, 148n7
sacraments/sacramentals, 46–48, 46nn12–13, 55
sacred powers, 167

Sacred Universe (Berry), 134n10, 140
saints, for the leaders and members of the church, 89
Samaria, term usage, 139
Samaritan woman, 123–25
sanctification, term usage, 55
Sandel, Michael J., 153
Sanhedrin, 182
Sartre, Jean-Paul, 59
schism (1054 AD), 48
Schleiermacher, Friedrich, 53n18, 55
A Secular Age (Taylor), 12n17
secular models, 40n2
self, term usage, 4, 5n6, 6
Septuagint, term usage, 184
service, 182
Sex, Ecology, Spirituality (Wilbur), 40n2
shalom, term usage, 181, 184
shaman, term usage, 170
Sheldon, Charles, 160
Singer, Irving, 119
Smith, Huston, 5n7, 107n1
social justice, 149–52
Social Justice Tradition, 102–3
The Song of Achilles (Miller), 4n3
soul
  formative journey of, 1–18
  term usage, 4–5, 5n6, 7, 17
soul, journey of being conformed
  church's response, 175–78
  contemporary response, 178–83
  following Jesus, 171–72
  key terms and concepts, 184
  reflection questions, 183–84
  way of Jesus, 173–75
soul, journey of being informed
  faith, pathway of, 57–68
  living wisely and well in perilous times, 21–36
  spiritual center, endorsing, 57–68
  spiritual center, finding, 19
  well-being, alternative ways to, 37–56
soul, journey of being reformed
  character strengths, maturity and, 114–15
  character strengths, model of, 115–17

character strengths, practices,
    112–14
ethical life guide, 107
gentiles, Paul's ministry to, 73–74
key terms and concepts, 86, 119
life of faith, hope, and love, 79–85
message to us from Paul, 74–77
Philippi, Paul's ministry to, 88–90
Positivity Project, 118
prayer for, 71
reflection questions, 85–86, 118–19
religions of human family, 118
Roman Empire, Paul's ministry
    to, 78
spiritual life, understanding of, 73,
    128–29
spiritual maturity, cultivating, 71
spiritual maturity, participating
    in, 88
spiritual virtues, 118
streams of living water, 107–8
strength of character practices, 107
soul, journey of being transformed
    Alaska, religion in, 166–69
    answers, searching for, 156–58
    divine mission in the world, 141
    divine presence as love, 123–25
    enlightenment, journey of, 158–63
    ethical mandate, 149–52
    human health, 155–56
    humankind, role of, 141–42
    key terms and concepts, 152–53,
        169–70
    love, priority and capacity, 144–49
    love of God and neighbor/self, 152
    mission in troubled world, 121
    natural world, caring for, 142–49
    peace in troubled world, 154,
        180–81
    peace of mind, 155–56
    reflection questions, 152, 169
    religious life and thought, 164–66
    social justice, 149–52
    spirituality, contours of, 163–64
The Soul of Christianity (Smith), 5n7
spirit/spiritual, term usage, 5–6, 17, 69
spiritual, term usage, 169–70
spiritual center, endorsing, 57–68

spiritual center, finding, 19–36
spiritual formation
    model of, 33–35
    phases of, 90–96
spiritual gifts, of Holy Spirit, 79
spiritual life
    pathways to, 125–26
    understanding, 73, 128–29
spiritual maturity
    biblical understanding of, 41–43
    cultivating, 71
    participating in, 88–90
spiritual practices, in faith formation,
    96–105
spiritual virtues, 118
spirituality
    in Alaska, 166–69
    term usage, 119
spirituality contours, 163–64
Stages of Faith (Fowler), 34n18
Stassen, Glen H., 119
staying the course, 16–17
stewardship of the earth, 138
Streams of Living Water (Foster), 97,
    98
strength of character practices, 107
The Study of Spirituality (Jones,
    Wainwright, Yarnold), 6n9
suffering, 59, 62, 154
Suleyman, Mustafa, 12n17

taboo, term usage, 170
Taylor, Charles, 12n17
Teachings on Love (Nhat Hanh), 153
Teilhard de Chardin, Pierre, 138, 139,
    140, 161
temperance, as character strength, 117
temptations, 22–24
Ten Commandments (Decalogue), 47
Teresa of Calcutta (Mother), 103
"The Holiness Tradition" (Foster), 99
The Kingdom, the Power, and the Glory
    (Alberta), 44n11
Theology of Liberation (Gutierrez),
    161
Thich Nhat Hanh, 39, 94n3, 153, 163,
    163n13
Thomas à Kempis, 18, 19n1, 97n7,
    106, 160

Tillich, Paul, 5n8, 8n13, 161
Tolle, Eckhart, 163
Torrance, Thomas, 160
Toward a True Kinship of Faiths (Dalai lama), 163n10, 163n13
transcendence, 117
transcendental monism, 139, 153, 164
transformation/transformed, term usage, 119, 178
tribal, term usage, 139
Trump, Donald, 180
trust, in God's presence, 79–82
truth, 179–80

Ukraine conflict, 156, 179
Unbearable Wholeness of Being (Delio), 24n7
United States, Bill of Rights, 149
Universal Christ (Rohr), 25n9
Unlimited Love (Post), 120

virtues
  in Positivity Project, 118
  spiritual, 118

Wainwright, Geoffrey, 6n9
Washington, George, 131
Watts, Alan, 163
way of Jesus, term usage, 35

The Way of Zen (Watts), 163
Ways to the Center (Carmody and Carmody), 167n19
well-being, alternative ways
  educational models, 37–45
  educational strategies, 45–54
  key terms and concepts, 55
  reflection questions, 54–55
  to soul, journey of being informed, 37–56
Wesley, John, 99
Wholehearted Faith (Evans), 87
Wilbur, Ken, 39n1, 40n2, 56, 138n14, 139
wisdom
  character strength, 116
  from patterns of nature, 168
The Wisdom of the Native Americans (Nerburn), 170
Wise Heart (Kornfield), 96n6
Wolsey, Roger, 70
world conflicts, 29–30
World War II, 157
The World's Religions (Smith), 107n1

Yarnold, Edward, 104
Yu, Jane Kim, 184

Zeus, 130

www.ingramcontent.com/pod-product-compliance
Lightning Source LLC
Chambersburg PA
CBHW062037220426
43662CB00010B/1540